Mo
Her Bipolar Memoir

Jo Carroll Lewald

*Enjoy,
Jo Carroll*

Copyright © 2012 Jo Carroll Lewald

All rights reserved.

ISBN-10: 1477573801
ISBN-13: 978-1477573808

Mom's Crazy Her Bipolar Memoir is dedicated to all those who lived it with me and the children pictured in the 1977 photo on the cover: Steven, Heather and Gina, Robert, Aleece, Carol and Drew. And to my love, Alfred.

CONTENTS

ACKNOWLEDGMENTS i
1 Electric Tracks 1
2 All Aboard 18
3 Atchison, Topeka & Santa Fe 28
4 Magnolia Blossom Special 45
5 Switchman 76
6 Babyland Bound 95
7 Sunset Limited 107
8 Coming Round The Bend 116
9 Couplings 134
10 Clickity-Clack 144
11 Sons of Pullman Porters 162
12 Flares on the Track 171
13 Shalom Zephyr 179
14 Great Western Flyers 199
15 Mourning Train 213
16 Midnight Express 231

ACKNOWLEDGMENTS

Mom's Crazy could not have been written without the help of my dear capable friend, Judith Marburg. She came to me one day, after my ECT treatments were finished and suggested a book should be written about my experiences. She had no idea my ECT treatments were only the tip of the iceberg. Judy patiently worked with me weekly for nearly a year to get this project started. And the book could not have been completed without the assistance of my talented niece, Rebecca Shelton Tombaugh, who spent many hours editing and my son Steven Wallace who badgered his friends to read my manuscript, cajoled me with bribes to finish my book and finally provided much needed technical assistance. My daughter, Heather Wallace, supplied the title. And my husband, Alfred has looked at my rewrites so many times I'm sure he can recite several versions of the manuscript from memory.

There are many psychiatrists along the way who helped keep me alive so this book could be written. Among them were Dr. Frank Silva, often called the father of psychiatry in Baton Rouge, Louisiana and Dr. Sarah Jones who still practices in Omaha, Nebraska. Two of the latest doctors to take up this challenge were Dr. Jack Barsman in Atascadero, California and Dr. Lou Ann Eads, Little Rock, Arkansas. After my first session with Dr. Barsman I came home and told my husband, "He's either the craziest doctor I've ever met or the most intelligent." My helpful husband reminded me these were not mutually exclusive traits. Dr. Eads, who is currently keeping me on as even a keel as I'll ever have, once offered me the option of ECT treatments. Tiffany Corjay, my psychiatric counselor in Hot Springs, continues to remind me I am a strong woman, and for that I thank her.

The reader needs to know shock treatments are still performed at the rate of about 100,000 annually in the United States. More are performed on women than men, but in my opinion this is merely because more women seek professional help. According to the National Institute of Mental Health 2.5 million people suffer with Bi-Polar Disorder. Funny thing is, I never have thought I suffered with it. I coped with it, I was aggravated by it, I struggled with it, but I never suffered with it. I suffer from bad knees and poor vision. I survived the label of Bipolar Disorder.

1 Electric Tracks

"Don't worry, dear. ECT – Electroconvulsive Therapy has been used on thousands of patients."

My young-looking doctor hadn't even called It "shock treatments." His soothing words and explanations about ECT were all for naught. Nobody but me was being strapped onto the table.

ECT, shock treatment—or whatever they called it—was happening to me. They were going to hold electrodes to my head and send a current of electricity through my skull. It sounded more like torture than treatment. I was nauseous and weak. My hands and feet felt numb from a mild sedative a nurse had given me. I felt threatened, like a trapped animal.

"Alfred, how do they know how much electricity to use?" I asked my husband. He had answered this question before, but I wanted his assurance one more time. "Maybe they'll fry my brain."

I clutched Alfred's hand tightly. I had finally managed to marry a man who passed more than a casual reality check. He'd always had a full-time job, he was well read and he could communicate with other people at most any level. But nothing mattered right now. I talked rapid-fire to chase my horrible fears away. Would I be alive to say anything to him tomorrow?

Panic welled up in me like bile. My throat felt full of cotton. I couldn't breathe or talk. Why go through with the shock treatments? I was going to die in the hallway, beside Alfred, before he knew it. Cold sweat immediately covered my body and, just as quickly, disappeared. I could talk and breathe again, at least for the moment.

"I'll be a moron when they're through."

"You've had these treatments before, Jo Carroll. Maybe you can't remember but you're always all right the next day."

"There's that smell again, Alfred. It makes me think of fried brains. My grandmother used to fix me fried calves' brains on Saturday mornings. I hope I don't end up as someone's breakfast."

Alfred usually came up with quips for any occasion, but he was too busy hiding his own nervousness. When he first came into my life, my whole perspective changed. What would happen now? Could these treatments cure my depression? What about Alfred and me? Would we still be able to lay in bed and share secrets no one else would care about? Why wouldn't anyone tell me the real truth?

Other patients waited, alone, all wearing the same pale-green hospital gowns and green-striped seersucker robes. I wondered if anybody was ever buried in this uniform. Everyone looked disoriented, like sick, old people in a nursing home. I was the only one with a hand to hold.

A big, metal steel door opened. I had to let go of Alfred's hand. Later, he told me he paced the waiting room, repeating the mantra, "They know what they're doing. They know what they're doing."

"Okay, Jo Carroll. It's your turn," the anesthesiologist said.

Two nurses, "Frick" and "Frack," as I called them, helped me onto the cold, metal table. Nurse Frick pulled the top of my gown down while Nurse Frack placed monitors on my chest. The fast, impersonal invasion made me shiver.

"We're not going to hurt you," Nurse Frack said. "We just want to monitor your heart."

I heard another voice speaking from behind my head. "Hello," said a doctor. He had wire-framed glasses and a blond-white mustache. He looked far too young to treat me. How did he know the ways of the world, much less my head?

"They tell me you're doing just fine," he said.

Sure, that's what they think! How would they know? Have they ever been here? I tried to raise my hands, but someone had already strapped my torso and limbs to the table. I couldn't move. I tried to scream, but my mouth formed only silent terror. Waves of fear pulsated from my heart. Just before I went under the anesthesia completely, I felt someone placing a band around my forehead. Two paddles, similar to those used on heart attack victims, were placed on each side of my head. At once, something took hold of my brain. My head started to spin. My body stiffened momentarily, and then relaxed.

The young doctor nodded to the technician at a nearby console. Everyone took a step back. The needle on the console jumped. Nothing moved except my toes. Medicine injected with the anesthetic relaxed my muscles. Only my brain cells had been affected in the electrically induced spasm.

The doctor glanced at the anesthesiologist who indicated all was well. The entire procedure, which had taken over 50 years to develop and refine, amid much controversy, had taken less than five minutes. The IV and restraining band were removed and an oxygen mask was placed over my mouth and nose for a few minutes.

When I awoke, the twin nurses were helping me off the table and into a wheelchair. Nurse Frick acted as if I was her daughter and had just come home with an "A" on a report card.

"You did very well," she said.

"Your seizure lasted 45 seconds," intoned the doctor. "That's very good."

Frick and Frack both chimed in.

"You should be so pleased."

"This was a good session."

Would I be alive if it had been a bad session?

"Now, you'll be able to go back to your room and have breakfast," said the doctor.

Breakfast? Didn't they understand? What kind of appetite did they expect me to have? My body had just been through electric shock, which left me with a trembling so intense my brain felt like liquid Jell-O. What, I wondered, was the difference in the amount of current between the electric chair on death row and the ECT treatment table at Richard Young Psychiatric Hospital? Why all their silly remarks? If the treatments were so wonderful, why did they treat me as though I was senile afterward? I just wanted to get back to my room and sleep.

Alfred kissed my cheek lightly.

"Hi, sweetheart. You okay?"

I tried to smile.

"I'm fine," I said.

Alfred pushed my wheelchair to my psychiatric unit. Being here for every treatment was hard on him. He looked professional and business-like in his suit, ready to go to the office. I wondered what he said when he came in the office late. Everybody knew his wife was in the loony bin. I wondered if they smelled the excess electricity and made jokes about burnt toast behind his back. He never said much, but I knew he'd canceled business trips to be with me.

This hospital wing was frightening and intimidating. I was on a ride that I knew I would be taking many more times before the series of treatments was complete. My head ached in a way I had never experienced before, as though huge varicose veins covering the outside of my skull were throbbing unrelentingly. I had never known anything like this. My head hurt so much I wanted to cry, but I didn't want to do anything to take a chance of increasing the pain.

I had never been able to overcome completely a feeling of desertion since Bruce, my first husband, left. Alfred, too, knew what it was like to be deserted. His first marriage dissolved without his desire or request. Maybe that was part of the reason he made sure I knew he was always there. His love and hope made me feel like nothing would go wrong.

"What's the matter, lovely lady? Am I taking the bumps too fast, or are you upset about something?"

"I don't want to do this anymore."

"Dr. Jones told you there was no other option. Your depression is too deep and the medications weren't working. Just be patient."

The doors to the psychiatric unit were locked, and only opened from the outside. I couldn't leave, use the telephone or get myself a soda without help or permission. Prison must be like this, only I would have committed a crime to get in. Why do I have to go through all this when I have not done anything wrong?

Once inside the unit, cigarette smoke engulfed everything but my bedroom. I laughed to think that a place could smell strongly of cigarettes and yet have a too-clean smell. Patients were allowed to smoke, but couldn't carry matches or lighters. Nurses and aides carried lighters around their necks to accommodate the smokers. I didn't smoke. In spite of all the different medications I'd taken over the years, I didn't seem to be addicted to anything, except perhaps my morning drink of carbonated beverage.

Back in my room, Alfred put his arms around me and held me gently. Of medium height and trim build, the main indication of his 50 years was a bald head. The fringe of hair and his moustache were black with a little gray. Behind heavy glasses, his twinkling hazel eyes appeared somber. I fit into the curve of his arm, my forehead resting on his check. I didn't want to get my hair on him. It was sticky from the residue left by the electrodes placed on my scalp.

"Listen, honey, I've got to run. I have a meeting at 10. Breakfast's in your room. You'll be okay."

"I'm not allowed to go to the pop machine before lunch. Would you get me a Coke before you leave?"

Alfred's answer was upbeat. "Sure," he said, but his body gave a tired sigh. I'd learned over the years to recognize when he had reached his limit.

"Never mind. I'm sure one of the aides can get it for me."

"Have a good day."

"You, too."

After a quick peck on the cheek, he was gone. Immediately, I felt a deep loneliness. The trains in my head left the station without passengers or freight. My doctors weren't sure how electric shock worked or exactly what it did in my brain, but they "Had an excellent success rate" using it, I was told. I read once that the treatment had only a 1-in-20,000 death rate. I wondered if it was less harmful if electric eels were used? I felt as though I had a terminal illness. Confusing thoughts bounced around in my splitting head and I had difficulty hanging on to them. What difference did it make if the shock treatments killed me?

Frightened and alone, I made a decision: I didn't care what my doctors recommended—I was not going to be plugged in again.

I quit thinking and made a stab at eating breakfast. The tin plate cover had been on so long the eggs were cold and had a funny, metallic taste. The toast was soggy from having been buttered several hours ago. I wouldn't have eaten the oatmeal, even if it had been hot.

I lay down on my bed, exhausted.

I had no idea how long I slept, but when I awoke, a dark rain was hitting the windows. My head pounded, but the veins had returned to their right and proper place inside my head. The afternoon group therapy session did not change my mind about my decision. The therapist, Janet, was direct. She didn't let the group ramble on.

"And, Susan, how can you be so certain your cancer is in remission?"

"There was a rainbow in my mashed potatoes last night."

"What?"

"Now, would God send me a rainbow right there on my plate if He thought I was going to die?"

I couldn't control a giggle. Susan had sold discount cosmetics out of the back of a faded-red station wagon she claimed was "Mary Kay Pink" until she had been diagnosed with lung cancer. Her whole life had been fantasy, but this latest version was funny.

I sat in the maple rocker at the back of the room and wondered, "Why am I here?" Other members were in worse shape than I was, why weren't they having these God-awful treatments? Intellectually, I knew ECT was not an effective treatment for all mental illness. I wasn't the only one in the room who was suicidal.

"I can't stand this," I thought to myself, for the umpteenth time. Why do they think I'm so weird? Because I have treatments and they don't? Some of them are so sick they're never going to get well.

"I'll tell you what I think," announced a tall, thin man. "I think you just got more grease on them spuds than the rest of us. Next time, why don't you try..."

Nora, who was sitting next to me, interrupted.

"Now let's look at all the angles here" she said. "If God wants to send us a message here, how's he going to do it? The damn nurses sure wouldn't let you talk to anyone on the phone who said he was God and I know I'm not getting all my messages."

"You're not even getting any, much less your messages," Mark yelled out. He was a good-looking man in his 40's, and someone I might have been attracted to in the past. His loud voice was all an act. He rarely contributed anything to the conversation that didn't reveal the dimension of his balls.

"All right, all right. I think we've gotten off track here," said Janet. "I said I'd like the group to help Susan deal with her vision. I haven't heard anything bright enough to write home about. Jo Carroll, what about you? Is your mind clear yet?"

"Jo Carroll ain't got nothing up there but a little static electricity," said Jimmy, leering and laughing at the same time.

"Shut up you turkey!" I shouted back. "You act as if I'd just come back from another planet. I'm not as sick as most of you, just 'cause different doctors treat people differently. How many pills do you take every morning Jimmy? Is it 15, or are they shoveling 20 down your throat now?"

"Jo Carroll, please," said Janet. "Do you have anything constructive to say?"

"Oh, sure," I said in high, whiny mimic. "I think God sent you personally a secret message in those mashed potatoes. You should look to heaven to guide you away from this evil place. But in the future, could you ask for gold at the end of the rainbow instead of some cheap mashed potatoes?"

My voice shifted to a growl.

"And next time, skip the mashed potatoes and ask for macaroni and cheese so none of us will have to listen to your crap."

I was tired of listening to other people's problems. I wanted my treatments to be over. The session continued, but I became lost in my own thoughts. Nobody seemed to notice my inattention. The next thing I knew, Janet was saying, "Well, I guess that will be all for today. See you guys back tomorrow."

When Alfred came to see me I was adamant: No more.

"Are you feeling a little better? You look better than you did when I left. Your head must not ache any more?"

Yelling at Alfred was hard for me. I had been gathering my courage all afternoon.

"It's too much, I'm not going to take any more of these stupid shock treatments. You don't know what it's like. I feel like I'm going to die every time I go down that damn hall."

My voice broke into a shrill.

"I feel worse now than I did before. It's not working! I want out!"

I waited for what seemed an eternity before Alfred responded to me. For once, his calming words had no effect. He reminded me of the doctor's prognosis without treatment. I didn't want to listen.

His body tensed.

"Jo Carroll," he said, "I think you're making a rash decision in the stress of the moment."

"Well, it's my stress, not yours. It's not you they're strapping down three times a week. I can't do it again."

"Think about what you're saying, what you're proposing, honey. Don't you remember how good you can feel? You're not going to feel that way again if you stop these treatments. Do you want to take that chance? I don't."

"I don't believe this is all that's left. There must be medications I haven't tried. And there are new ones coming out all the time. This medieval torture is ridiculous, unnecessary, and I'm not going to put up with it."

I began pounding on his chest. Alfred held my wrists to keep me from hurting him.

"I can't believe how childish and selfish you're acting," he shouted. "It's not like you. Go find someone to talk to, do something about the aches, relieve the stress. Talk to your doctor, the therapists. You know what they'll recommend. Think about what you're saying, about all the ramifications of stopping treatments."

"I am thinking about it," I screamed. I shook my head back and forth in short, jerky motions. "It's not you that has to sign the paper before every treatment giving them permission to burn my brain. They don't bring those papers to me to sign because it's as safe as eating a Popsicle."

"Jo Carroll, You're being ridiculous."

I saw his mouth and eyes make a hard line.

"Do what you want," he said. "But if you persist and don't finish your treatments, I'll leave you. I love you, but I don't see any other choices for me. You're not the woman I love when you're in a deep depression, medicines aren't doing the job and your doctors tell me shock treatments are the only alternative left. The choice is up to you."

Tears stung my eyes as he walked away. I didn't have to ask him what he meant or to repeat what he said. He had given me an ultimatum I would have to deal with. The long days at the hospital were unbearable and the nights were hell. My treatment put too much pressure on Alfred to visit me every single evening. Most of my friends who knew where I was didn't know they could visit someone in a mental hospital, or were afraid to see me. I could hear it in their voices on the phone. Did they imagine people in strait jackets or wild-eyed madmen drooling at the mouth?

The evenings when I expected no company I dawdled and poked around in the cafeteria as long as I could. One night, I wandered over to the table where Marilyn was sitting drinking a cup of hot tea, void of any sugar or cream.

"Does it bother you if I sit with you and eat this piece of pie?" I asked her.

"No, of course not. You're not the one who has problems with her weight. I am. I could never think of eating any dessert, much less that peach pie. I have to count every calorie."

"Don't be silly. You're so thin your rings are falling off your fingers."

"I'll pretend I didn't hear that, Jo Carroll. After all, you're one of the few people around here who ever talks to me."

Marilyn, a victim of anorexia, first caught my attention several days earlier. She was engaged in an activity designed by her therapist to make her aware of the exaggerated way she looked at herself and her weight. Marilyn was sorting magazine pictures of people with various body structures and weights. Into a category labeled "heavy" she had placed slender, almost gaunt, fashion models. Under the "normal" heading she grouped photographs of starving African children. Marilyn was convinced she shouldn't exceed the weight of her bones.

"If you accept me with all this electric static in my head, I can appreciate you even though you think you qualify for the fat farm."

We both laughed and lingered at the round dining table as long as possible, leaving only after a cafeteria employee shooed us out.

I never watched television at the hospital. Focusing was too hard, the pictures moved too fast and the stories didn't make much sense. I didn't have the concentration to read either. Some friends sent books, but they lay untouched in a pile by my bed. My spare time was spent hanging around the lounge room with other patients trying to overcome the boredom.

"Hey, Jo Carroll, pull up a chair and take over my hand. I have to go back to the desk," said a nurse named Mabel. I didn't particularly like her because she treated all patients like they had an IQ of 50.

"No, thanks."

Knitting was more to my liking this evening. I walked to the nurses' station to get my unfinished sweater. I had to leave my knitting there because the needles were considered a possible hazard. As far as I was concerned, the yarn was potentially more problematic than the flexible, plastic round needles. But I kept those thoughts to myself, otherwise the nurses might get the idea I planned to do something dangerous with the soft blue-green yarn. I was making a sweater for Heather, my oldest daughter. I picked a color that matched my eyes, and therefore, hers. Maybe Heather could help get me out of here. She understood me. She'd always been on my side. All I had to do was convince her. Telephones were wonderful, and connected me to any part of the world, even from inside an institution for the crazies.

I dialed her number.

"Heather?"

"Yes, Mom."

"Listen carefully. I've discovered something. The nurses aren't really nurses here. They don't talk like nurses. They don't dress like nurses."

"Mom, you're in a hospital. If they weren't nurses they wouldn't be there. Has somebody done something to you?"

"No. You don't understand. Something is wrong here."

"Mom— "

"They want to give me more shock treatments."

"Mom— "

"They explain it to the family like it's all okay, but..."

"Mom, answer me, damn it!"

"Yes?"

"Do they hurt you?"

"Not physically, but you never can tell where they're going to put the wires next."

"Oh, Mom..."

My agitation increased with every word.

"They say it's okay, but how can they tell what's going on in my brain?"

"The treatments are supposed to make you better."

"Better, bitter."

I began to cry.

"I just want out of here."

"Mom, where's Alfred?"

"I don't know," I said, stubbornly.

"Mom, you're not telling me the truth."

"The truth is supposed to set me free. Just come and get me out of here."

"I can't, Mom. I love you."

The phone was silent. Heather was gone without even saying goodbye.

I didn't call anyone else. I didn't want another conversation like that. I felt unsettled, so I pushed the phone conversation away and tried to knit 1, purl 2. I was working on the sleeve ribbing. Two hours passed with hardly anyone bothering me. Glancing up, I saw Emily, a young nurse, heading my way. Emily always knew how to smooth over the rough edges of an evening.

"Knitting? Boy, you're going to be finished with that before you leave here."

"I hope I get paroled before then," I laughed.

"Ah, you don't think this place is like a jail, do you?"

"Well, my bedroom at home doesn't have security screens on the windows and the doors aren't locked from the outside. And I heard my new roommate is supposed to be Bobbie McGee. That's enough jail for me. Are you on the night shift?"

"Nah, I'll be going home at 11."

"Could you sit down and talk to me for a while?"

"Sure."

I didn't know what I wanted to say. I just wanted companionship for a little while. I stared at my hands as I spread my fingers wide.

"Do you think I'll ever get well?"

Emily looked at me and grinned. Her slight overbite mocked me.

"I said, do you think I'll ever get well?"

"Jo Carroll, you, of all people. Everybody asks me that. But you should know better. Look around you. You were in bad shape when you came in here, but look at you now. Listen to yourself. Can't you see it? Can't you tell?"

"I don't know. Sometimes I do and sometimes I don't. I just want out."

"You're much better, but it won't do you any good if you go home before you're completely well.

I closed my eyes. The trains in my head were screeching around familiar curves. I'd heard the same rhetoric from everyone around me and I didn't want to hear it again.

Around 9:30 pm, the medicine cart came around. Pills to control the general population were handed out, but I didn't have to take my sleeping pill until 11 p.m. Hospital patients were not confined to their rooms, even at night, unless they threatened to harm someone. I'd already spent several sleepless nights on the couch in view of the nurses' station. In the middle of the night, when I couldn't sleep, the depression was gone, and the "what ifs" came and stole my brain. What if I was institutionalized for the rest of my life? What if one of these treatments wiped out my entire memory? What if the courts reversed an earlier decision and decided I was an unfit mother after all?

I was going to try another technique to meet the Sleep Goddess my demons had successfully been keeping at bay. I ambled down the hall and entered a small therapy room where the relaxation exercises had already begun.

"Jo Carroll, lie down on that bare spot of carpet next to the window."

"Here?"

"That's fine. Okay everybody just let all your muscles go. Make believe you're floating in water. Water is all around you and you don't have to do anything to hold up your body."

That was the wrong image for me. I hated being in the water floating on my back. I always felt like someone was trying to drown me. But, I was here. I'd try. I attempted to make my muscles relax, but my efforts obviously weren't working. I had a cramp in my leg.

"Jo Carroll, what are you doing? Please lie down."

"I have a cramp in my leg. I'm rubbing it."

"Lie down or leave the room. The rest of us are doing a relaxation exercise."

Feeling like a chastised child, I tried to ignore the tightness in my calf and lay down. Being a good patient was important to me. I confused being a good patient with time off for good behavior. What I had been doing wasn't working. I could hear the soft snoring of several people around me. They were obviously relaxed.

"Okay, that's all for tonight. See you day after tomorrow. If one of your buddies has fallen asleep wake them up so they can go to bed. I looked around and did not see anyone I considered a buddy. I got up and went back to my own little cubicle in my room. I let my clothes fall to the floor and slipped on a nightgown.

The nightgown was a constant reminder I was in the hospital. Nightclothes of any kind were not my norm. I'd slept naked ever since my first husband had left me. It gave me a sense of power, a feeling I could do anything I wanted with my body. I didn't have that kind of control here in the hospital. They checked you with a flashlight once an hour—a definite invasion of privacy—and I didn't want my hand to be in the wrong place or any bare parts showing to some unknown night nurse. I glanced at the empty bed against the far wall. The hospital did not have private rooms, but I managed to be without a roommate for a couple of weeks. I didn't know if I liked that. I didn't have to be afraid in the middle of the night that some crazy woman would come over and try to strangle me. On the other hand, someone to talk to as I was falling asleep might be nice.

Tears trickled down my cheeks as I slid into bed. I hoped sleep would come easily. Some nights, I just stared at the ceiling and eventually wandered out to the lounge hoping to find someone to talk to. The night before an ECT treatment, I didn't sleep at all.

I couldn't bring my soft fluffy pillow from home because of the fire regulations. I didn't remember this one being so lumpy. I reached underneath and pulled out a box of chocolates.

I looked at them blankly for a minute. I removed one and took a bite. The taste was sweet and comforting. Then, I remembered, of course, Morris, the editor of the Jewish Press, where I used to work, had trotted down the steps in the hospital several days ago with the box of chocolates in hand. His visit was a pleasant surprise. He cared about me as a person, which was nice. Second, and more important to my ego now, he didn't think shock treatments would turn me into an imbecile and I wouldn't be able to write articles any more. He still wanted me to work for the paper when I got out of the hospital. I rolled his encouraging words in my mind.

"Take your time," Morris had said. "Don't rush, but I have some stories in mind for you. I haven't told the people in the office where you are because I wasn't sure if you wanted them to know. But people are asking why your material hasn't been in for a while, they miss your byline."

Remembering his promise of continuing employment at the newspaper had a soothing effect. I went to sleep easily.

The next day, I looked around for reading material while waiting for lunch. I leafed through the usual tabloids and settled on a women's travel magazine describing how to go to the exotic ends of the earth on money you saved out of the grocery budget. The article nudged my dormant writing genes to the surface. I tucked it under my arm and pulled it out again after lunch. My concentration was so intense, Marilyn tried three times to get my attention.

"Jo Carroll, we're supposed to go to the gym for exercise now. Don't you remember?"

I looked at her blankly. Actually, I'd hoped no one would notice I wasn't there. The hospital had a large, well-equipped facility for our daily dose of physical activity, considered highly beneficial for the mind as well as body. I was of the opinion I would have to run 200 laps around the gym to even begin to clear the synthetic cobwebs medical science had brought to my brain.

"I guess I can go use the walking track."

I knew if I didn't find any activity some jock hired by the hospital would try to teach me the latest version of push-ups. I had the track to myself. Usually, at least one person trotted around at a good clip, trying to beat the odds of a return visit to the psycho ward. After 20 minutes of brisk walking, I let my body return to where my mind was—the magazine with more allure than travel.

Later, I called Alfred at his office. I verbalized how I felt for the first time.

"I was reading a magazine and suddenly I realized I was able to concentrate. I was really interested in it. I can write like that. I have written like that."

I reluctantly added, "Maybe the treatments are working. You're right, sweetheart. Of course, I have to continue with the treatments. It's just that I'm so frightened. What if..."

I could almost hear Alfred grinning on the other end of the line.

"I know it scares the shit out of you. It does me, too. But what if they do work? They have a 90-percent success rate. The odds are with us."

I felt a surge of excitement. I giggled like a child.

"The food is so awful here. Bring me a burger or something decent to eat when you come, okay honey?"

"You haven't sounded so cheerful for ages, sweetheart. You can be my date for dinner. What flavor shake would you like me to bring you?"

"Surprise me," I paused just the right number of beats. "You know what I like. I love you."

That evening, we sat cozily in my room eating gourmet fast food. If all continued to go well, I had only one more week of treatments.

"Heather said she would drive in Thursday to make sure everything was shipshape at the house," said Alfred. "I guess she doesn't trust me to take care of it."

Alfred had arranged for Heather to come for a prolonged visit when I was released from the hospital. We'd had a heated discussion over this. I didn't want to admit I needed my oldest daughter to come take care of me. I hadn't had surgery, and as far as I knew, I could still walk and talk like a normal person. I wasn't 80 years old. Why did anyone have to come and take care of me?

But, as usual, Alfred prevailed.

"You know how much I have to be out of town," he'd said. "Gina is a bright, mature young lady and a big help, but honey, she's just a junior in high school. We're fortunate that Heather's in a position where she can come to stay. Let's take advantage of her willingness and accept her offer. I know I'll feel more secure when I'm gone, knowing that she's there for you to lean on if you need her."

I looked up at him. I would be home soon recovering from this episode of manic depression. Tears streamed down my face.

"Do you want me to make a shopping list so there'll be food in the house?" I asked.

We fell into comfortable small talk until he had to leave.

"I can't wait to have you in my bed. I've really missed you," he said, and kissed me firmly on the mouth.

After he left, I sat quietly for a while, basking in the remembered warmth of his presence. I'd been in the hospital for more than four weeks. I was at the end of the ECT treatments. I was feeling relatively good most of the time and wanted to get on with life. I could hardly wait to lay on top of him in our big, gray bed, to snuggle my head into that special place in his neck and know when I went to sleep, he would be beside me in the morning.

Another week went by and tomorrow was the last scheduled treatment. I had a weekend pass and, if all went well, Monday morning they'd check me out for good. I would still be attending weekly therapy meetings and support groups, plus regular appointments with the psychiatrist. My calendar was filling up and I hadn't even spoken to my friends about doing lunch. A normal life loomed ahead. I could hardly contain myself. I could go home on Friday and eat whatever the hell I wanted.

But right now I just needed to get through the next meal without gagging.

Breakfast had always been a difficult meal for me to eat and having to face hospital cafeteria food so early in the morning was ten times worse. The nurses frowned at my Southern-style beverage of choice, Coca-cola. They didn't understand that nothing cuts the humid air of the morning like the syrup-sweet mixture from Atlanta. I no longer lived where my friends called Memphis a "northern city," but some habits were hard to break.

"Eat," said the server shoveling scrambled eggs and sausage on my plate. "You have to eat so the medication won't make you weak."

"Don't make me take so damn much medicine and I won't have to eat your awful food," I sniped back.

After I ate, I went back to my room for my daily ritual of staring at my typewriter. No one had a computer. I had wanted to keep a diary of what happened to me since I'd first walked into the doors of the institution almost a month ago. Every morning, even after a treatment, I'd sit in my chair and start with a new sheet of paper. But the typewriter stared back at me. My diary didn't seem to be forthcoming.

Instead, I found myself writing a history of everything that had happened to me in the last 20 years. Everything that had brought me to this point, the frantic pace of my life that ran the tracks from a tiny town in Kansas to the Southern coastal hamlets of Mississippi, from an artist colony in the Ozark Mountains to utter poverty in Louisiana, and finally plunging to the ground near the banks of the Missouri River in Nebraska. The fear of forgetting my background, history—my very being—drove me to the write it down while I could remember. The doctors said memory gradually recovers, but, when pressed, they would say anything to ease their patients' minds. What if they were wrong? What if I couldn't remember why I'd had the abortion? What if I couldn't remember the suicide of two 21-year-old boys I'd loved with all my heart and soul? What if I couldn't remember why I married a man knowing he was gay? And what if I couldn't remember seducing Alfred, my best friend's ex-husband?

What if, God forbid, I had to undergo another series of treatments in the future?

I didn't want to lose my memories.

And, I wanted to figure out why, in this era of modern medicine, I had to undergo shock treatments.

2 All Aboard

The phone rang several times before I managed to answer it. The bedside clock said 8 a.m. I was sleeping late. My two children, Heather and Steven, didn't have school that day and I was not scheduled to work at the bank.

"Oh, Jo Carroll! Help me, please, come to the house, I can't get Bill up!"

The caller's voice was so weak I could hardly hear her.

"What do you mean?" I asked.

"This is Francis," she said. Francis was the maid who had cooked and cleaned for the family of Bruce, my husband then. Bruce was one of five boys, and Bill was the youngest. Bruce's parents were out of town, and Francis, who'd practically raised Bill, was staying at their house.

In high school, Bill organized a rock-and-roll band. They wore Beatles wigs and played in joints where female performers wore tassels and not much else. He hadn't thought much about college, and then the draft board called him. He never talked about the time he spent in Vietnam. He'd been back home from the war almost six months and hadn't looked for a job. But he loved to spend time with my children and was always fun to have around. I knew he had a girlfriend who enjoyed listening to him play the guitar, but I'd never met her.

"Just please, come right away!" said Francis.

I pulled on whatever clothes I had lying on the floor, shoved jeans and T-shirts on my two sleepy, protesting children. I knocked on my neighbor Julie's door to ask if she would watch them. My car flew across town to the Wallace's house, which sat on a narrow brick street. I recognized Dr. Brown's car. "Brownie" had delivered my two babies, and his daughter, Lynn, was the maid of honor at my wedding. The front door was open, but that was no cause for alarm. In this neighborhood, people rarely locked their doors. The screen door banged closed behind me.

"Francis! Francis! I'm here. Where's Bill?"

The living room, where I had enjoyed many good times, was silent and cold. I hurried into the kitchen. Francis was seated in the breakfast room, crying softly. Her tears made her wire frame glasses nearly slip off her nose. She grabbed the edge of her apron to wipe her face. Francis got up, wound her skinny arms around me tightly, sobbing between broken words.

"I...called Bill...for breakfast...I called and called...I couldn't wake him up so I started to go up...I didn't know what else to do. He wouldn't wake up. His breakfast was getting cold, but he wouldn't get up. Dr. Brown and Dr. Fast came."

Her words whirled around in my head and didn't make sense. Why did she have to call two doctors? I loosened Francis' grip. The Wallaces had years ago turned their attic into a knotty-pine, paneled dorm for all of their boys. I wanted to go upstairs and see Bill, but both doctors blocked the way.

"When did you last see Bill?" asked Dr. Fast. He was a doctor I didn't know very well, but he had the prettiest wife in town.

"What do you mean?" I asked. "Isn't he upstairs? Is he gone? I don't understand."

Dr. Fast looked at me with an accusing sneer. Something was wrong and nobody was telling me. What was wrong with Bill? Why was he still upstairs? Had someone burglarized the house? I felt limp. My knees gave way and I slid back onto a kitchen chair. I felt lightheaded.

"Jo Carroll, I asked when you last saw Bill?"

An ache in my stomach made his question hard to answer. I couldn't think. I couldn't speak. His words didn't make any sense.

"Did you hear me?"

"Yes," I answered, slowly. "I talked to him on the phone about 11:30 last night. He's going to come over and eat with me and the kids tonight since Bruce is out of town, I asked him what he wanted for supper."

"Was it usual for you to talk to your brother-in-law so late at night?"

I stared at him. What could be the matter? Why was he asking me all these stupid questions? Why didn't they just tell me what had happened?

"Bill and I talk all the time. Usually not that late at night, but my husband and his parents were gone. He comes over and plays with the kids all the time. Please tell me, what's this all about?"

"Jo Carroll," I heard Dr. Brown's soft voice. He put his arm around my shoulder. "Do you know how we can reach your in-laws? Where are Ruth and Wayne?"

"They're in California. Francis has the number. Please, what about Bill? Was he shot? Let me go upstairs. He might need me."

"No, Jo Carroll. You need to stay in the kitchen."

I sat quietly, fighting to stay conscious, as I listened to Dr. Fast dialing the phone.

"Wayne, this is Spencer, in Atchison. I hate to call you with news like this, but we've found your son Paul dead on the second floor of your home. Brownie's here with me, and we haven't yet been able to determine the cause of his death."

The words "dead" and "death" became sharp pains, like someone driving iron spikes into my head. The pounding got louder until I couldn't hear anything and I lost consciousness.

Memories came flooding back into my mind. I remembered being at the hospital in Atchison, watching my grandfather, Harry, unravel knots in an invisible handkerchief and hand me imaginary rings. Harry drifted in and out of consciousness for more than 24 hours. But, somehow, he felt my presence beside him on the hospital bed. In the closing hours of his life, he kept handing me those invisible rings, trying to give me something that didn't exist.

I always called Harry by his first name. He loved to buy me jewelry, special gold lockets and pretty bracelets. After I was married, he taught me how to plant tomatoes and make gravy, the extra-thick, mild kind oozing over mashed potatoes.

We were close. He told me he loved me a "bushel and a peck and a hug around the neck," and when I went home he'd always call out, "I'll see you in the funny papers if you don't see me first."

I lived across the street from him all through my school years. I paraded boyfriends in front of him. I laughed with him when my pet pigeon used to chase his huge, yellow tomcat under the porch. He was afraid for me to go barefoot, which I loved to do. So he would spit on my feet, if I dared step on his porch without shoes. I got so mad I'd always go get the hose, rinse my feet and climb the steps again. His arms stretched out for a giant hug.

"You know I ain't got nothing 'gainst you. I just don't want you gettin' hurt," he said.

In the hospital, I kept looking and listening to the monitors keeping track of his heart. IVs hung from a pole on the other side of his bed and the tangled tubes came together in a needle on the back of his brown hand, weathered by years of farming and carpentry. The whole medical contraption jiggled every time he moved his fingers.

"What's he doing?" Bruce whispered to me. "Why does he keep doing the same thing?"

I sometimes thought my life with Bruce wasn't all a marriage should be. But what else was there? We'd been married eight years, had two children, two cars, an aloof Siamese cat and a friendly Dalmatian, and we lived in a tract house in Atchison, Kansas. I worked part time as a bank teller and Bruce worked for a community action program. Why didn't I feel like our life was perfect? A stranger might think Ivory Soap would want to feature us in a commercial.

But I couldn't stay on top of things. I couldn't seem to catch my breath. Yet, Harry's death seemed part of the natural order of things. He'd lived his life, had a child, watched his grandchildren grow up and had even gotten to enjoy his great-grandchildren. His life was like his Bible. He sat in his Morris chair every night and read a little to himself, and finally he was done. The book was closed.

I leaned over to answer Bruce. "My grandmother used to keep her diamond rings knotted in a hanky and pinned to her bra," I said. "He's trying to give me those rings."

Nana, my grandmother, had been dead almost 10 years, and the rings had been given to my mother many years ago. Harry looked at me through watery eyes as he untied the invisible handkerchief again. I tried to get him to stop. Tears running down my face, I accepted the beautiful rings from him, over and over.

The lines and numbers on the monitor began their final erratic movements as Harry began to gasp for breath. The machines were screeching as the nurses rushed in the room. Bruce stayed by Harry's side and held his hand. I left and joined my grieving parents in the waiting room. I loved my grandfather dearly, but I couldn't stay and watch him die anymore than my mother could.

A few days later, I found myself driving to the small funeral parlor in Horton. The winter chill and threat of snow had not kept people away from Harry's funeral. He was well known and loved, and many came to bid their final farewell. I stood with Bruce watching the procession of people, as if through an old cracked mirror. I wanted the reflection to be bright and whole again.

In the weeks that followed, my daddy helped me cope with Harry's death. Bruce and I lived down the street from my parents. I'd run up to their house and jump in his lap while he was reading the newspaper, just like I had when I was a teenager. His hand would smooth the top of my hair and he would lean over and give me a quick kiss on the cheek. He'd never been thrilled with my marriage to Bruce and eyed my relationship with the whole Wallace clan with considerable caution. But, when I needed him, he gave me love and support. Daddy knew we were anxious to leave the area. Bruce had talked to him about the possibility of looking for other jobs. We had considered moving, not down the street—but away from Atchison—out of Kansas completely. We wanted to try our wings in a place neither one of us had lived before. We would be on our own, and not be subject to the rumor mills of a small town. After my grandfather's funeral, my daddy had pulled me aside, saying, "Jo Carroll, honey, you don't want to move. Families need to stay together, to give each other support. You have a nice family, a nice home. Be happy here."

I wanted the warmth of Harry to be back. He had given me a thread of stability that I didn't want to lose. I felt pressure, an undeniable tenseness. But I couldn't identify its source or deal with it. I couldn't explain it, but I knew I couldn't bear this feeling any longer and stopped by the office of Dr. Wayne Wallace, my father-in-law.

Dr. Wallace was Bruce's father, and a family practitioner, like almost every other doctor in Atchison. He was Harry's doctor and he had delivered my sister-in-law's babies. Everyone who knew him called him "Wayne." I often stopped in his office to leave a message or pick up something. But I had never been inside as a patient until, one day, after Harry's death, I suddenly realized I couldn't stand the way I felt any more.

The waiting room of Dr. Wallace's office was full of patients waiting for their appointments. A low hum of conversation filled the air. On the wall, I saw a clock I had cross-stitched for him. I felt uncomfortable. I checked in at the front desk and Juanita, his nurse, then whisked me through the waiting room and into an examining room without asking a question.

The examining room was typical, brightly lit and spotlessly clean. My father-in-law saw me right away. He came into the room in his starched white jacket and perched himself on the end of a chair.

"I guess there are advantages to being family," I quipped, trying to downplay my presence. I just sat there, not knowing what to do next.

Dr. Wallace saw right through me. Not only was he trained to observe people, but he had seen me sit at his kitchen table many times. He knew I was usually babbling on about the kids or my project of the moment. Now, I was silent.

"What's the matter, Jo Carroll?" he asked.

I hadn't seen this compassionate side of his nature before. Tears streamed down my checks. I looked at him, unable to choke out any words.

"I don't know," I finally managed to mumble. "I just don't know. I don't feel good."

"Do you have a fever?"

"No."

"Does your body ache?"

"No, it's nothing like that. I just feel confused or something. I can't really explain it."

"Are you having trouble concentrating?"

"Maybe. I guess so. I just feel like half of me is going in one direction and the other half is going off by itself."

"You do a lot of volunteer work. Are you taking on too much?"

"I don't think so. I don't know. Sometimes, everything I do just seems to take me in circles."

"Are you and Bruce getting along okay?"

"I guess so. We really don't have any fights."

"Does he know you're here?"

"No one knows I'm here. I didn't plan to be here. I was just driving by and couldn't stand it any longer. I know it sounds silly, but, at times, my mind feels like there are hundreds of railroad tracks, sometimes running parallel, sometimes crossing each other and going over and under and around. Every track seems to carry a string of cars and I have been trying to keep them all going on the right tracks, in the proper direction, at the correct speed. These trains are always rushing down the tracks. Wrecks are always a possibility."

Dr. Wallace took hold of my hands.

"Dr. Sahni, a psychiatrist, has just opened an office in my building," he said. "I think you should talk to him."

Dr. Wallace was an old-fashioned doctor who believed all medical problems could be cured by traditional methods such as antibiotics or surgery. I was amazed he even knew a psychiatrist, much less rented an office to him. Dr. Wallace was of the same generation as my mother, who always taught me that, if I just toughed it out, I could handle my own problems. When I had problems that didn't go away by themselves, I would blame myself and say, "I must not have toughed it out enough."

"Okay, if you think it would help," I said. "But I don't know what I'd talk to him about."

"Don't worry about that. He's right next door. Let me call him and see if he has some free time now."

A few minutes later, Dr. Wallace came back into the examining room.

"Dr. Sahni can see you right away. Don't worry, it's probably nothing serious."

I went into Dr. Sahni's office. One entire wall was windows, another was decorated with an Oriental rug, but the room was still dark and eerie. A small man with swarthy skin and an accent, leaned back in his chair.

"Please, Jo Carroll," he said, motioning in the general direction of a comfortable chair by his desk and a mustard-colored leather couch nearby. I didn't know if I was supposed to slowly sink into a faint on the couch or sit upright in the chair. I choose the chair, but didn't hold my composure for long. I started to sob, "I really don't know what I'm doing here."

Dr. Sahni let me cry, without interjecting a word, until I calmed down.

"Tell me what is bothering you," he said.

I repeated what I'd told Dr. Wallace. "I just don't feel good."

Dr. Sahni waited in silence for me to answer, but I was quiet.

"What do you mean?" he asked.

After an hour of questions and replies, Dr. Sahni wrote a prescription for an antidepressant and handed it to me.

"I've decided to accept you as a patient. Do you have any questions? Isn't there anything you want to ask me?"

I looked at him blankly.

"No, I don't think so."

"Not even how you are going to pay for this?"

Before I could reply, he continued, on, "Because your father-in-law is renting me this space at a reduced rate, I'm not going to charge you anything. But you should have asked me how much it would be."

I wondered if he hoped I would then convey this favor to enhance his image with my father-in-law. But he embarrassed me so much, I never fully trusted him.

My sessions with Dr. Sahni were a help, but when my mood swings were severe, I'd spend several days in bed, hiding from the world. The trains were speeding around in my head as I tried to cope. At first, I didn't pay much attention to this behavior and called them my "vapor days," recalling the descriptions in books of the Victorian Era when women were prone to what was a catch-all diagnosis described as "female hysteria." Bruce told me I was just lazy.

Back in the Wallace's kitchen, I regained consciousness. I opened my eyes and saw Dr. Brown was leaning over me. I grabbed his hand. His hand had reassured me many times and I needed him to reassure me now. He rearranged the cool cloth on my forehead.

"Where's Bruce?" he asked.

"He's at a special conference in southern Missouri."

"Can you call him and have him come home right away?"

Before I could answer, Dr. Fast asked, "Do you have a funeral home you usually use?"

I burst into tears. A funeral home wasn't a place one usually used. It wasn't like the cleaners or the corner market

"No, I don't. Can't some of this wait?"

"No. There's going to have to be an autopsy and coroners like to know who's going to be handling the arrangements."

The doctors in Atchison took turns serving as coroner and Dr. Fast had pulled the duty this time. An inquiry into the death of the young son of another doctor wasn't going to be easy.

"Don't you know why he's dead?"

"We're not certain. We want to make sure. Let's go into the living room and talk before they take the body away."

"Body?" I asked myself. Why can't he just say "Bill?" He's still "Bill." He will always be Bill.

"What was your relationship with Paul?"

"Everybody called him 'Bill.' Paul was just his first name. I loved him. He was a little—"

"In what way did you love him? Did you have a sexual relationship with him?"

"No. Of course not. He's my brother-in-law."

"That doesn't exclude other relationships. He was an attractive young man."

I started to cry again. I couldn't get used to hearing Bill's name in the past tense, and the doctor's implications unnerved me.

"He's like a little brother to me. That kind of love. Why are you asking me all these questions?"

"Do you know if he was troubled by anything? Was anything bothering him? Did he owe money to anyone?" His questions came so fast I couldn't answer. I didn't know of any problems, and I'm not sure I would have told even if I had.

The next day, the Atchison newspaper reported Paul William Wallace, 21, son of Dr. and Mrs. Wayne Wallace, died from aspirating his own vomit. Not a pretty death, but certainly an explanation more acceptable than suicide. Years later, when Brownie casually said to me, "I don't think Wayne ever got over the suicide of his son," I learned how the two physicians had conspired to cover up the true cause of death, which was an over dose of sleeping pills.

Bruce came home before I could go to sleep that night. We held each other and cried. He had never imagined outliving his little brother. Later, as we walked through the rows of coffins, I couldn't make any sense of us picking out something we'd like to bury Bill in. Death carries so many details I had never thought about. We'd rather he not be dead, not be buried at all. Numbly, I went through all the preparations for the funeral, helped along by the pills my psychiatrist gave me.

Unlike my grandfather's funeral, Bill's funeral was a small, family affair. Not many young people wanted to acknowledge the death of a peer, and Dr. Wallace didn't want the preying eyes of patients seeing his grief. We had selected a plain, walnut coffin. Unadorned, the finely polished wood gleamed. The casket seemed too beautiful to be confined underground. That we were burying Bill seemed impossible. It couldn't be him. Maybe somebody had made a mistake. But everyone seemed to be so accepting. They kept saying, "This is the way Bill would have wanted it."

I wanted to scream, "Bullshit! Bill wanted to live! He had his whole life ahead of him!"

At the time, I had no way of knowing that, one day, I would understand why he wanted the cold, dark safety of the ground, where he would hurt no more and nothing would ever bother him again.

3 Atchison, Topeka & Santa Fe

I was alone in the Kansas City hospital room. Nothing hurt, but I couldn't stop crying.

A middle-aged doctor came into my room. His white jacket was stretched and buttoned across his large, round belly. He was the doctor who, earlier, had told me, "No one will be able to tell you've had an abortion." The procedure, he said, was relatively simple and corrected a number of problems, including cleansing the uterus from an unwanted fetus.

"What's wrong?" he asked. He stared at me, waiting for an answer.

"I...don't...know..." I said, between sobs.

I was barely 27, and already felt like an old woman.

The doctor continued his questions. "Do you hurt?"

"No," I said. I crossed my legs and squeezed my thighs together as tight as I could. I made the same motions with my arms across my chest. I didn't want to hurt.

Life with Bruce had fallen into a pattern. I worked two or three days a week at the bank. Bruce went to work at the community action agency, although he no longer kept the late hours. I didn't know if I cared. Our conversations were limited to the kids. Our social life was nonexistent because I didn't trust any of the women who had been in our circle of friends. I suspected Bruce was having an affair. The signs were classic: I didn't wear much lipstick, but I found a new tube of bright red when I cleaned out the car. Sometimes, Bruce's shirt collar smelled like perfume, and the scent wasn't mine. I'd wake up in the middle of the night and he wouldn't be there. Terrified, I'd lie in bed and wait for the sound of the garage door, but all I heard was the clickity-clack of the trains in my head.

"Where were you?" I'd ask later. "I was afraid something had happened to you."

He would answer, "I couldn't sleep. I went for a walk," or "I told you Tom and I were going for a beer. You were half asleep. You just don't remember."

But most of the time I heard, "You're just imagining things. I was in the bathroom. Turn over and go back to sleep."

Bruce often brought home people who worked in his office. One night, he turned up with two members of VISTA, Volunteers in Service to America, a Peace Corps-like organization, but just for the United States. Alan was intelligent, but rather spacey, and he looked like he could have been related to John Lennon. His partner, Roger, was shorter, but by far the better looking of the two. He had long, dark, curly hair and a California tan. "Long Beach," he told me when I asked where he was from. His voice was raspy, and his eyes never stopped looking at me when he talked.

I invited the two to stay for dinner. I had a large pot of vegetable soup simmering on the stove. The four of us ate and talked like we had known each other for years. We discussed the war in Vietnam, the CIA, the Chicago Riots, the Kennedy assassinations and Martin Luther King's death. There was little we weren't trying to solve that night. We considered ourselves liberals beyond compare. We were going to save all the peoples of the world.

The evening was fantastic, as all my conversations lately had been with the older neighborhood women, who talked about snotty children, what to cook for dinner and the recipe on page 43 of the Good Housekeeping.

"Jo Carroll," said Roger, "I can't believe you're not helping with this project." He bit the skin of his left forefinger.

"I don't have the time," I said. "I work at the bank part time and I have two kids."

"That's a bunch of crap. Everyone finds time for what they really want to do. Don't you care about the kids around here who don't have enough to eat?"

"I didn't say I didn't care."

Bruce looked around the circle the four of us made as we sat on the floor. "There's plenty of us working on this. Jo Carroll doesn't need to get involved. She's got her hands full."

"Whatsa matter, Bruce? 'Fraid of a little competition in the family?" teased Alan. "Think she can just handle the old barefoot-and-pregnant routine?"

"No. She hasn't been feeling good lately, and I don't want her to get overloaded. She knows she can do anything she wants to."

I glared at Bruce. I hated for him to make even the vaguest reference to my seeing a psychiatrist.

"Until we can get some better jobs lined up for some folks, Jo Carroll could be some help by teaching some evening classes on how to stretch a food budget," said Roger.

I grinned. Roger had noticed I had a brain.

After dinner, Roger put on his worn, red plaid jacket to leave.

"Where on earth did you get that coat?" I laughed. "Some poor, unsuspecting logger in the north woods must be running around freezing to death."

Roger turned his head and winked at me. "Maybe we can make you a clothes consultant, too. Wanna come by my apartment tomorrow afternoon about 2 p.m. and talk about the classes?"

The next morning, after Bruce left for work, I called Dr. Sahni and canceled my appointment. I still saw him, but the visits were more as a medication check. I'd never talked to him about any of my marital problems. Professional ethics aside, he was too close to my father-in-law to even chance it. I lied about having a sick child. I felt guilty, but Roger was better than that stupid doctor.

Roger's apartment was in the basement of a yellow stucco house that had gone unpainted too long, with bikes and toys on the grassless front lawn. This house was in a row of homes that backed up to the Missouri River bluff. A path around the side led to his door. I felt like a little kid standing in front of the Principal's office. I wasn't sure what I was doing. My trains carried no answers.

I knocked lightly. When no one answered, I knocked a little harder.

"Just a minute."

Roger answered the door wearing khaki shorts and pulling a T-shirt over his lean body.

"Sorry I took so long. I was taking a nap. Come on in."

His apartment looked like a college dorm room, with books and papers scattered all over. Empty glasses and a half-eaten sandwich shared the dining table with an old manual typewriter.

"Excuse the trash, we don't clean up in here very often. Here, let me get this junk off the couch so you can sit down. Would you like something to drink? Beer, water? How about a Coke?"

"I don't drink beer."

"You don't drink beer? I never knew of anybody who didn't guzzle a few now and then. Is that some kind of Midwestern thing?" He got a Coke out of the fridge for me.

"No, silly, I just don't like the taste of it""

Roger sat down on the couch next to me. He explained the community program, and how I would fit in. I didn't pay much attention to what he said. I looked at his eyes so I'd remember their color. I turned my head upwards and he kissed me. The nice, soft, gentle kiss made my knees weak and scared me. He was only five years younger than me, but suddenly, he was The Graduate and I was Mrs. Robinson.

"Roger, I have to go home."

"Whatever you say."

"Maybe we can discuss this over the phone."'

"Sure."

Now, as I lay in the Kansas City hospital, my throat felt the dryness from the anesthetic tube. Down below I could feel some blood leave my body; it was warm and felt heavier than the flow of a normal period. Had they scraped too much from my insides? Slight cramps pulled at my insides. I wanted to pull up my gown and look, but the middle-aged doctor was asking me another question.

"Did someone force you to do this?"

"No."

I knew I felt some deep emotion, but it wasn't guilt from removing an unwanted fetus from my body.

"Then why are you crying?"

"I don't know."

My head was spinning with thoughts of all I had to do, and all I put Bruce through, just because I found a young man from California attractive.

After the first kiss with Roger at his basement apartment, several days passed before I returned his call.

"Still need some help?" I asked.

"Sure do. Bruce said you were a little under the weather so I didn't know if you'd be able to."

"What if I meet you at Jerry's Cafe this afternoon at two?"

Jerry's Cafe was a thriving restaurant specializing in home-cooked meals and heavenly pies made by his wife. It was located on a side street just across from the Exchange National Bank, where I worked. I told myself seeing Roger at the restaurant would look like a business meeting. My hot tea and Roger's coffee came in heavy, white ceramic mugs, the kind cafes had had for years. Even when the cups were empty, they gave your hand a comforting, warm feel, and a waitress was always standing around ready to give you a refill. Jerry continued to use these old cups, even when other small restaurants turned to plastic. Roger talked about the program for a while and then folded his hand over mine.

"Are you okay?"

"Yes. Why?"

"I don't believe you. If you're okay, you must've painted half moons under your eyes."

"Roger, let go of my hand. It's nothing. Really."

"It's got something to do with you and Bruce doesn't it?"

I looked into his eyes. They were the same color blue I remembered.

"Everyone in the office knows he's been seeing other women. We couldn't figure out if you knew or not, or if you knew and didn't care."

"I don't know whether I care or not. Sometimes I think if I really knew the details I'd throw up." I looked around. This cafe was smaller than I remembered. Was the waitress ready to refill our cups, or was she trying to listen? If I wanted to continue to talk to Roger, we needed to get out of this place. My daddy could walk in any minute and want to sit down with us.

"I can't talk here."

"Want to come to my place?"

"No."

"Nothing's going to happen. I think you need a shoulder right now."

Tears rolled down my face. "Okay, but I can't stay long."

He laid enough money on the table to cover our bill. We went out the back door and walked across the parking lot next to the grain elevator looming over my car. The drive to Roger's apartment was short, and, once inside, he led me over to the couch and took both my hands into his. He sat silently for a long time as my tears flowed freely. He put his arms around me and I laid my head on his shoulder.

"He's not worth it, you know. You're such a free spirit, why do you let him do this to you?"

My composure was completely gone. "I don't know. I don't think he means to hurt me."

Roger put both his arms around me. I started to cry again and he kissed me. I didn't object when his tongue slid into my mouth. He picked me up and carried me to a windowless bedroom. Yanking off an old, yellow chenille bedspread, he laid me down on the bed and sat beside me, stroking the side of my face softly with the back of his hand.

"I don't want to do anything you don't want to do," he said.

The insides of my thighs ached. My breath came in short gulps. I hoped I wasn't going to pass out. As he pulled my shirt over my head, my protest sounded more like a moan than a scream. I decided I was more capable than Roger of undoing my bra. I watched as his clothes slid off a little more quickly than mine. His chest was warm and I wrapped my arms around this body that was new to me. The trains in my head weren't telling me anything and even if they were I wasn't listening. He was a strong, young, athletic lover, and afterwards, he held me in his arms. Making love with him was like a shot of adrenalin mixed with two parts ego. I didn't want to think about whether this might ever happen again. I kissed him again, but neither of us said anything.

I left in a hurry to pick up Heather from preschool.

"Mommy, look what I made."

"Oh, that's a great picture. Who's it supposed to be?"

"You and daddy. You have the long hair and daddy has the glasses."

I thought to myself, "That's all I need, a husband who's obviously fooling around with someone else after dark, me having a romance in the afternoon with a younger man, and my child drawing a picture of her mommy and daddy living happily ever after. What the hell did I think I was doing this afternoon?"

Steven bounced into the house from school just as the phone rang. "I won't be home for supper tonight," said Bruce. "I'm going over the final draft of the Nelson grant."

"I thought you'd finished that."

"I did, but it has to be redone."

"Who's with you?"

"I'll be working by myself most of the evening. Kiss the kids good night for me and don't wait up."

I hung up, but I didn't believe him. I was convinced someone was there with him, but my own guilt prevented me from saying anymore.

"Mom, what's for supper?" asked Steven.

"How about chili dogs?"

"Yeah!" exclaimed Steven.

"Yeah!" said Heather, who was always Steven's echo.

I thought to myself, "At least the kids approve of me."

That night, I put on too many covers to compensate for Bruce's absence. I cried until no tears were left. The trains kept carrying the same messages. Where was Bruce? Why had I kissed Roger? Why couldn't I do anything on my own? I didn't want to take the medication Dr. Sahni had prescribed, but long after midnight, I gave in and chugged a couple of pills. At some point, Bruce slid into the bed beside me. The alarm clock awoke both of us.

"Where were you last night?"

"At the office, like I told you. Putting the final touches on a grant seems impossible sometimes."

"I called your office, but no one answered."

"Well, I was there. Sometimes if the calls go through the switchboard at the front desk and there's no one there, it doesn't transfer like it should."

While he went to shower, I decided to stay in bed for the rest of the day. I didn't have to go to work. Maybe, if I stayed in bed all my problems would disappear. When he came back from the bathroom, I told him what I wanted him to do.

"All you have to do is drop Steven off at school. The carpool picks Heather up for the Y today."

"Okay. Do you have the flu?"

"No."

"Have you taken your medicine?"

"Yes."

I limited myself to one-word answers. I wanted him out of the house as soon as possible. I wanted to crawl back under the covers and hide. But my day in bed did nothing for me but make me want to spend the next day there, too. The second afternoon, I heard my bedroom door creak. I looked up to see my neighbor, Suzy, peeking her head in.

"I didn't hear the doorbell."

"I didn't want to wake you. Bruce was concerned. He wanted me to check on you, see if you were doing okay, if you needed anything."

Suzy dyed her hair a mouse-brown color. She wore glasses that never slipped on her nose, and her face looked like a cosmetic ad for flawless beauty. Her husband couldn't afford the clothes with the kind of labels she wanted, so she went to her parents whenever she wanted to go shopping.

"Can I change your sheets or anything? What if I fluff your pillows?"

She leaned over and pushed at my pillows with her spindly arms. Her perfume was overpowering and made me sick. It was the same scent that was in our car. Instantly, I knew why Bruce had sent her.

"Suzy, do you always wear that kind of perfume?"

"Oh, yes. It's kind of my signature. I even wear it to my boys' ball games."

Suddenly, I had figured out what was going on: Her husband drove a truck and was often gone for two or three days at a time.

"Get out of here," I screamed. "You bitch, get out of here before I call the cops!"

"Oh, Jo Carroll, you're so sick. Let me call Bruce, or maybe you need a doctor."

I picked up the glass of water on the floor and hurled it at her.

"You fucking bitch! Get out of here! Get out of here!" She ran out of the room and, by the time the front door slammed shut, sobs racked through my entire body. Unable to control myself, I thought I was going to faint. I reached for the phone and dialed Bruce's number.

"I think you'd better come home right now."

"Is something wrong? I have a ton of papers to go through today."

"Just come home, right now."

"Are the kids okay?"

"Yes. This has nothing to do with the kids."

"Jo Carroll, you're being unrealistic. If this isn't an emergency I'll be home in a couple of hours. If you're going to lie in bed all day, one of us has to bring home a paycheck." He hung up without another word.

Instantly, I had strength and boundless energy. I got up and dressed, changed the sheets and put in a load of dirty laundry before the carpool arrived with Heather.

"How was your day, sweetie?" I lifted her up to sit on the kitchen counter.

"I don't know why they call it a 'carpool' if you don't get to wear your swimming suit."

"Maybe when you're older they'll let you swim at the indoor pool and then you can wear your swimsuit under your parka. Now, why don't you go play in the backyard and wait for Steven. He should be home in a few minutes, then the two of you can walk up and talk to Grandpa.."

My parents lived five houses up the hill. In the winter my father was home early. He'd contracted to build most of the houses in our subdivision, and he loved being close to the kids. I didn't know if he was prouder of his construction or his grandchildren, as he gave them equal time.

I still didn't know what I was going to say to Bruce. Getting mad and yelling was unlike me. When the phone rang, I expected the caller might be Bruce with an excuse why he wouldn't be home tonight.

"Jo Carroll?" said Roger. "I haven't heard from you for several days. I hope everything is all right."

"I'm sorry. I have to go, Roger," I told him.

"No, wait a minute. I hope I didn't overstep my bounds the other day. It was one of those things that happen. I'm sorry."

Nobody had apologized to me in a long time. I lost my struggle for control and the tears began to flow.

"Are you all right? Are you crying? It was no big deal."

"No, I'm fine. My mind is just somewhere else right now."

"I was really serious about the classes."

I drew a deep breath, desperately trying to maintain some composure. "I'll call you back tomorrow," I said. My hand shook as I hung up. My head filled with racing trains. I could feel the uneven clickity-clack of rough tracks. My head, my whole body, ached.

The phone rang again and, this time, the caller was my mother. I had to maintain control to have a calm, rational discussion with her.

"Jo Carroll, your daddy and I would like to keep the kids for supper and sleep over. You know we always keep PJs here for them, so that's no problem."

"Okay, mom, but listen, make them eat some supper before they get dessert."

"You know I always make them eat right. By the way, I saw Suzy on the street and she said you hadn't been feeling well. Why don't you pick up the phone sometimes and call your mother. I shouldn't get information like that from a neighbor. It's not like I live in another country."

"I know, mom, I'm fine now. Don't worry." I tried to keep the edge from my voice.

"Is it the medicine that foreign doctor gave you?"

"No, mother. It's not the medicine. I was just a little tired. It'll be wonderful if you and daddy keep the kids tonight. Thanks."

I wiped away the remaining tear, and turned to find myself face to face with Bruce.

"I want you to take your medicine and go to bed. I'll take care of the kids," he said.

"The kids are at my folks, I'm not sick and you can just go to hell!"

"I don't understand you. I sent Suzy over here to help you and you turn into a raving wild woman. I think you're really going crazy, off your rocker."

"I feel better now than I've felt in a long time. Don't you dare tell me I'm crazy! You send your lover over here to try and find out what's wrong and I catch on. You're crazy for thinking I'm so stupid."

Bruce covered his mouth with one hand and laughed. I picked up the closest object on the counter and threw it with as much anger as I had ever known. The butcher knife stuck three inches into the kitchen wall. I let out a scream and pulled on my hair so hard with both hands that strands were left between my fingers.

Bruce went to the wall and touched the knife, making sure it was real. With one hand on the wall, and the other on the handle of the knife, he worked it out of the wall with up and down motions. He pricked his finger with the tip that had just been withdrawn and a small drop of blood appeared. He put his tongue to his finger, tasting the blood and shook his head. Deep sobs came from my throat, and then nothing.

We didn't speak to each other. He went into the living room and turned on the TV. I went to the bedroom, lay down on the bed and stared at the ceiling.

An hour passed, and Bruce stood in the doorway. "I guess we ought to talk about this."

"What makes you think you can talk to me? I'm crazy, remember?"

"You know I don't really think you're crazy. Maybe a little upset, a little depressed, but never crazy. As long as you take your medicine and get plenty of rest, you'll be just fine."

"Bruce, that's not the problem and you know it."

"What do you mean?"

"I mean Suzy!"

"You're imagining things."

"Give me a little credit. I'm depressed, not dumb."

We stared at each other for a long time. He wore glasses as thick as Coke bottles, and I could never seem to remember the color of his eyes from one day to the next. Finally, his gaze dropped to the floor.

In a low voice he said, "What do you want to know?"

I lunged at him from the bed, screaming. He tried to put his arms around me, but I beat on his chest with my fists as hard as I could. His arms caught me and I collapsed, sobbing. We sat on the floor, neither of us knowing what to do. I didn't want to hear the details of his affair, and he didn't want to tell me. The pain in my chest was so deep and so intense I thought I was having a heart attack.

He began to kiss my ear. He wanted to make love and go to sleep, as if he could erase all that had happened. But Bruce went to bed alone, and I scrubbed the kitchen from top to bottom. I was not a clean-freak, but I had to keep my mind and body occupied. I was almost finished with the floor, and the fumes of Mr. Clean were beginning to eat through the outer layers of my eyeballs.

I looked up and saw where Bruce had put the knife on the counter. It had come with a set of knives an unknown cousin had given us as a wedding present. Harry had taught me how to sharpen it. I didn't want anyone to see it. I couldn't stand the thought of using it to cut a chicken or dice a steak again. I took a rag I had been using on the floor and wrapped the knife in it. Then, I found some newspaper to wrap around the rag. It looked the way my mother was forever wrapping her garbage. My knife package found its place in the middle of the trash barrel.

I think I could have killed Bruce, or myself, or, perhaps, both of us. I certainly had no remorse at how close the butcher knife had come, but I couldn't stand to touch it another time.

Just before dawn, I crawled into bed and slept next to Bruce, but I felt further apart than I had ever dreamed possible.

The next morning, Saturday, was business as usual. By the time I got up, Bruce was puttering around down in the basement.

"Don't you think we ought to get the kids? It's almost 11."

"Are you going to tell them?"

"Tell them what? That their father doesn't love me? That he likes Timmy's mother better than he does me? I'm not telling anyone, but you have to stop. You have to promise to stop seeing her. You can't see her ever again."

"Okay. I'll call her and tell her."

"No. You can't call her, you can't see her. Nothing. It's over."

"Be reasonable. I have to tell her."

"I'm being completely reasonable. I'm not serving you with divorce papers. I don't want you ever to talk to her again."

"That's impossible. She and her husband come over to our house all the time."

"Not any more, they don't."

"All right, fine, if that's what you want."

"And I don't want you to touch me for a long time. Not until I say I'm ready. And I can't guarantee how long that will be."

"What if I say 'no?'"

"Then I want a divorce."

His eyes began turning funny colors behind his glasses, and I realized he was crying. "I didn't mean to hurt you," he whispered.

After the first time Roger and I made love, we no longer limited ourselves to his apartment. We made love in the park on the moonlit grass. Once, we stripped naked and made love in a farmer's creek. If we were in the privacy of his apartment, we sometimes smoked a joint. This was the '70s, the time of free love, and, if I couldn't be in San Francisco, I was going to wear flowers in my hair in Atchison.

When I put on my favorite plaid skirt, I couldn't button it. I stepped on the scale and saw I had gained 10 pounds. I blamed the extra weight on the medication Dr. Sahni had put me on. Then, I missed a period, and vomited two mornings in a row. I didn't have to see a doctor to know I was pregnant. I called Dr. Brown's office and made an appointment. I didn't tell anyone.

"Well, Steven and Heather are going to have someone to play with," he said, handing his instruments to his nurse.

I closed my eyes. Roger was a clean young man. I knew I didn't have any diseases. AIDS was years away from scaring everybody. I never even thought about pregnancy. Roger must have assumed I was on birth control pills. I had tried them, but they had too many complications. I had also tried an IUD, but shortly before I met Roger, I had it taken out because of bleeding. I wasn't having much sex with Bruce, so I'd picked up some contraceptive foam in the drug store. Sometimes, I used it with Bruce, sometimes I didn't. I never used any contraceptive with Roger. After all, free love didn't have any consequences and the boxcars on my trains were filled with so much crap, the thought of getting pregnant just seemed to be sidetracked.

The only sexual advice my mother had ever given me while I was in high school suddenly echoed in my mind. "Don't do something with a boy you shouldn't or you'll live to regret it the rest of your life," she said.

"Dr. Brown, could I speak to you privately?

He lifted his eyebrows. "What's the problem?"

"Bruce and I don't want any more children."

"Why didn't you go to Wayne?"

"He might not understand."

"And you think I do?"

"Yes."

"Does Bruce know yet?"

"No!"

"You have to tell him," he said, firmly, but fatherly. I wondered if he had this rapport with all his patients, or if he was treating me differently because his daughter and I had roomed together at college one summer.

"I'll tell him tonight. I was just scared. I wanted to be able to tell him what we can do about it."

Dr. Brown wrote a note on a piece of his stationery and handed it to me. "You don't know how lucky you are. Kansas has just passed new laws regarding abortion, and as long as you can get statements from two different physicians that the pregnancy will endanger your health, you can have a legal abortion. I'll give you a letter and you can probably get one from the psychiatrist you're seeing. I'd recommend you go to the KU Med Center in Kansas City. A lot of the smaller hospitals, like in Atchison, can't get permission from their boards to do them. And, well, you might not want all the talk that this town can generate."

I left his office relieved, but I didn't know how I was going to tell Bruce. What if he questioned me too much? Could I pull it off? I sent the kids to my parent's house for dinner and sat down to wait for his car to pull into the driveway.

"Bruce, could I talk to you for a minute?"

"Can it wait? Dad asked me to come help him move a piece of furniture."

"No, it can't wait."

"What's wrong? You look a little tired. Are you okay?"

I took a deep breath and realized I loved Bruce, and I might be ruining our marriage. "I'm pregnant."

"Are you sure?"

"Yes, I went to Dr. Brown today."

"I thought that foam you were using was supposed to be pretty reliable."

"I thought so, too."

"We haven't made love that many times lately. When's the due date?"

I hadn't even bothered to ask Dr. Brown that question and I ignored Bruce's.

"I don't want this baby. Our marriage is holding on by a thread now. I couldn't handle a pregnancy."

"Maybe it would bring us closer together."

"That's no way to save a marriage and you know it."

"Do you want an abortion? Do you think we can get one?"

When he said "we" I knew I was home free. We were together. Maybe we still had a future in all this mess. "Brownie gave me this name and number at the KU Med Center."

Bruce put his arms around me, the greatest sign of affection he had shown me in months. He would never need to know he probably hadn't had anything to do with the fetus to be aborted. We went to bed that night and held each other, too scared to do anything else.

At KU Med, two women had shared the room at the hospital with me. One was an unmarried teenager, and the other a married woman with too many years between her children. As I lay in the bed between them, they talked across me about how the abortion would change their futures. The teenager could finish her education, and the older woman wouldn't have to deal with another baby. I didn't know what was going to happen to me. The abortion had messed with my head, more than my body. I hadn't worried about the actual procedure, but what if, somehow, Bruce found out the truth? Would he leave me? Would he take the children with him? Could I support myself financially if I had to? Could I feed and clothe my children without his help?

The middle-aged doctor asked me another question. "Is there someone here to pick you up?"

"Yes."

He looked at the skinny, blond nurse who had accompanied him into the room, then glanced at his watch. "Dismiss her."

The ride home from the hospital with Bruce was bumpy and quiet. Every few minutes, he'd ask me if I felt okay, and every few minutes, I'd feel guilty about not telling him he didn't have anything to do with this. Then, his tone changed.

"I had an interesting call yesterday from a guy down in Mississippi. They're getting ready to build a bunch of housing for people who got wiped out in a hurricane. He wanted to know if I could come to work for them right after the first of the year. What do you think?"

I let out a squeal, "It's perfect, Bruce! It would give us a fresh start, a new beginning. We could go where nobody knows anything about us and just start over. We could get away from both our families and just be on our own."

"Well, I don't know how perfect it'll be, but we should consider the offer. It's a place called Gulfport, a little town on the water. The money is better than here, but they can't promise the job would last more than a year."

After parking in our driveway, Bruce came around to help me, pulling me toward him.

"What do you think? Should we give it a try?" he asked.

"I think we should give ourselves another try and Mississippi might not be a bad place to start. Do it."

As soon as Bruce left for work the next morning, I called Roger. "I need to see you."

"Sure. Come on over. I got some great stuff. A friend of Alan's brought it back from California night before last."

We took a walk from his apartment to the river. The path was overgrown with weeds, and littered with soda and whiskey bottles covered with ants scrambling for bits of anything that would keep them alive.

I began telling Roger I had taken a pregnancy test, but he became furious and interrupted.

"I thought you were on The Pill."

"No, I couldn't take it."

"Why? You're not Catholic. Goddamn you! I can't believe this. You stupid little bitch."

4 Magnolia Blossom Special

Here I was, in the middle of a parking lot covered with seashells, instead of gravel. Millions of seashells lay everywhere I looked.

This wasn't Mississippi. It was Heaven.

I reached down, scooped up a handful of shells and put them in my pocket. With so many, no one would ever miss the few I'd taken. In the middle of January, I could hardly believe we had left two feet of snow behind in Kansas to move to Mississippi. Only days before, the movers had come and taken our possessions south. We said goodbye to our parents. My daddy was more than upset. He kissed and hugged the kids "one last time" at least 100 times.

When he leaned into the car to give me one more farewell kiss, he said, "Jo Carroll, I can't stand for you to leave. I'll never see you again."

"Don't be silly, Daddy. It's not the end of the earth. It's only Mississippi."

Gulfport had the greenest foliage I'd ever seen, and the white, sandy beach ran along the ocean. Everyone kept telling me this was not really the ocean, just the Gulf of Mexico. But I grew up in Kansas, and it looked and smelled like the ocean to me.

Bruce and I were going to go out to dinner with a bunch of people he worked with at his new job. He took my hand and I followed him into the restaurant. Our table was near the window. I missed most of the first half of the conversation from staring outside, trying to see what the water looked like in the moonlight.

"Jo Carroll, are you enjoying the climate? Do you think you can get used to living down here?" asked Mu Lie, one of Bruce's new coworkers. She was perfectly put together and elegant. Her black hair was pulled into a bun, accenting her dark eyes.

"Do you like the food here?"

Answering all her questions at once, "Yes, yes, and yes!" I said.

I wanted to tell her I'd found Paradise.

Bruce and I had moved into a large, partially finished house just a block from the beach. I'd never seen anything like the white brick with white mortar oozing out, accented with bright, pink trim and pink double doors leading to an entry with a white marble floor and a white brick fireplace. The master bedroom had a king-sized bed, complete with red velvet headboard and spread. The room was the size of a roller rink. The place even had a little guest cottage in back. I thought a prostitute might still be hiding in one of the back closets, but actually, the property was owned by a couple who made millions selling Amway. They rented this castle for less than the payments so they'd have a quiet place to retire in their old age. As we moved in, Steve and Heather ran in and out, asking a million questions,

"Is this our bathroom? All to ourselves?"

"Can we go to the beach every day?"

"Who lives in that little house out back?"

"Do we have to go to school right away?

Then, a different voice surprised me.

"Hi! I'm Linda, your next-door neighbor!"

A woman, a few years younger than me, a little too plump, with tangled, blond hair and friendly blue eyes, came in with three children trailing after her like ducklings.

"Why don't you come over and I'll tell you anything you need to know," she said. "You can't possibly want to unpack any more boxes today."

"Not really, but I need to. How about tomorrow?"

"That's great. Just come over whenever you want. If my kids get in the way today, just send them home. And don't let the dog scare you. Boots would just lick you to death."

Her tan-and-white boxer dog, Boots, followed her home, but the kids stayed.

Bruce had been helping one of the movers set up Steven's bed, but he came over to me after Linda left.

"Who's that?" he asked.

"Our friendly next-door neighbor."

"She looks awful."

"Oh Bruce, if a woman doesn't have the right-sized hips, you think she's terrible. Give her a break."

"You give her a break. I'll be at work tomorrow."

I hated the stacks of boxes the movers had left, but I had a good feeling that Gulfport was going to be a new start. My trains had a destination. The kids were full of energy. Bruce seemed anxious about his new job, and the people were making a fuss over him. I had never felt better. I'd even stopped reaching for the little white pills.

Linda's kids went home, and our kids, exhausted from all the running around and excitement of moving, fell fast asleep in their bedrooms. No noises came from anywhere. That huge bed waiting for us. Nothing to unpack, nothing to set up.

"I think we ought to try it out, don't you?" Bruce asked. We undressed and lay down, looking up at the red velvet, tufted eight-foot headboard looming over us.

"Think it will fall down?"

"Not if we move to the other end of the bed."

The tension of the trip, not to mention the past months, dissolved in the passion of the night. The bed had a slightly musty smell, a smell I soon came to associate with anything that had been in the South over two months.

The next morning, Bruce yelled from our bathroom.

"If we ever get a divorce, you get the kids and I get conjugal rights."

I laughed.

I had a busy day. Not only did I have plenty of unpacking, but I had to enroll the kids in school, get to the grocery store, and I wanted to have time left over to stop at Linda's.

The school, appropriately called "Mississippi City," sat in a peaceful setting with magnolia trees lining the sidewalk. Steven went into the second grade without a murmur. He was a little shy, but the pretty, black-haired teacher took his arm and led him right into the classroom.

The room was located on an outside passageway and I could watch through the windows and see her introducing him to each student. He would be fine.

Heather had been enrolled in kindergarten in Atchison, but Mississippi schools began with first grade. I wanted to put my daughter in the first grade. I knew she was smart enough to do the work, and I wished not to have any children at home.

"I'd be willing to give it a try," said the principal. Her Southern drawl sounded strange to me. "But you'll have to talk to the teacher. It's her last year before retirement, and I know she doesn't want any extra hassles in the classroom."

"I'm sure Heather wouldn't be a hassle. When can I talk to her?"

"Right now. Let me introduce you."

Heather pulled on my hand.

"Will I get to go to school, mommy? I promise, I promise I won't be a hassle."

"Of course you get to go. Mommy just has to talk to the teacher first."

Outside the first-grade door, a poinsettia grew as tall as the roof, its blooms almost blocking the door. We knocked and an elderly woman in a practical, dark-colored dress appeared.

"Yes?"

"This is Mrs. Wallace. She's here to talk to you about enrolling her daughter in your first grade."

"I already have a full classroom. I don't see how I can take her. This is the middle of the school year."

"She's been in an advanced kindergarten and she can read," I pleaded.

"I can read," Heather interrupted. "I can read my brother's books."

"I don't have time to take her today. Bring her back tomorrow for a two-week trial, but if things don't work out she'll have to start over next year. You understand?"

"Oh, yes ma'am. Thank you."

I'd only lived here for a few days, but I'd already learned the words, "Yes ma'am" could work wonders.

I hit the local grocery store, Winn-Dixie, to stock up on canned goods, but, before I could unpack them, Linda was on my doorstep with her youngest daughter, Carol.

"Why don't you take a break and come over?"

I hesitated only a moment.

"I guess everything will still be here when I get back..."

Heather and I followed Linda, who carried Carol sidesaddle on her hip, between the crushed branches of the azalea bushes, down the path leading to her house. Boots met us as we entered through the rear patio doors. I was shocked by what I saw inside. My housekeeping left a lot to be desired, but this house was the pits. Toys lay scattered all over. An odor of cigarette smoke and soiled diapers hung in the air. The room was strewn with clean and dirty clothes and the walls had obviously been decorated by the children.

"Mae," Linda yelled, "Y'all come get Carol."

A tall, skinny, black woman appeared in the doorway. As Linda introduced me to her housekeeper, I tried not to stare. What on God's earth did this woman do?

Mae padded over to Carol and gathered the chubby, dark-haired child in her arms. Then, she put her hand out to Heather.

"Ya wan' ta come play too, honey?"

"Mommy?"

"Go ahead, you'll have fun and I'll be right here if you need me."

The three of them disappeared and I soon found out Linda had a wealth of vital information to share. She told me where to buy the correct brand of peanut butter, where the public schools were—although her kids went to the best private schools—what TV channels had the best news and where to shop for clothes that didn't look like Midwestern ski outfits. She never mentioned the mess in the house, but she did tell me Mae worked for her full time and could watch the children if we wanted to go to lunch.

We went to lunch the next day at the Broadwater Marina, just across the street from the Broadwater Beach Resort, with its wide, arched canopy, where movie stars and politicians mingled. I felt like a native when I didn't put the shells from the driveway in my pocket.

Linda requested a table overlooking the water. As we followed the maitre d' to the table, I tried not to stare at the huge diamond on my new friend's hand. I was sure I hadn't seen it yesterday. And her expensive summer suit and up-swept hair gave no hint of the casual, next-door neighbor I thought I was going to lunch with.

Linda lit a cigarette as soon as we were seated, and the waiter, handing us the menus, asked if we would like a drink. Atchison had hardly prepared me for ordering drinks before lunch and I hesitated. Linda ordered a Bloody Mary, and the waiter turned to me.

"And you, ma'am?"

"The same."

The only drink I could remember the name of was a gin and tonic and I didn't know if you were supposed to order one before lunch.

Waiting for the drink, I asked to see Linda's ring. It was big and beautiful, and classy and gaudy, all at the same time. Sort of like Linda, I thought, as I looked at her.

"Isn't it gorgeous?" she asked. "I inherited it from my father. Alfred would never give me anything like that. He's too tight. I'm having a shrimp salad. What would you like?"

I looked at the tall, white menu and couldn't even find the shrimp salad. In fact, I'd never tasted shrimp salad. All the shrimp in Kansas came in fried, flat, round pieces with tails.

"That sounds good, I'll have one too," I said.

"So, your husband's office is on the Sea Bee base. He's not military is he?"

She continued talking before I'd finished shaking my head "no."

"I didn't think so. You don't look like that kind to me. My family is from New Orleans. Uptown New Orleans."

Linda paused.

"Have you ever been there?"

"I don't know. Is Uptown part of the Quarter?"

Linda giggled a funny little laugh and leaned back in her seat while the waiter placed our drinks in front of us. Two shrimp salads, she told him and she lifted her glass to me.

"To our new friendship."

"To my first friend in the South."

Our glasses clinked.

"Well, now, where were we? Oh, yes. Uptown is an exclusive area in New Orleans where the wealthy live."

Linda giggled again.

"That's not exactly right, but it's an old historical district where lots of rich people still live in huge houses. My sister has one. I'll show you some day. I have another sister in Kansas. Didn't you say you were from Kansas?"

Again, I only had time to nod.

"Her husband is doing his internship there. After he's through they'll move down here some place and live in a gorgeous house. I'll probably be stuck in this dump the rest of my life."

I didn't have the slightest idea what she was talking about. We sat, sipping drinks before lunch at a restaurant with a maitre d', while a maid looked after the kids in a house overlooking the Gulf of Mexico. I stole another peek at her ring. I must be missing something.

"Linda, it's beautiful here. Why don't you like it?"

"Oh, this is a hick town and I'll never get out. Wait till you meet Alfred. Then you'll see what I mean. We own a furniture store, but it'll never make any money. When I grew up, I never had to worry about anything. I went to school at Newman, drove my own convertible. Now, Alfred won't let me spend money on anything."

Trying to relate to something she was saying, I asked, "Is Newman a Catholic school?"

This time, she didn't giggle, she let out a belly laugh.

"No, just the best, most expensive private school in New Orleans, probably the whole South. Before the turn of the century it was a Jewish Orphanage. You know I'm Jewish? Really, only part Jewish."

"How can you be part Jewish?"

"My mother wasn't born Jewish. She converted. My father was Jewish. My father died when I was four and my mother died of cancer when I was a teenager. I slept in the same room with her. It was terrible. When I went to college, I was just looking for someone to marry. I wish I'd looked around a little longer."

"Why? What's wrong with your husband?"

"You won't ask that after you meet him." Her giggle came back. "Oh, I love him and all that dumb stuff. He's just not what I wanted to end up with. Just wait. You'll see."

Our salads were served and I was grateful. I didn't like hearing about other people's marital problems and I was afraid she'd expect me to talk about my marriage, too. And, I was hungry.

The next few days passed routinely and uneventfully. Bruce went to work, the kids went to school and I unpacked boxes and filled the kitchen cupboards. Linda helped me discover pecan rice, kidney beans, eggplant, artichokes, and cookbooks with recipes calling for cayenne pepper.

She made regular visits to my house, leading her kids through the azaleas. After supper one evening, I started to return a dish of hers and ran into a strange man. He frightened me. He wore old Madras shorts and a T-shirt barely covering his belly. I didn't think anyone used the shortcut but our two families.

"You must be Jo Carroll." His voice was deep and his complexion was very dark. "I'm Alfred."

"Oh, I was just returning this. Could you give it to Linda for me?"

"She's not home. I came home for supper and she and the kids were gone. She knows I like to eat as soon as I get home on Wednesdays because sometimes I go back down to the store and do the books. Is she at your house?" He glared at me. "Do you know where she is?"

"No, I'm sorry."

"If you see her, tell her to come home. I need to eat."

My first impression of him was that Linda was right. He wasn't the greatest. He was rude. Why couldn't he fix himself something to eat?

Before I went to bed, I made a banana cream pie, fixed the kids' lunches and made sure everyone's clothes were laid out for the next day. I wanted everything to be perfect. This was a new start and I was going to make it work. No more vapor days for me.

But perfection didn't last long. At 2 a.m., the phone rang. My mother could barely get the words out between sobs.

"Your daddy died about an hour ago...his heart couldn't take it any more...it just exploded."

I didn't want to believe her. He didn't have a history of heart problems. He'd been depressed about my leaving, but I didn't think anything physical was wrong with him.

Bruce was already awake and holding me before I ended the phone call. I grabbed clothes and started packing. I called Linda and asked her to care of the animals and help herself to the fresh pie. By 6 a.m. we were boarding a plane in New Orleans headed for Kansas. All the way back, the trains in my head repeated his parting words to me, "I'll never see you again. I'll never see you again."

Psalm 23 was recited at his funeral. When I heard "For Lo, though I walk through the shadow of the valley of death, I will fear no evil..." my eyes filled with tears.

The stay in Atchison was short. Saying goodbye to my mother was much more difficult the second time. Without my daddy standing beside her, she looked lonely and afraid. I thought I saw small wisps of white peaking through her head of heavy, black hair. As I reached to brush her hair back from her face, my hand accidentally caught in one of her diamond earrings. She reached for my fingers and held tightly.

"You know, these will be yours someday."

"Mom, I don't even think about things like that. You're going to be wearing them until they're worn out."

I gave her one more tight hug and caught her perfume, "White Linen," mixed with a slight scent of expensive clothes that need to be dry-cleaned. I had to rely on Dr. Sahni's magic pills to leave her.

I don't know precisely when, but I stopped reliving my father's funeral long before the shock treatments started. His death was so unexpected, painful, and filled me with so much guilt. I had no need to remember any more. His body was buried atop a hill outside Atchison. Someday, my mother will be buried beside him, making two graves I won't visit. His spirit and memories are deep within me, not in that cold ground.

After the funeral, Bruce and I decided to drive the old station wagon we had left in Atchison back to Gulfport. It was painted school-bus yellow, and we shoved all our luggage and anything we had left behind scarcely more than a month ago into it. Steven turned eight on the trip back. We stopped in Little Rock and spent the night with friends of Bruce's, John and Kaye.

We arranged to have a surprise birthday cake. John and Kaye were a prosperous couple. Their two new cars, matched in model, different only in color, sat beside each other in the driveway. Inside, a dark oak Mediterranean-style dining table was set with china for Steven's birthday. The gas logs in their fireplace made their living room look as manicured as their lawn must have looked in the summer. Their modest house looked perfect. John, who had been one of the first to volunteer for Kennedy's Peace Corps, was starting a successful career as the assistant city manger in Little Rock. They didn't have any children, but they had that "TV family" look I hoped we could achieve in Mississippi. The magazines were in the magazine holder, the towels were folded on the rack in the bathroom, the throw rug by the front door didn't have any wrinkles in it. Everything in this house appeared to always be in sync.

Although I was a thousand miles from Kansas, once I settled on the Coast, I found many of my interests remained the same. In high school, my drama teacher had pulled me from my wallflower position and made me the star of the senior high production of "Our Hearts were Young and Gay." I became hooked on the attention. After high school, some of my favorite escapes from reality had been on the stage of the Atchison Little Theater Productions. And, while some of my friends learned to play bridge, I learned lines for my current production. In Gulfport, I tried out and landed a small part in a theater production. And, when that was over, I immediately found myself in rehearsals for a Biloxi production of "Cat on a Hot Tin Roof." I had thrown away Dr. Sahni's little white pills. I had lots of energy. My trains were on a positive track.

We even went sightseeing locally, but never stayed overnight anywhere without the kids.

"Bruce, New Orleans would be so much fun. Do you think we could find a few days to go there by ourselves?"

"Why? Besides, you don't have anybody to leave the kids with."

"We need to get away, just the two of us. It would be romantic. I'm sure Linda would keep them just overnight."

"We'll see."

Bruce began to travel on business more. The traveling bothered me, because I felt we were growing close and I didn't want him to be gone so much. We were rediscovering what we had in common. Years ago, when we met at a party at his apartment in Lawrence, just blocks from the University of Kansas, the physical attraction was what had first drawn us together. During a summer session, he decided to drop out of college after his classes ended. I was taking classes at nearby Baker University, a Methodist college. I was floundering about what to do next. During our first trysts, we discovered we liked to laugh together, to take impromptu rides in the country, walk in the woods, and just joke about life in general. I think our time together was a way to get away for the both of us, so we didn't have to make choices about the future. When we went back to our parents' homes in Atchison after the summer sessions were over, I found my daddy had bought a boat. He and mom were spending their weekends at Sugar Lake, just across the Missouri River from Atchison. Bruce and I joined them. I learned to water ski, as my new love steered the boat. We both liked the feeling being on the water gave us, which was an extension of the thrill of making love.

Our lovemaking and closeness to the water had returned in Gulfport. I collected carton ends from the Kool cigarettes Bruce smoked, sent them in with a small check, and received a Styrofoam sunfish sailboat complete with a giant "Kool" spelled out in green on the sail. The boat was light enough to carry from our house to the beach, and large enough for both Bruce and I to sail in the shallow waters of the Gulf. We laughed, realizing we had to remember to keep the drain plug in, and quickly learned the difference between a tiller and a rudder. We tasted saltwater many times as the boat tipped before we could bring it around. Sometimes, we took the kids with us, enjoying a picnic on the beach. We tried not to dunk the children in the water too much as we inched up and down the shoreline in the shallow tide. I didn't smoke, but later, in bed, after making love, when Bruce lit up one of his long, thin Kools, I'd take a drag and inhale memories of the ocean.

We always liked going out to eat at little inexpensive restaurants, and we discovered an Italian place on Pass Road in Biloxi, where red-checkered cloths covered tables lit with wine bottles holding an ever-dripping candle. Bruce stuck to the meatballs and spaghetti with red sauce, and I devoured pasta topped with sautéed oysters, fresh from the Gulf. Neither one of us drank much, but occasionally Bruce would have some bourbon, and I would sip Chianti.

Between business trips, Bruce and I took advantage of the big house and gave parties. He invited the people he worked with. They were quiet and serious, and their conversations centered on inexpensive housing projects for Hurricane Camille victims. I invited my theater groups. They danced in the foyer, necked in the bedroom and drank in the kitchen. I came to adore Gordon, the director of "Cat," and his Southern wife, Anna. She was from the Mississippi Delta and sounded like she drank honey every morning for breakfast.

But Linda was the one I saw and gossiped with every day. She was always over at the house, and didn't like Bruce any more than I liked Alfred.

"I don't know how you put up with him being gone all the time. If you ask me, I think he travels more than the U.S. Mail."

"Oh, it's okay. It's just part of the job. He has to do on-site inspections."

Actually, I hated Bruce being gone, but I was loving life in the South. I fell in love with the humidity, which softened my skin and curled my hair. I was delighted to learn the huge tree in my front yard was a Magnolia, and I became delirious when it began to bloom.

One afternoon, I settled myself on the red velvet cover of the giant bed and watched the news on TV. A station in Louisiana was showing a very pregnant young woman on the steps of the State Capitol explaining why she should have the right to sell flowers in the French Quarter.

"It's a racket," she said. "I have to have a license, but the big florists have everything wrapped up so tight I can't get one. I couldn't afford one anyway. Now, you tell me, what am I supposed to do?"

She seemed angry, but the reporter remained calm and asked what she planned to do.

"I'm here to get them to change the law so people like me can make a living without having to be wealthy enough to afford a building first."

I didn't know who she was, but I liked her style. I didn't recognize her accent, but this Flower Child certainly wasn't from San Francisco. The next afternoon, while sitting on her patio, dodging Boots and Carol, I mentioned the newscast to Linda. She broke into laughter.

"That's Alfred's sister, Susan. All we ever do is get her out of trouble."

I couldn't imagine the young hippie woman being related to uptight, chauvinistic Alfred. They couldn't have had the same parents.

"Are you sure? She was real pregnant."

"That's Susan. Her baby's due any day."

"She and Alfred seem so different. They don't even have the same accent."

"I don't know where Alfred gets his accent. He was like that in college. I guess he wants to sound like he's from somewhere else."

As soon as I opened my mouth, I knew I'd said the wrong thing. Linda wasn't aware that, at times, I could hardly understand her because her Southern drawl was so thick. And, while her sister-in-law, Susan, slurred her words, she managed to do it with a "twang." When Alfred spoke, he sounded like he'd just come from the East Coast for a visit.

"I guess it's hard to figure out the accents because I don't have one," I told Linda.

"Well, maybe not when you lived in Kansas," she laughed.

Later that afternoon, when I walked through the azaleas to my new home, I realized I had made my own friends here. My trains had passengers on them.

I began to see a lot of Anna. She hadn't been married long, and the couple lived in Gordon's bachelor cottage on the beach. She'd had an interior designer redo the inside, but it was small, and the outside resembled an old, roadside motel. This didn't stop them from entertaining lavishly. Soon, an invitation for one of their parties came in the mail. I knew Bruce was going to be out of town that night, but I accepted anyway. Anna wouldn't care if I came alone.

When I arrived, Mr. James, an old, black man who sometimes worked as their butler, served Oysters on the Half Shell from a gleaming silver tray. Whole strawberries, heaped in a sparking, crystal compote sat on a table waiting to be eaten. Guests clinked delicate glassware, and the champagne flowed.

I sat down on a snow-white couch that only someone without children would dare own. Anna squeezed in next to me.

"I'm so pleased you could come. Is that Bruce out of town again?"

"Yes, he'll be back day after tomorrow."

"I'm glad you didn't sit home alone tonight. Life's too short to spend it waiting on somebody, especially when he's spending all his time with Yankees."

"Anna, I'm a Yankee."

"Gracious me, Jo Carroll. I never thought of you as a Yankee woman."

That was the best compliment she could have given me, and after that, our friendship blossomed. We went to lunch, talked on the phone, sat in bars listening to music, and solved the world's problems.

But Anna worked, and I didn't. The kids were in school all day, Bruce was out of town, and I was bored.

"Bruce, what would you think about my going back to work?"

"Sounds like a great idea."

"What kind of job could I find down here? Do you think I could work in a bank again? I don't think I want to be a teller, though."

I bubbled with energy and enthusiasm, delighted that Bruce hadn't put immediate obstacles in my way.

"Look in the paper and see what kinds of jobs are listed. You'll have to find something where you could be home when the kids get home from school. This isn't Atchison and your mother doesn't live two doors away."

"I could have a housekeeper, like Linda does. Help is cheap here. Even if half of what I made went for the housekeeper, I'd still be ahead. Besides, I get lonely."

"You have the kids. What's there to be lonely about?"

"I get lonely when you're not here. A job would make me feel better."

"So find one. Just make sure the kids are taken care of."

The next morning, I talked over my new plan of action with Linda. She wasn't happy about it.

"What do you want to work for? You can stay home and do anything you want. If you're really bored, there's a lot of volunteer work out there. You won't make much money, and babysitters will take up most of it. Believe, me, I pay Mae a lot, but we couldn't get along without her. We could never afford her if I didn't have money from my father's trust fund. Alfred doesn't make enough to pay her."

"I don't get it. Why do you stay with him, Linda? He doesn't treat you right, he's always angry, always yelling at somebody, and he doesn't make enough money to suit you."

"I don't know. If you think Alfred yells, wait 'till you meet his father. Nothing's ever right, and he yells instead of talking, even when he's not drinking. They never fall very far from the tree, you know? Alfred's not an alcoholic yet, but he will be. Everyone says it runs in families."

"I don't know about that, but I wouldn't live with him if he were the last person on earth. Have you ever thought about a divorce?"

She waved her hand in my direction and giggled.

"Of course not, silly. Besides, there's the kids, the house and the business. Who would get what? I'd just like to get rid of him on Sunday afternoons."

"Why?"

She leaned forward to tell me her secret.

"He always wants to do it, and he'll do it any way I want him to."

Her famous giggle was back.

"That sounds nice."

"It is, except sometimes, frankly, I just as soon watch TV. It's more interesting."

The tone of her conversation made me feel uncomfortable.

"Listen, I gotta go. I need to read the paper. Maybe a job will just pop up."

And, it did. I made arrangements to interview at Coast Federal, a savings and loan office located in downtown Gulfport. I interviewed with Rob Barber, the president, and walked out of the office with the job as his secretary. A job in Paradise. I couldn't wait to get home and tell Bruce.

"That's great, Jo Carroll. That's terrific."

He spun me around and gave me a tight hug.

"I think that's great you want to work. I don't see what some women do all day. Look at what's-her-face next door. All she does is stuff her mouth and watch TV. I don't know what her housekeeper does either, her kids are always in the street when I come home."

"Oh, Bruce. I know you don't like her, but she's awfully nice to me, especially when you're gone. Do you suppose you might be home more next month?"

"Maybe. I don't know. I really don't know how long this job will last. Maybe you'll be the only one with a job soon."

"Are you serious?"

"When we moved down here, we both knew it wouldn't last forever. The government's not as eager to release grant money for housing as it once was. Seems like they think they've solved the hurricane difficulties and the integration dilemma all at once."

"Do you think you could find another job here on the Coast? It's so beautiful, I'd hate to leave."

"You could stay, even if I didn't."

"Without you? Don't be silly. I like it, but not that much!"

"Well, you don't have to worry yet. I forgot to tell you, I have another trip next week. Make sure you have a sitter hired before I leave town if you're going to start that job on Monday."

"I wish you didn't have to go. Linda invited us over for dinner next week."

"Please, don't make any arrangements with them that include me. I can't stand the sight of her and he can't talk about anything but his precious New Orleans Saints. Every other word, it's Archie-this and Archie-that. I had to ask him who he was talking about."

I scurried around to find someone to take care of the kids while I worked. I found Lucy. She had a Jamaican accent, and claimed she could cook, clean, take care of my children, and do it for a price I could afford. She wanted to be able to stay over in the guest house sometimes, because she didn't have her own car, and taking the bus every day was too much. I agreed immediately. Now, I'd have someone to stay with the kids when Bruce and I wanted to go to New Orleans. Lucy's references were almost as good as her cooking, and she started immediately.

A short time passed when, one night, my mother called to ask if she could come for a weekend visit.

"Sure, mom," I said. "You'll love it here. The house is less than a block from the beach. It'll do you good to get out of Atchison for a while."

"Can I bring someone with me?"

"Of course. You can always bring anyone you want to my house."

There was a hesitation on the other end.

"Mom, are you still there?"

"Yes, dear. You don't know who I want to bring. It's your Uncle Joe."

"I'd love to see him. Does he have business in New Orleans or something?"

"No, we've been seeing each other, dating, I guess. We'd like to come down together, as a couple."

I could hear the nervousness in her voice, and I responded quickly. For some reason, I didn't want her to think I disapproved.

"That's fine, Mom, Just tell us when you're coming and we'll pick you up at the airport."

"That's sweet, dear. We're flying into New Orleans, but we're going to rent a car, so you don't have to bother. But, we do want to stay with you."

"I love you, mom."

"Yes, dear. See you soon."

I hung up and plopped down in the nearest chair. Bruce walked in from the living room.

"Guess what?"

"Our new maid has decided to open a restaurant in our kitchen?"

Bruce had discovered Southern food, and thought Lucy was the best thing that had ever happened to our bland meatloaf menu.

"Mom and Uncle Joe are coming for a visit."

"Is he the one who got drunk at your Dad's funeral or the one who kept getting sick to his stomach while his wife hovered over him?"

"The stomach one."

"And he's coming with your mom? How come?"

"She told me that they've been seeing each other. Dating."

"Is he still married?"

"I think so. They want to stay with us."

"That will be interesting. All we have is that king-sized bed in the guest house, I'm not sure I want Lucy to give it up for anyone."

Bruce was getting angry.

"What are we going to tell the kids? That grandma and Uncle Joe are suddenly a hot item?"

"Don't be ridiculous. If we treat it like a normal event, so will the kids. They'll like Uncle Joe. They won't pay any attention to who sleeps with who."

"Is that because so many of your theater friends sleep with whoever they want to, whenever they want?"

"Bruce! What are you talking about?"

"I see them. They're always hanging all over each other. Don't you think I know what's going on? I bet sometimes they go for more than two at a time. Do you ever join them?"

"How could you!"

"I was just wondering."

"Oh, shut up. I don't care what your nasty mind is thinking. She's my mother and I want her to come. I don't care if she brings the milkman. And, if some of my friends sleep around, I don't know anything about it, and you know I don't. So whatever you're trying to say, just cut it out!"

"Look, I'm sorry I brought it up. I know you're not doing anything. I just think your mom has a lot of nerve asking. I bet she wouldn't take him to see your brother."

My brother, Jack, was always the smartest, the brightest child. He was eight years older than me, so he was always "there." I don't have early memories of our relationship, just snippets here and there. I think, mostly, I remember our childhood from the black-and-white reflections of pictures our mother took with her Brownie box camera.

In one, we're both sitting in the grass, and I'm about 4 years old, and holding on tightly to my doll, and he's sitting next to me, with his golden trumpet in his hand. He played the trumpet in the high school band. I played the saxophone. I never got beyond second chair, not even when Jere Pederson graduated a year ahead of me and vacated the seat. Then, Anita Hamel, who was younger than me, got first chair because the band director thought she was better. But Jack played first chair, he was the best. Jack was always the best.

While we were growing up, my maternal grandparents, Harry and Nana, lived across the street. And, although Nana adored both of us, Jack was the best. She had a bright red spot on the bridge of her nose. One day, I asked her what it was, and could the doctor do something to remove it?

"Oh, no," she said. "Your brother accidentally scratched me when he was a little baby, and I'd never do anything to remove the mark. It's a mark of love."

I never had the feeling of protection from my brother when I was growing up, but, one Saturday afternoon, he caught me sitting at the movies holding hands with a boy he didn't approve of. Jack's job was to come retrieve me from the Saturday afternoon matinees at the local movie theater, and that day, he'd come a little early.

"I'm not going to tell mother you were sitting with Larry," he told me.

When my mother and Uncle Joe drove up the driveway several weeks later, I ran to meet them. They flew into New Orleans, spent the night in the French Quarter, and drove over to the Coast. I hadn't seen my mother since my father's death, and I held on to our hug long and tight. She was the first to break away.

"Oh, Jo Carroll, I can't believe I'm here," she said. "Look what the rental agency gave us to drive, a Cadillac El Dorado. They tried to give us a little Pinto, but Joe let them know who he was. Then they changed their minds quickly."

My mother patted his arm affectionately with her right hand and looked at him with her large brown eyes in a way I'd only seen before in old Sophia Loren movies.

Joe was the manager of a steel plant in Kansas City, but in his spare time he dipped into politics. He was currently the mayor of Raytown, a small, suburban town just outside Kansas City on the Missouri side. His blue blazer and gold cuff links, even on a vacation trip, reflected how he viewed his position.

"Mother, I'm going to put you and Uncle Joe in this little guest house we have out back. It's not very big, but it has a new king-sized bed, and we don't have any extra bedrooms in the house. Is that all right?"

I was trying to ask my mother what her current sleeping arrangements were with my uncle without sounding rude, but I was more embarrassed than she.

"Of course," she said. "Anywhere you want to put us. Is that big huge tree in your front yard really a Magnolia? I recognize the leaves, but I've never seen one that tall before."

My mother had skipped over the question of sleeping arrangements as casually as if I were asking her whether or not she wanted her toast buttered. She'd made some choices in her life and they were not to be questioned. Her focus on the tree was real. She walked over to rub the shiny leaves with her fingers.

"These might make a great arrangement on the dining room table," she said. "You could put the blossoms in the middle and the leaves down each side."

Joe brought their luggage into the guesthouse, while my mother and I entered the house through the kitchen.

"Now, we don't want you to cook tonight, we're taking you out to dinner," she said.

"Oh, thanks mom. Bruce should be home a little early tonight and I know just the perfect place. I know you love seafood and it's hard to find a place that doesn't serve good seafood."

"Now, we want it to be a nice place, expense is no problem, and, of course the children will come with us. Where are they? I can hardly wait to get my hands on them. Do they like school here? Does Steven has a place to shoot his BB gun? Is Heather still so crazy about her Barbies? I have a new one for her in the car."

By now, we'd made our way into the giant living room with the terrazzo floors and white fireplace.

"What do you think, mom? I couldn't believe we found such a place to rent and just a block from the beach."

"Joe, we're in here. Oh, it's lovely dear. Do you think you'll buy it?"

I just laughed. "Oh, I have no idea, mom. Here, you two, come and sit down and tell me how you got together. Would you like something to drink?"

"No thanks," Joe answered for both of them as they held hands like teenagers. They talked about the flight down, the beautiful drive along the coast from New Orleans, everything, except why or how they were together.

The kids came bounding in from school and tore into the presents mom had brought them. Bruce came home and we made dinner reservations. Steven and Heather insisted their grandmother sit between them at dinner, while I sat between Bruce and Joe across the table. When the waiter came to take the drink orders, I looked up, surprised when I heard my mother order Cutty and water. She raised her eyebrows and smiled at me.

"Just one of the joys of life your Uncle Joe has taught me," she replied to my unasked question.

We finished with fabulous gooey desserts for the children, coffee for me, the only way I like it—with Kahlua and whipped cream, Baileys for mother and Joe, while Bruce settled for another Pepsi. We called it a night and headed home. I kissed my mother at the door to the guest house and decided at that moment she was more than an adult, and, for whatever she's been through by the sudden death of my daddy, I shouldn't question her actions now.

As Bruce and I got ready for bed, he kept shaking his head.

"I just can't believe your mother brought him here. Isn't he still married?"

"I don't know. I didn't ask her. She's my mother, and I love her, and she seems happy, and that's all that matters to me right now."

We awoke the next morning to sounds of children running and screaming through the house. Linda's three had seen someone go into the guesthouse and had decided to investigate. My mother told me later that she and Joe had awakened to five children, Steven and Heather had decided to wake up Grandma and Uncle Joe, and of course, when the neighbor kids showed up they joined the welcoming party. All five children had gathered around the sleeping guests in the bed and shouted "Boo!" My mother and Joe laughed about the incident for years after they were married.

"When I woke up, I thought I'd entered the land of munchkins," Joe used to say as he slapped his hand on his knee.

The next few days were filled with shopping, dining and trips to the beach. I could see my mother was clearly in love, and my uncle treated her like she was a fragile statue on a pedestal. When my thoughts would occasionally return to memories of my father and mother together, I swallowed hard and tried not to judge my mother. What would my life be like without a husband? Wouldn't I be tempted to reach out to someone who treated me like Joe treated my mom?

Heather clung to my mother when it was time for them to leave.

"Oh, Jo Carroll, can't you put her on a plane to come visit us this summer? We could meet her in Kansas City. She's such a big girl now. Wouldn't you like to come see us, baby doll?"

Spring came and went, and soon the time came for school to be out. Steven was going to a YMCA camp in the Mississippi Delta, and I had decided to let Heather fly to Kansas City, where she could spend a couple of weeks in Kansas with both sets of grandparents. The arrangements were perfect. Bruce and I could sneak over to New Orleans.

We loaded the kids' stuff in the car and took Heather to the airport for her big solo flight to Kansas. We were going to deliver Steven to the Y camp which was located just a couple of miles from Kosciusko, Anna's hometown. She and her husband, Gordon, were going to meet us there and introduce us to Anna's family.

I gave Bruce a little love pat on his behind, but he didn't respond. I thought he must be getting one of his migraine headaches. I had witnessed this debilitating condition since the first week we were married. Often, his father would have to come to our home to administer Bruce a shot. He hadn't had one in a long time.

"Bruce, if you don't feel good, I'll drive."

"No, I'm fine."

I leaned over to kiss him, but he kept his lips pressed together like steel. I touched his forehead with the back of my hand.

"I can take the kids myself, if you're not up to it."

He ignored me, and instead was trying to catch Heather. As she ran around the car door, Bruce threw her up in the air, bringing her down again with a quick hug.

"Daddy's going to miss you. Will you send me a postcard?"

"Sure, daddy. Let's go. Where's my stupid brother? Where's my cat? I don't want Carol to play with my cat while I'm gone."

Steven wasn't talking. Two weeks at a camp, where he didn't know anyone, was not his idea of a good time, and he was the last one to get in the car. After many hugs and kisses at the airport, Heather finally boarded the plane with a giant note pinned to her dress. A friendly stewardess was holding her hand. Once we were back on the road, Steven settled down in the backseat for a nap, I started up a conversation with Bruce.

"How was your trip?"

"What trip?"

"The one you came home from yesterday."

"Okay."

"Do you think we'll be able to live in Gulfport for a while?"

He ignored my question.

"Look at the map and see how far the turnoff is from Kosciusko."

"It's still a long way."

"I know that. I just wanted an idea of how far I have to drive before we turn off."

The tone of his voice told me to stop talking. I read him the map's directions and turned on the radio to my favorite country music. We didn't speak for a long time, then I drew my finger across his leg gently.

"Are you mad about something? Did I do something? You know we don't have to go to meet Anna and Gordon if you don't want to. We could always call and say we're tired or something."

"It's okay. Nothing's wrong."

Steven looked sad when we left him at the camp. He dug one shoe into the dust and wouldn't go anywhere near the kids who were signing up for different activities.

I put my arm around him and tried to reassure him. He wiggled out of my reach and stuck his lower lip out. The time came for us to go. Bruce and I both managed to get a slight hug from him.

"Now be sure to put on plenty of suntan lotion and keep your hat on when you're in the sun," I reminded him as we started to leave.

"I don't want to stay at this dumb camp. I don't know why I couldn't go get on an airplane and go someplace, too. Heather has all the fun."

"Trust me, Steven, by the end of the two weeks, you won't even want to come home."

I kissed the top of his head and we left.

In less than 10 minutes, we were back on the main road to Kosciusko. "Bruce, please, before we get to Anna's, tell me what's wrong."

"Nothing's wrong. You're just imagining things."

"That's not true and you know it."

"I can't talk about it right now."

"Why not? You haven't touched me since you came home yesterday. Please tell me what's wrong. I have to know. It's driving me crazy."

"I don't want to get into it right now. We'll talk tomorrow."

He took my hand and gave it a squeeze.

"Promise?"

"Yes, I promise."

Kosciusko was a small town where the skyline contained only church steeples and the county courthouse tower. The statue on the front lawn of the court house was a Confederate soldier, with the words, "Lest we forget" engraved on its base. I decided I didn't like everything about the South.

Anna's mother was waiting for us on the front porch. Bruce and I both put on fake smiles and followed her into the house. It was filled with family pictures, comfortable, overstuffed furniture and well-worn antiques.

Dinner was at the uncle's home, just a few doors down the street. The front steps led up to a wide porch with a swing at one end, and a wicker table and chairs at the other. The smell of Magnolias couldn't have been heavier. My mind was in two places at once. The warm Southern hospitality surrounding me couldn't be ignored, but I was frantic about what Bruce was going to talk to me about. I was scared of what he might have to say. I glanced into the living room at an antique fainting couch and wondered who had vapor days in this house. I didn't know whether to cling to Bruce's side, or ran to the bathroom.

Instead, I followed the aunt into the kitchen where Anna and the cook were fixing fried chicken for dinner. I shut my mind to whatever was bothering Bruce and inhaled the delicious smells of the kitchen. Rice, string beans and squash all simmered on the stove. Anna was making sweet tea.

"Can you help me with this? Just put some ice in the glasses and take them to the table."

The meal started with Anna's uncle saying grace. We all bowed our heads and joined in with "Amen." Anna's young attorney cousin, his blond, pregnant wife and their squirming 3-year-old were seated across from me at the table. I attempted to make polite conversation. I pushed my food around and asked for seconds of iced tea. I tried to catch Bruce's attention, but he seemed to be preoccupied with the silver flatware. I couldn't do anything, much less eat, until I found out what was his problem.

The evening grew late, and we were too far from home to drive back to the Coast that night, so we stayed at a motel in Kosciusko. I ignored my instincts, and thought of every other thing that could possibly be wrong. Had Bruce lost his job? Did his mother have cancer? Had he gambled our savings away?

"Bruce, please, I know you said tomorrow, but I can't sleep. Tell me what's wrong."

"Just turn over and go to sleep. You'll be fine. I'm too tired tonight."

I started to cry and went into the bathroom to wash my face. I wasn't in there long, but by the time I came out, Bruce was asleep, or at least pretending to be. I crawled into bed beside him and put my arm around him. I felt like I was holding a statue. I cried all night, big gulping, silent sobs, with salty tears running down my cheeks into my mouth. By morning, I felt like one of the trains in my head had run over me.

We dressed in silence, filled the car with gas and started home. Once back on the main road Bruce finally turned to me.

"Do you have any medicine with you?"

I didn't know what he meant.

"For your headache?"

He shook his head "no."

"You mean my stuff? No. I don't have any left. I don't need it anymore. Why?"

"I guess now's as good a time as any to tell you. There's someone else in my life."

Our conversation paused. I didn't want to understand what he meant.

"What do you mean? In your life?"

"I've been seeing another woman."

I think I screamed, I don't remember now, but Bruce pulled over to the side of the road.

"I didn't want to tell you like this."

"How did you want to tell me?"

"Jo Carroll, I don't know what to do about it."

"I do. Just like before. Stop seeing her."

"It's not that simple."

"Do you love her?"

"I don't know."

"Do you love me?"

"Yes, I'll always love you."

"Then it's that simple."

"No, you don't understand. It's more complicated than that."

He pulled back onto the road. This time, my tears were not silent. Finally, I managed the painful question.

"Who is she?"

"You don't want to know."

"Yes, I do. If you don't tell me, I'll find out from somebody else."

"I don't think you know her. Rosemary Hanson."

I turned the name over and over in my head. I didn't remember her at first. Then I thought of a woman from Bruce's office in Atchison who had walked into a restaurant wearing the same dress I had on. Hers was green, mine was blue, but they were from the same Butterick pattern. But she could not be her. I must have the wrong name with the wrong face. She lived in Atchison, and Bruce hadn't been there in months.

"What does she look like?"

"She's hard to describe. Short, blond hair."

"Does she work in Atchison?"

He didn't answer. So, I screamed in his ear.

"Where does she work?"

"You don't have to yell. Nothing's been decided."

"What do you mean 'nothing's been decided.' Are you still seeing her?"

I was still screaming.

"Where? How? When do you see her?"

"I'm going to pull off and get a Pepsi, Do you want anything?"

"When do you see her?"

He didn't answer.

I stared out the window while he pulled in front of a grocery store. He came out with two cold drinks and handed one to me.

"Here, I think you need this."

I opened my car window and threw the full can of soda into the air.

"I want to know where you see her."

"It's not like you think."

"What do you mean, 'it's not like I think?' You just told me you're seeing another woman. What am I supposed to think?"

"We're in the same line of work. I see her at conventions."

"Don't give me that crap. She's a fucking bookkeeper, and you're a housing specialist, or don't you do that any more?"

I tried to make my trains backtrack through every town that Bruce had made trips to in the last six months.

"Was she with you in St. Louis?"

"Jo Carroll, please don't do this to yourself."

The rest of the trip was made in silence. I couldn't get up enough nerve to ask him what I really wanted to know. When we were almost to Gulfport, I finally asked the question.

"Have you ever kissed her?"

"Yes."

My tears began again. All I could do was cry. My chest hurt. I thought I was having a heart attack.

"I don't know what I want to do."

"What does that mean?"

"Just that. I don't know what I want to do. I haven't decided if I want to be with you or go to Rosemary."

I was in shock, afraid to ask any more questions. Both of us had been with lovers in the past, but that was over, or, at least I thought it was. I don't know what I thought. Nothing made sense. I'd felt so good. Now, I seemed to have a funny pressure pushing down on my shoulders. A blackness seeped into me and took over. When I looked up, we were turning into our driveway.

"Did you remember Mu Lie is coming over to fix us supper tonight? She said she'd bring everything. Bet she brings shrimp. I told her that was your favorite."

"Bruce, are you crazy? I can't have anybody over tonight."

"Why not?"

"Look at me. I'm a wreck, inside and out. We have to talk. I can't leave it like this. What am I supposed to do?"

I followed Bruce into the house, my voice increasing in volume with every step.

"What have I done wrong? When will you tell me if you're leaving?"

"You don't get it do you? You haven't done anything. I don't know what I'm going to do. And, in the meantime, we have to just get up every morning and brush our teeth. Nothing's going to happen overnight."

My mind spun. I tried to think of something, anything, I could say to him. I was sure nothing I had ever said to him was as important as the words I would say now, but nothing came out of my mouth.

"Jo Carroll, are you listening to me? We need to pick up the toys the kids left in the living room before Mu Lie gets here. I bet her apartment at Gulf Shores looks like a showplace. I don't want her walking into a mess here."

I spun around and tried to scream "I don't care," but nothing came out of my mouth. I sank to the cold marble floor and sat there waiting for something to change. I didn't think I could take another breath. Everything was getting darker.

I felt Bruce's hands gripping my arms as he pulled me to a standing position.

"What's wrong with you? I didn't say I was leaving you for sure. I'm not going anywhere tonight. In the meantime, we have company coming for dinner. Go splash some cold water on your face. I'll set the table."

For once, I didn't notice the faint rotten egg smell of our well water. After I pressed some powder into the dark circles under my eyes, I hunted in every old purse I could find for one more magic pill. I didn't find any. I was on my own.

The pit of my stomach hurt and a weight pressed on my chest, a knot formed at the top, near my heart. But, when I heard the doorbell, I managed to put on a plastic smile and went out to give Mu Lie a peck on the cheek.

"I've got some fresh, jumbo shrimp I want to fix for you this evening, but first, let me sit down and have a drink with you. Bruce, a little scotch on ice with just a splash of water, please. Oh, Jo Carroll, I didn't bring any flour, but I was sure you'd have some. My goodness, girl, that little trip to take your kids to camp must have worn you out. Don't worry, you won't have to do anything but just sit and enjoy tonight. Treats on me."

"That sounds great. I'm awfully tired."

I tried to lie and smile at the same time. As she talked to me about her home in China, I tried to think ahead about how to answer questions I wasn't even listening to. Suddenly, in the dark madness of my mind, I thought I had the answer to save my marriage.

I grabbed her hand and pulled her face close to mine.

"Will you help me?"

Startled, she looked me straight in the eye and gave my hand an extra tight squeeze and nodded "yes."

Before Bruce could return with the drink, I led her back to the bedroom. With Mu Lie seated motionlessly next to me on the red velvet spread, I folded my arms across my chest and rocked back and forth in pain. When Bruce knocked on the door, she told him to wait in the living room. I barely knew this woman, but I poured out what I knew of Bruce's latest desires. I told her I loved my husband and wanted him to stay with me.

"If he's still here, I'm sure nothing serious has happened between them yet. Would you like me to talk to him? Maybe I can help."

"Oh please, would you? I don't know what to do."

"You don't have to do anything. Just leave everything to me. Sit here and I'll talk to Bruce. Then I'll show you how to fix the meanest fried shrimp in town."

She returned in two minutes with a glass full of ice and gin, which she pressed into my shaking hands.

"Don't be impatient. We'll be a few minutes."

I sat on the bed for an eternity. I had been stupid to say anything to her. What could she say to Bruce that could possibly make any difference? My husband knew me better than any man on earth. If he didn't want me, who would?

A long time passed. I wondered if they'd left the house without telling me. Then, the bedroom door opened.

"It's not as bad as you think. Bruce said they hadn't actually done anything yet. You still have time to work it out. Stay with him for as long as he needs. I'm sure everything will be all right. Be patient. You'll both come through this fine."

"But he loves another woman."

"And, he still loves you. That means you have a chance."

I stared blankly at the bed for a moment, and when I looked up, Mu Lie was gone and Bruce was kneeling in front of me.

"You know I don't want to hurt you."

"Does that mean you're staying?"

"It means I know I have to leave you, I just don't know when. It could be tomorrow. It could be as long as a year."

With a low moan, I asked him, "Why?"

"Because she loves me."

"I love you."

"But not the same way she does. No one's ever loved me the way she does."

"Do you love her?"

"I don't know."

"Do you love me?"

"Of course."

By now, neither the questions nor the answers made any sense. While Bruce watched, I took off a pair of flats and put on my tennis shoes.

"Where are you going?"

"I don't know. For a walk, I guess."

"Now's no time to be going out alone. Let me walk with you."

"No, just get out of my way and leave me alone."

Without looking back, I walked out of the bedroom and through the front door, down the short block to the steep cement bank that led to Highway 90. Just on the other side of the highway lay the white sand beach that ran for 27 miles down the Mississippi coastline. The sun had set but there was enough light for me to see the traffic. Not that I cared. It would have been the easy way out. I started walking down the beach. The sound of the wet sand crushing under my shoes was so loud, it hurt my ears. Everything about me hurt, even my hair.

The beach was empty. There was no one to bother me. Any decision I made was my own. I took my shoes off and walked in the edge of the warm Gulf water. I knew the water was shallow a long way out, but I wondered just how far. I walked straight out until my clothes were wet to my waist. I sat down on the sandy bottom. Water came up to my chin, and, every once in a while, a gentle wave would push it into my mouth, leaving a taste of dirt mixed with salt.

"If I had just tried harder...," I told myself.

I thought about Bruce, and myself, and what a failure I'd been.

I put my face down in the water and left my eyes and mouth open. I couldn't see anything, but I felt a small crab crawl across my hand.

5 Switchman

By the time the sun rose the next morning, I had walked down the beach far enough to see the lighthouse in Biloxi, the one that had been painted black when President Lincoln died.

I brushed the sand from the bottom of my damp, salty feet, and put on my tennis shoes. I needed to turn around and walk back. I'll never know why I chose to live through that night. Maybe the reason was just the simple fact that it was too hard to drown myself in shallow water.

Bruce was asleep with his head under the pillow. He woke up when I entered the bedroom.

"Where were you all night? I waited and waited. You could have at least called. Mu Lie went to all the trouble to fix that fabulous shrimp, and you didn't even let us know where you were. I almost called the police."

I didn't pay any attention to what he was saying. I took a long shower, got dressed and went to work. Around noon, I walked down the block from Coast Federal, where I worked, and found the nearest pay phone. I didn't want my co-workers to overhear my conversation. I knew I needed help, but I couldn't afford the fancy psychiatrist Linda saw in New Orleans.

I looked up the number of the nearest public mental health center, inserted my coin, and called.

"I'm sorry, ma'am, everyone's out to lunch. Can I take your number and have someone call you back?"

"No. I'm at a payphone. Isn't there someone I can talk to?"

"Well, there's a guy, John Curtis, a counselor who eats his lunch here sometimes. Hang on, I'll see if he's here."

I listened to the silence on the other end of the line, and hoped she didn't disconnect me. I couldn't make it through another night with Bruce in bed beside me.

Over time, John Curtis proved to be indispensable in my life. He was my idea of middle-aged: balding, with black, greasy hair. His cheap, polyester slacks with an overly long belt indicated that his lanky frame had once carried considerably more.

"You can't wait until Bruce makes up his mind about what he's going to do," John told me. "You have to take some action now. That's clearly your only choice."

At our first meeting in person, he'd asked to record my sessions. This was before a small, discreet tape recorder could be hidden under the desk, or set unobtrusively in the corner. John's tape recorder was a huge, monstrosity of a machine, with miles of naked tape waiting to gobble up every word I said. I hesitated to reveal myself permanently on tape, but John convinced me the recording was no different from doctors taking notes, and, he would be able to go over our conversation later, in case he missed something. He assured me that no one, but him, would ever hear the tapes, so I said, "Okay."

John couldn't prescribe medicines himself, but he got me an appointment for me with a doctor who had no qualms about writing one prescription to alleviate my depression, and one for sleeping pills. He instructed me to take the sleeping pills only when I needed them. To me, that meant whenever I wanted to sleep.

I took John's advice and made plans to move out of the dream house on the beach. The house only seemed to contain nightmares now.

The day before I moved, I ran into Alfred, trying to catch Boots, his dog had run away again. He took my arm gently, like he was helping an old lady cross the street.

"Bruce is a fool," he said.

I smiled silently, and shrugged my shoulders. I didn't have anything to say.

I found a two-bedroom apartment, not big, but all I figured I could afford. Gordon and Anna helped me move.

"I don't know how you're going to unpack," said Gordon. "There isn't room for anything but the boxes."

When I told Bruce I was moving he tried to convince me to stay until he decided to move out. I didn't see any future in that. Eventually he agreed with me and left the house at the same time. He even stayed the first night in the apartment. Later, he would tell me I could never charge him with abandonment because I was the one who left him. He hung around town for a month, taking me out on dates, trying to get up the courage to leave, or maybe he just hadn't finalized where he was going to meet his lady friend.

Meanwhile, I tried to sort out my life. I should have been tired, but I wasn't. My trains ran non-stop, 24 hours a day. I unpacked, and found room for almost everything, including my beloved antique barber chair. I placed it in the kitchen and sat, while I talked to everyone I knew about everything, except my fallen-apart world.

The two kids shared the room where I put Steven's bunk beds. I took Heather's double bed for myself in the other bedroom. I couldn't handle the thought of sleeping by myself in a king-sized bed, which felt big enough to swallow me whole.

I had to find homes for our cat and dog, because the apartment complex didn't allow pets. I felt guilty, so I ended up buying Steven and Heather everything alive that the mall pet store sold in a cage. We had white mice, which made terrible squeaky noises as they mated in the bathroom night after night. The parakeet soiled more newsprint than the paper boy could deliver, and the gerbil looked like his uncle had been a rat. One day, when I was flying exceptionally high, I came into the kids' room and found the bird on its back, feet in the air, a sure sign it needed immediate disposal. I looked around the room and saw the gerbil, shedding enough hair to make a blanket, and the mice getting ready to make more babies. I couldn't take it any more. I saw myself as the mother in "The Effect of Gamma Rays on Man in the Moon Marigolds." The bird immediately went into the trash outside, and the caged animals were released at the edge of the woods, with the hope they would find something to eat, or something to eat them.

When Steven and Heather came home from school, I gave them the news.

"First, we have to leave our nice house and move to this crummy apartment, and change schools again, and now you go and get rid of my pets," said Steven. "I even have to share this lousy old room with my sister!"

His voice held all the anger and indignation a confused eight-year-old could muster.

"I'm sorry, Steven, I couldn't stand the smell any more."

"Are you sure my bird was dead?"

"I'm sure he was dead. Maybe, someday when we move to a house, we can get a dog and cat again."

"Maybe, maybe, maybe," Steven muttered. "Why can't you ever say for sure. Besides, it still stinks in here. This whole apartment stinks. Where's the cage? Maybe we can get a new bird."

They were too young to understand I couldn't deal with anything extra. To everyone else, I appeared to have an inexhaustible source of energy. I was still active in the theater, and I worked full time in a demanding nine-to-five job. I went out with my friends. My laundry was clean, my children were fed, taken shopping and read to. But I hadn't an ounce of strength left over for myself. Even more so, I was fast using up my reserves. Twice a week, I went to a therapy group led by John Curtis and another counselor. But no one recognized my symptoms, or made a proper diagnosis. I thought the only reason I couldn't do something was that I didn't try hard enough. Everyone told me to slow down and relax. But I couldn't do that. Life had screwed around with me long enough. I had to use all the time I had left to turn things around my way, to make things happen. I couldn't waste a minute.

Although we were still legally married, Bruce was living in Indiana with Miss Butterick Pattern No. 3789. So, I decided I wouldn't allow myself to wilt away, and, carefully and methodically, as though I were picking out the right outfit to buy, I dressed and went to a fancy bar that was known to have a good band. Hot pants were in and, since my legs had always been my best feature, with that combination, I picked up a young engineer named Bill from Alabama. After a couple of dances, and a couple of drinks, I gave him my phone number and disappeared. He called the next day to invite me to a concert the following weekend. I agreed, gave him my address, but not the details of my life. After all, it was just a date.

Saturday night, before he was scheduled to arrive, the babysitter from upstairs came with her three young brothers.

"Can they stay here until my parents get home?"

Her request seemed reasonable. I returned to the apartment's tiny bathroom to finish getting ready. I'd told Steven and Heather I was going out on a date, and they seemed as excited as I was. The doorbell rang and, before I could get to it, Heather swung the door open and looked up at Bill.

"Are you going to be my new daddy?"

"Oh, Bill, you're here. We'll leave right away. I know you're anxious to get started."

He'd only had a quick glance into my apartment, but he would've been blind not to see the six children, and I hadn't even told him I had been married. He was a lot younger than I thought, at least five years.

We drove for some distance, talking about our tastes in music, but long before we reached our destination, Bill turned to me.

"I want to ask you one question."

What the hell, I thought to myself, here's where he turns around and takes me back to my apartment.

"Okay," I said.

"I don't want to get real personal, but how many of those kids are yours? Not that it makes a difference or anything."

I took a big gulp of air, and didn't seem to be able to swallow.

"Come on, I don't really care, I was just wondering."

"Just two are mine. The one little girl, Heather, who greeted you so friendly like at the door, and the red-headed kid in the back, Steven."

"The tall one?"

"Yes."

He could figure out my age from that, and take me back to my apartment, if he wanted to. But he didn't. He thought I was fun, intelligent, and sexy, and he had a king-sized water bed in an upstairs apartment on Mobile Bay in Fairhope, Alabama, that soon became familiar to me.

Bill had dreams of my sending the children off to relatives, moving me to Fairhope, and waiting for him to return from work, so we could make love through those long, Southern summer nights. But, even before the first day of winter arrived, I didn't intend to spend anymore of my life waiting for a man.

I soon learned, if I planned carefully, I had enough time and energy to date more than one guy at the same time. Gordon and Anna introduced me to Merle, a young Air Force captain, who lived in the apartment complex across the road. This time, not wanting to repeat my mistake with Bill, I shook hands with him and spoke first.

"Hi, I'm Jo Carroll. I have two kids, Steven, 8, and Heather, who's 6."

My information didn't faze Merle. He started to appear at my apartment, accompanied by "Shags," his large, mutt-of-a-dog, with loads of unkempt, white hair. Steven thought Shags was the greatest, and vice-versa. And, soon, I heard, "Mom, can I go over to Merle's to visit?"

"Did he ask you?"

"Well, not exactly, but the last time I was over, he said I could come back any time."

"Okay, but be back in an hour, and don't get in his way."

Merle was a short, stocky redhead from Monroe, Louisiana. He came complete with a Northern Louisiana twang, and a face full of freckles. He was a speech pathologist at nearby Keesler Air Force Base, and I often wondered if all his patients ended up sounding like they had Louisiana licenses plates on their cars. He never called ahead, and dropped by frequently, usually with something of interest to show or tell the children. Once, when he and Anna were visiting at the same time, she noticed my wall-to-wall counter of dirty dishes. I'd been flying high for quite a while, and, when I was in a manic mood, mundane things, like housework, were low on my priority list.

"Merle, let's you and me clean this kitchen for Jo Carroll."

"That's not exactly what I had in mind when I came over."

"That doesn't matter."

"I think my dog needs to go for a walk."

"Never you mind about Shags. Jo Carroll, you look exhausted. Go to bed while we clean up in here."

I argued a little, but not too much. The apartment was so small, it had no hallway, just a small square off the living room with doors to the two bedrooms and bath. I fell across the red-, white-, and blue-flowered bedspread that I'd bought as a symbol of my female independence after Bruce left. I still have it, and use it to cover picnic tables on outings, as it reminds me that things and people do survive. But, then, I fell into an almost drug-like sleep that was typical in the middle of a high when I finally let myself go.

I awoke to a clean apartment, but I was still alone with my trains.

About this same time, another guy started hanging around. I met Kin at a party given by the Biloxi Little Theater, and found him quite charming and attractive. I'd already had a few drinks, and was feeling relaxed and loose, when Kin asked me to dance. He was a marvelous dancer, not just the "one, two, back-and-forth, can-I-hold-you-tighter" type. After about the third dance, he commented that he was getting a little chilly.

"I'll warm you up, baby," I said, snuggling in as close as I could.

"What did you say?"

He looked down at me and laughed.

I batted my false eyelashes and repeated myself.

"I'll warm you up, baby."

He took a long look at me.

"You're serious, aren't you?"

"Yes."

"Let's go out on the back porch and talk."

I readily agreed. After all, wasn't this a prelude to what I had in mind?

Kin took me to a wooden corner seat on the overcrowded porch, brushed aside several plastic cups, and sat down beside me.

"I need to tell you something," he said, taking my hand gently in his.

I was sure he was going to tell me he was married.

"I'm gay."

"Oh, I'm happy, too," I gurgled back at him innocently.

I wasn't ignorant or naive, I knew what homosexuality was. But, I had lived in a highly heterosexual world all my life, and had a stereotype image of someone who preferred the company of the same sex. This guy simply didn't fit my image of a gay man. When he started to explain, I became very embarrassed. Of course, I understood, I nodded. Of course, I knew what he was talking about.

"Is there anything you want to ask me?"

"No, I don't think so. You're a nice guy. Thanks for being honest with me."

So, that was that. I crossed Kin off my potential romance list and we became friends. He would take me out to a café, and I would have a cup of tea, while he had coffee, laced with three spoons of sugar, and as much cream as the cup would hold. His right hand always held a cigarette. Sometimes, he went with me and the kids to a movie. He became somewhat of a fixture at my apartment, sort of like a big brother.

My life settled into a hectic routine with kids, work, theater, and an assortment of male friends and couples occupying my days and nights. My trains raced and puffed, sending out warnings, which I ignored.

Driving down the Coast Highway one day, I asked my bright third-grader to read the signs for me. He couldn't. At first, I thought he might have inherited his father's poor vision, but he couldn't read the huge sign even when we were almost on top of it. I thought he must be teasing me. After all, he had all "A's" on his report card, even in reading. When we got home, I called Anna, whose field was Special Education. Maybe she could suggest something. Horrible guilt feelings hopped on one of those trains in my head. Maybe Steven was having trouble because Bruce and I weren't living together.

"If you're not doing anything tonight, why don't you bring Steven over to the house. I've got some simple tests that might uncover something. In fact, I haven't seen you in a while, bring both kids and come early. We'll have dinner together."

"I don't want this to be a big deal. He could be faking it to get some attention."

"Don't worry about it. I'll have him and Heather play some games for me, and they'll never know we're even testing him."

Anna frequently worked at home, and she and Gordon had made a playroom with swinging balls to be hit with colored sticks. Papers, colored pencils and numerous games littered a table. After supper, Anna took the kids to the playroom, while Gordon and I relaxed with a drink he'd introduced me to, a White Russian, equal parts of vodka, Kahlua and cream.

"Do you think it's anything serious?" I asked Gordon.

"Probably not, but I might want to test his hearing, just in case."

I was nervous. I didn't need anything to be wrong with my kids.

"Is that expensive?"

"Don't worry about it. I'll do it at my office at Keesler. Do you need another drink?"

"No, just some fresh ice in this one."

I seldom drank anything to the bottom of the glass.

Anna opened the playroom door and the kids came bounding out in front of her.

"Gordon, why don't you take them to get some ice cream."

The sound of the departing car could hardly be heard over their excited yells at the surprise treat of double scoops during the week. I was nervous, afraid Anna was going to tell me that Steven had an inoperable brain tumor.

"Jo Carroll, I think Steven has some kind of difficulty with his motor skills, especially when it comes to reading. He doesn't see letters or words the same way we do. Heather may be having some problems too, but not as severe."

"Will he be all right?"

"Of course. It's not like he has a disease. He needs to have further tests, and, if I'm correct, we need to teach him to read a different way. He's a bright boy. He'll be fine."

Anna's preliminary diagnosis was correct, and Steven's retraining began, with his sister tagging along part of the time. Anna handled the situation beautifully. She told his teachers that he was a special test case for a new program in Mississippi, and he would have a private tutor three times a week to teach him reading skills. As a result, Steven was never labeled as a Special Education student, nor was he put in a separate classroom.

At the same time, I discovered the paper boy at the complex was dealing in more than just newspapers. I moved out of the apartment and into a house in a subdivision, where the kids could have normal pets, like a cat and a dog, and we could at least look like a regular family. All these changes added more trains to the tracks in my head, and I was convinced they had to move faster and faster if I was going to get anywhere or accomplish anything.

I began seeing Merle a lot more often. Sometimes we went to Anna and Gordon's for dinner. Other times, we took a picnic to the beach or took long walks with the kids. Merle was dependable, but didn't seem sexually attracted to me.

I had stopped taking medication at this point, and quit going to counseling, but I was continuously experiencing those vapor days I'd felt in Atchison. One day, Merle came to the house and found me curled up in Heather's bed clutching one of her dolls.

"You look awful. What's the matter?"

"Nothing. I guess I'm just tired."

Being "tired" was an excuse I'd used all my life, and I didn't see any reason to change it. Besides, the truth might scare him away.

"Why don't you let me take the little rug rats home with me to Monroe some weekend so you can get some real rest."

"Are you sure you want to?"

"You know I wouldn't suggest it if I didn't mean it."

"Sometimes, I think you come to visit me just so you can play with my kids," I teased him.

He grinned.

"Well, maybe sometimes. But I was thinking of asking if you want to go out to eat next Saturday night, maybe have a drink after at that new bar in Ocean Springs."

"Are you asking me for a real date?"

He reached down and smoothed the pillow, as he gave me a peck on the check.

"I didn't think I had to ask you out. We're together so much, either here or at my place."

Now, he was teasing me. He was well aware of our age difference, not to mention the enormous responsibility of my two children. I knew that asking me out was a big deal to him.

"What'll I wear?"

"Dress for me, not the kids," was his response.

The unanticipated dinner invitation temporarily lifted me out of the doldrums, and I rummaged through my closet all week trying to find the perfect outfit. Flats, not heels, for sure. Merle and I were the same height. Something sexy, but not loud and flashy. I didn't want to overdo it. I settled on a ruffled blue blouse with a short skirt to match, and found a pair of gold hoop earrings I hadn't worn in a long time. If I wanted this to move beyond a four-way friendship with my children, I would have to look both classy and alluring.

I sent the kids to a neighbor's house so they wouldn't be around when Merle came to pick me up. I didn't want any distraction to mess up our first real date. He was a few minutes late, and more than a little nervous. Friendship seemed easier for him than dating.

"Where are we going?"

"What?"

"Aren't you taking me out to dinner?"

"Sure, but it's a surprise. Where are the kids?"

"I told them they could spend the night with friends. You just have me tonight."

"Great! Let's go then."

We didn't turn toward the beach, and instead drove down a road which followed the edge of the woods, and turned west. Merle wasn't talkative, but he held my hand as he drove with the other.

"Where are you taking me, New Orleans, or California? Remember, the kids are only spending one night away."

"Have you ever heard of the Marlborough Man's place?"

"You mean the one that belongs to the guy on the billboards? You're kidding! I've heard a lot about it. Is that where we're going? Do you think he really has that tattoo on his hand?"

Merle grinned.

"We can check it out. I've never been there, but everyone says the food is good."

"I'd just like to see him."

The restaurant, actually more like a cafe, was one I'd heard about ever since I'd moved to the Coast. It was run by a former Marlborough cigarette model who still maintained his image as a tough cowboy who could attract the women, and some said, men, too. His mother supplied the down-home-style cooking, while the restaurant specialized in fresh seafood.

We both ordered the crab-stuffed flounder. Merle talked about the houseboat he had just moved into, how he'd built it with his dad in Monroe, and brought it to the Coast to live on while he served as an audiologist at Keesler. He'd named the houseboat "Moon Shadow," but I never found out why. He tried holding my hand across the top of the table, but the attempt at romance didn't work. He wanted to be close, but not too close.

"Let's get a drink in Ocean Springs. That new bar has music, and maybe I'll even dance with you."

"Sounds good."

The new bar did sound good, but going home and hiding under the covers sounded even better. I kept that thought to myself. After all, hadn't I been looking forward to this evening? Merle was acting a little strange, and I didn't quite know how to take him. We drove down Highway 90, along the coast to Ocean Springs, a romantic drive with moonlight dancing on the water. I snuggled next to Merle, and he put his arm around me. I had a nice, comfortable feeling, but nice and comfortable weren't enough. I didn't know what I wanted. I did know I wanted to feel good, and I wanted it to hurry up and happen. I liked my relationship with Merle, but it wasn't moving fast enough, I needed more from him.

The small bar was jammed with people.

"Look, Merle, there's Kin. He has some empty chairs at his table. I bet we could join him. Let's go see."

He took my elbow and steered me in the opposite direction, but the room wasn't that big, and Kin had seen us. He pushed aside tables and people, and there he was, standing in front of us.

"Hi, y'all come over and sit with us. None of these dumb people are going to leave for a long time, and you'll never be able to find a seat."

Kin extended his hand to Merle.

"I'm Simpson Kinard Fite. I don't know if we've met before." He beamed at me. "Jo Carroll calls me 'Kin,' if you're a friend of hers, feel free to do the same."

"I think we have met, but I can't remember where."

I could. Their paths had crossed at my apartment. After Kin had left, Merle expressed his dislike for him. He didn't think Kin being around Steven and Heather was a good idea. I didn't pay any attention to his advice.

We joined Kin and his friends at a long table. Merle bought the first round of drinks. Kin ordered a Rusty Nail, a combination of Drambuie and Scotch on the rocks. I'd never seen Merle drink anything except beer, but this time, he ordered Jack Daniels on the rocks. I stuck with my taste-good White Russian.

I'd wanted to dance with Merle, but before I could convince him, Kin had taken my hand and was leading me to a vacant spot on the wooden floor. A long time had passed since I had danced with him, and he was wonderful, all the right steps, and swirls, his hand strong against the small of my back, and a steady flow of pleasant conversation. We were away from the table for two or three songs and, by the time we came back, Merle was on his third drink. He leaned over to me and spoke in a too-loud whisper.

"Thought this guy was queer. You sure looked like you were having a good time out there."

"You know Kin and I are friends. Why don't you dance with me?"

"No, I don't want to dance. You go dance with who you want to, and I'll drink whatever I want to."

I was angry. Merle didn't have any hold on me, and besides, Kin was just a friend. Why was he so upset? And, why did he have to pick tonight to start drinking? I let Merle drink, and I spent my time on the dance floor with Kin. His favorite song, "Color My World," played over and over, and the crystal disco ball spinning overhead was whirling almost as fast as my head. Kin's body felt warm and good next to mine, but the conversation was limited to the theater.

When we got back to the table, Merle was too drunk to make any sense, and much too drunk to drive. Some of his friends came by and said they would take him home. I took his keys, planning to return the car in the morning. He certainly wasn't going to need the car that night.

One more dance with Kin, and I was ready to go home. The house would be empty, but I needed some sleep before the kids hit the door in the morning.

I picked up the car keys and my purse and started to leave. Kin put his arm around my waist.

"Aren't you going to offer me a ride home? I only live a mile and a half from here. Do you mind?"

"Of course not."

I unlocked Merle's car. Kin climbed in the passenger side as I slid behind the wheel. His home turned out to be a large, white, cement block garage to the side and back of a friend's house.

"Want to come in for a minute?"

"No thinks, I don't think so. I'm tired. The kids will be home in the morning and I've got to get this car back."

"I don't think Merle's going to be up early to use it. My place really looks different, much better, on the inside. Come on in, Jo Carroll."

What the hell, I was already there. What would a few extra minutes hurt?

Inside, his converted garage was like a dream scene. Projects from different community theater plays hung from the high ceiling. Various colored nets decorated the walls, and all the furniture was painted purple. Before I had gone three steps, my head hit a giant bunch of artificial fruit.

"Sorry about that. It's left over from an old Carmen Miranda party. Let me help you into this chair. How about some wine? I know I've got some here somewhere."

"No, I'm just going to stay a minute."

Ignoring my protest, Kin went off in search of the wine. I looked around. Three paper mache flamingos peered out from behind a Victorian folding screen. Theatrical props were everywhere. What did he do with all this junk?

Kin's bracelets jangled above me. He was standing over me, holding two jelly jars full of red wine.

"Let's drink to fun and theater and dancing."

We drank toasts to everything. I was having a fantastic time, but the time was late, and I needed to go home. I stood up and discovered I'd drunk one too many toasts. I would be stupid to drive Merle's car drunk when I'd taken it away from him because he was drunk.

"Kin, I want to go home, but I need to go for a long walk first. I don't think I can drive right now."

"Had too much to drink? Happens to the best of us."

"Yeah, I didn't realize it. I think I need to sit down again."

"Why don't you lie down on the bed for a few minutes? Get your head together."

Kin's queen-sized mattress lay in a corner on the garage floor, partially hidden by a large easel. It was covered with a plain green throw, and hard to see in the dim light.

"Maybe for a minute."

I sat down on the bed, then put my head on the pillow, hoping to keep it from spinning so much.

"Get comfortable, close your eyes and take a little nap. You'll feel better."

This wasn't where I wanted to spend the night, but I was too lightheaded to argue. Kin looked the other way while I wiggled out of my little short skirt and pulled my top off over my head and got under the covers. I wished I'd learned to wear a slip, but I was vain enough to be pleased my lace bra matched my panties.

The next sound I heard in the darkened room was Kin snoring softly. I had no idea how long I'd slept. A small window high over the bed shed enough light from the street lamp to allow me to see I was sharing the covers. What was I supposed to do? I was uncomfortable about being half-naked, but I didn't want to wake my uninvited bed partner. Still dizzy, I rolled over on my side, facing away from Kin, and went back to sleep.

Somewhere between dawn and daylight, I felt his hands on my back, unhooking my bra. He slipped his fingers around my breasts from behind and pulled my body toward his. I discovered he was naked and ready. It felt good, but what was happening took a minute for me to understand.

"Are you sure you want to do this?" I asked.

His reply was a whisper.

"Shhh."

He turned me around and kissed me hungrily, holding me to him with one hand while the other slid my panties down. Memories of my initial attraction to him flooded my mind. We had a hot and passionate morning. My new lover didn't seem different or strange. He aroused me and responded to me as if his whole being had been waiting for this moment. In all his lovemaking, I did not detect a hint that he'd ever even considered any other kind of sexual encounter.

Finally, we lay silent and exhausted. He took my hand gently.

"You're the first, you know," he said. "You're the first woman I've ever made love to

I returned Merle's car to the parking lot where Moon Shadow was docked, and Kin drove my car to pick me up.

I didn't cycle into depression for weeks. His friends asked how I did it, how I turned him around. A few were happy for him, a few were not.

Kin became an energetic, ardent, devoted lover. A complete romantic, he wrote poems to me and read them on the beach, in the kitchen, in bed.

And he talked for hours about his past, how he'd begun his freshman year at Ole Miss in 1956, with a full math scholarship.

"You never would have recognized me as a frat rat."

School became secondary, and he'd suffered a breakdown in his junior year. Sent home to Biloxi, he'd hidden in his bedroom for a year. On the advice of a psychiatrist, his father started taking him to the state mental hospital once a month.

"We'd start out about four in the morning in order to be there on time. I had no say so whatever in the matter. It was horrible. My father shoveled me into the car and off we went. There were no preliminary talks at the hospital, no anesthetic, no nothing. They just strapped me down and started the electric shock. They called it treatments. My head ached for days."

When Kin told me about his shock treatments, all I could think of was that it was cruel and unusual punishment and it reminded me of electric cattle prods used to move a cow into the right stall. Why would they use this method on a human in the 1960's. Why did his father take him there?

Kin continued on.

"Later, I went to the public library trying to find some information about what they'd done to me. I couldn't find anything. It was like shock treatments never existed. One old encyclopedia mentioned an 18th century doc who'd wrapped electric eels around his patients' heads. Other than that, there was nothing. Zip.

"Between visits to the hospital, a friend started coming to see me. He had a sailboat and we'd spend long, lazy afternoons on Back Bay. Everyone thought I was getting better because of the electric jolts. I knew differently. I knew I'd found myself in a relationship that was making me a complete person.

"After the affair ended, I refused any more shock treatments and moved to New Orleans. I decided theater was more to my taste than math and found myself a job. Adjusting to night life in the French Quarter was no problem, and I was happy again. I found an older lover, and when that fell apart, I moved back to the Coast."

His past didn't turn me off, just somehow turned on my fascination. He left me love notes everywhere. They were signed "ily," his version of "I love you." Arrangements of wildflowers and vegetables on my dining room table often awaited my return from work, and a scented candle always burned in the bedroom.

Kin had been somewhat of a fixture in my home even before our romantic involvement, so he was no stranger to the kids. He hadn't moved in yet, but the fact I was sleeping with him was obvious to everyone.

Anna was skeptical about my new romance.

"I just want to make sure you're not doing something that could hurt your kids."

"How could Kin possibly hurt my kids? He adores them and they are crazy about him. He's encouraging their interest in some art projects, and we hardly do anything without them."

"What if Bruce found out?"

"Found out what?"

"Jo Carroll, I'm not dumb. Neither is Bruce. Be careful."

One night, Kin had bad news. He'd been fired from his job as a clerical assistant for an architect in Ocean Springs.

"I don't know what more the son-of-a-bitch wants. I can't find another job in Ocean Springs, and riding a bike to work anywhere else on the Coast is out of the question. I guess I'll have to move back in with my folks. I don't see any choice. Damn!"

"Move in with us, Kin." The words spilled out of my mouth without thought.

"You and the kids?"

"There's plenty of room. You could get a job in Gulfport, and I wouldn't have to drive home by myself."

"I like to sleep in my own bed."

"Wouldn't have you without it."

Kin had been living with us for about a week when Merle called.

"Can I come over for a few minutes?"

"Sure, I haven't seen you in ages. Where've you been?"

"Didn't you get my cards?"

"No."

"After that night at the bar I got to thinking. I guess I was too uptight about everything. I couldn't bear to share you. I took a month off and went to Hawaii. I've always dreamed of going there and I had a lot of leave built up. Anyway, I sent you and the kids a bunch of cards."

"We never got them. When do you want to come over?"

"Right now."

"Give me 20 minutes."

"It will take me that long to get there."

I looked in the living room where Kin was playing Monopoly with Heather and Steven. This was decision time.

"Kin, could you take the car and run an errand for me?"

"Just let me get my shoes on. Care if the kids go with me?"

"I was going to suggest it."

Kin and the kids had barely gone out the back door when Merle rang the front door bell. His arms were full of packages.

"What's all this?"

"I picked up some things for you and the kids in Hawaii. Where are they?"

"They'll be back soon."

I felt like a child with a birthday as I unwrapped the presents Merle had brought me. When I got to the grass skirt, I stopped.

"What's this?"

"What does it look like? Go put it on."

"No, I don't think so."

"Come on. You're not still mad at me are you? I missed you. I didn't know how much you and the kids meant to me until after I left. Jo Carroll, I love you. Let's get married."

"Merle, don't say anything else. I need to talk to you."

Before I could explain anything to this fine, young man, Kin and the kids walked in the back door, making our living arrangements evident to Merle. No doubt remained when Kin then decided to extend some hospitality.

"Merle, can I offer you some coffee? It's fresh, not left over from this morning."

Merle looked at me with hurt that quickly turned to disgust.

"No thanks. I was just leaving."

"I'll walk you to the car."

"That's not necessary."

Faster than Merle walked out the door, my depression ran in. A message from one of the trains racing around my head told me I'd hurt him, and I shouldn't have. I ignored that freight train and hopped the express telling me my relationship with Kin would bring me more happiness than I'd ever known. He never criticized me. He was warm, loving and faithful. He was fun and great with my kids. And, no one had ever taken care of me and fussed over me the way he did.

How or when Kin and I decided to get married is lost in the fog of my history. Maybe he asked me.

More likely, I asked him.

6 Babyland Bound

I'd never seen so many roaches in my entire life.

Kin and I rented a little house off campus at the University of Mississippi in Hattiesburg, where both of us were enrolled, but we forgot to look in the back bedroom. It was alive with the flying bastards. They'd eaten the wallpaper and almost through the walls.

Our wedding had been hosted by Anna and Gordon at their home in Gulf Shores.

"I want you to know I'm doing this for you, not him," Anna warned.

Our one-night honeymoon was spent at the Cornstalk Hotel in New Orleans. Kin took pictures of me posed nude in front of the fireplace, and we toasted our future with cheap champagne, while I ignored the frantic whistles blowing from all my trains.

Now, the U-Haul was sitting in the driveway, and Steven and Heather had already pulled their bikes off the back, and were exploring the neighborhood.

"Kin, I can't move in there. It's too gross. I can't sleep in a room like that!"

"I'll take care of it."

"How?"

I knew I was going to have to take charge if this marriage was going to work. I came to that conclusion early on. This bedroom was a prime example of Kin's idea of taking care of things. He would have closed the door to the infested area, put the two kids in one room, and bought lots of bug spray, which might never have been used. He needed to have smooth sailing all the time. Ripples were scary to him. But that bedroom was scary to me.

"Never mind," I said. "Why don't you start unloading the truck, and I'll call the landlord."

I fumigated the room and closed it off. The smell was horrible, but it was overpowered by the odor coming from the roof tar factory next door. The next day, a crew arrived to tear out the bedroom walls and install new paneling.

"You know, anybody who says they don't have bugs in the South is either blind or lying," I joked with the carpenters.

"Yeah, lady, but I ain't never seen them as bad as this!"

I agreed. I had no doubt in my mind this was the worst place I had ever lived, but it would have to do. Our only income was my child support, and Kin's grant to finish his degree.

I had decided to go back to college too. I told myself all students lived like this, but motherly guilt haunted me. I tried to make sure the kids were involved in all sorts of activities. They swam on the swim team and ran relays with the track team. Steven was a Webelo in Scouts, and Heather became involved in church activities with Anna's niece, whose father was a minister.

My illness appeared dormant for the time, but I was hanging on by the skin of my teeth. I directed a play Kin had written, and basked in the glory of the newspaper article that described us as a "husband and wife team." Taking care of my family, attending classes, and keeping up with assignments, not to mention coming home to that awful little house, took everything I had. My hands were full, and I couldn't risk looking to any kind of future. Would I ever have the energy to find out what I wanted, what was right for me?

The best part of my life in this small, Mississippi college town was my new friend, a woman named Alicia Ellis. She and her husband, Randy, had known Kin before and welcomed us into their midst. They and their two young children lived in a small house in the country. Randy, who'd had one lung removed when he had tuberculosis, was going to school on a disability grant. They had no money to budget, and lived on food stamps, but somehow Alicia always had surprises for my kids. She'd show them a wildflower blooming in the woods, or find some baby rabbits in the vegetable garden.

Alicia and I developed a deep, close relationship. Everything about her was special to me. She managed to make their tiny house into a warm, inviting home, where she and I would sit for hours and talk in the autumn heat. When the dark days came, I knew I could go to Alicia. She called those days "demons," and she'd had her share. We talked about the "darkness," and the "blackness" we both knew. I had never talked to anyone else who had this same intense depression.

"I feel like I'm in a deep, dark pit," I told her. "The sides are steep and slippery and they're closing in on me. The blackness is dripping down on me. It gets heavier and heavier on my shoulders until I can't stand up any more. Then I huddle in the pit, scared and alone.

"It's like an awful nightmare, but I'm not asleep, so I can't wake up. But, sometimes it's worse, Alicia. Sometimes, I don't even care enough to make the attempt. The trains in my head come to a dead stop and everything is still and dark. That's when it's really terrifying. What if sometime something happens and the blackness never lifts?" I asked Alicia.

"It doesn't, Jo Carroll, not completely. We have to keep struggling. If we stop trying to escape, it will take over, and we'll be lost forever."

Depression became a bond between us. Alicia knew. She understood.

She never asked me how, why, or when Kin and I got together, she just accepted it. She accepted my children, too, as though they were long-lost and sorely missed relatives.

Kin and I were having financial problems. Our budget wasn't working out and bills were overdue. One of the few foods we could readily afford was cabbage, but even it was limited in the number of different ways Kin could fix it. I decided we needed to move into the university's married-student housing to save money. We bribed some younger students with my prized barber chair, and they helped us move to our cheap, dinky new quarters. To fit ourselves into the cramped space, and to pay off some bills, we sold most of my furniture, keeping Kin's only contribution to our household, the queen-sized bed. Autumn became winter, we settled into the apartment, attended classes and lived hand-to-mouth. Love was the only item that didn't destroy our budget.

I found myself staying in bed all day, too sick to lift my head from the pillow. This time, the problem wasn't in my head, as my trains were on track. Kin brought me warm tea, the only thing I could keep down, and flitted about me nervously. I didn't want to think about why I felt so awful.

"Honey, I'd better get you to the clinic. I don't think I've ever seen anyone so ill."

"It's okay Kin. I know what it is. Just get me some crackers. I'm pregnant."

He grabbed me, and I couldn't tell if he was crushing me in anger or in love. As he drew back, I could see his eyes were wet with joy and tears.

"You mean it? Are you sure? Really sure? How do you know? Oh, Jo Carroll, it's a true love baby. I'm so proud! Me? A father?"

He danced with himself into the other room, clearly ecstatic with the idea.

But the time had come for me to talk to myself. I knew I was pregnant. I didn't mistake the symptoms. I had been pregnant three times, and I knew nothing else made my head and stomach turn on me quite like this. I hadn't planned on having another baby. We certainly couldn't afford another child, and Heather and Steven were all I needed. Kin loved them, too, but hearing him singing in the next room made me realize they weren't enough for him. Okay, this baby, and no more. I would have my tubes tied after this birth. After all, how would I ever find out who I was, and what I wanted, if I kept having children?

I did not have an easy pregnancy. It brought both joy and depression. By the end of the second month, I'd dropped out of school.

I frequently vacated my dismal apartment in favor of Alicia's big, iron bed with soft, fluffy feather pillows. She wiped my forehead with a cool cloth, fed me warm, comforting soup that Randy had made, and assured me that everything would be all right. This was, indeed, a love child within me, she told me.

When May arrived, the summer heat had come early and Kin's graduation was upon us. Although he was proud of his accomplishment, his diploma was just a piece of paper, and attracted no job offers.

I was homesick.

"Kin, let's go to Kansas. We could live with my mother while you look for a job in Kansas City."

Mother had married Uncle Joe, and they now lived on the family farm in Kansas just outside Horton, the same town where I had lived across the street from my grandparents. Kin, a true Southerner, whose blood froze at the mention of anything north of Memphis, didn't want to go.

"I could look for a job in New Orleans. Or maybe California. I've always wanted to live on the West Coast. Imagine raising a child in Hollywood."

A quick, flamboyant gesture with his arm nearly toppled our only decent lamp. Whenever we talked about the new child-to-be, Kin was even less realistic than usual. He was convinced his child was destined for great things, a star on the walk in front of Grauman's Chinese, or her name in lights on Broadway.

"Be realistic, Kin. You don't have a job. I can't work right now. We don't have any money. How many choices do we have? Besides, I'd like Dr. Brown to deliver the baby."

"Is he good? I don't want anyone near that child who's not the best."

"He's gentle and he cares."

I didn't want to tell Kin I needed to be in a place where I felt safe. I wanted to be someplace where he was employed when this child was born. If we went back to Kansas and stayed with my mother, I felt our chances would be much better. I was trying to force my trains to follow the right tracks. I wanted everything to be all okay.

Depression and anxiety had begun to control my life again. I knew I couldn't take any medication while I was pregnant. I hated to leave the comforting friendship I had developed with Alicia.

I had to do some talking, but I finally convinced Kin to move to Kansas. Once there, however, staying at my mother's home wasn't the panacea I had pictured. I was glad that Steven and Heather were spending the summer with Bruce.

Kin began the long and tiring process of looking for a job in Kansas City, which was a 90-minute drive from Horton. The leftover money from my divorce settlement from Bruce bought us a Volkswagen van, in which Kin commuted to Kansas City. Because of Mississippi laws I'd had to wait a year for a divorce from Bruce and by that time, I didn't wait for him to file. I filed on my own. We'd had some money in a saving account from the sale of our Atchison house, and the judge awarded me that. The absolute last of our funds bought Kin a suit, the first one he'd owned since his college days.

Kin was trying hard to change his lifestyle in preparation for our expanding family, and the new responsibilities that went with it, but my mother wasn't buying any of it. I hadn't realized mother and Joe hated Kin, until we shared a house with them for three months. I knew they didn't have any idea he lived a gay life before our marriage, but there was definitely something about him they didn't like. The feeling was mutual, and hard to disguise.

"I don't know how he thinks he's going to pay for the baby," she said. "Joe and I have our own life to get on with."

The farm house, though modern, didn't have air conditioning. On hot summer nights Kin escaped the heat by sleeping on the comparatively cool linoleum of the kitchen floor. Usually, he'd come back to bed before my mother awoke, but several times they'd stumbled into each other in the early morning hours. Kin and his purple jockey shorts were more than my mother could handle.

"You're my daughter and I love you, but he's no relation," she said, "and if I ever catch him sleeping on my kitchen floor in his underwear again, he's out. For good!"

I was in the middle, uncomfortable, and uneasy. I loved Kin. I loved my mother. And, I could see both points of view. She liked the privacy of her home, and couldn't understand how her daughter could have flipped over this unstable vagrant. Kin had lived in such an unorthodox world, usually ignored convention, and did what was comfortable. Trying to play mediator was tricky, taxing, and not what I wanted to do.

Kin accepted a job as an English teacher in Kansas City, and, with a little help from Uncle Joe, we moved into a big, old house in a middle-class neighborhood. My darkness temporarily retreated. Everything seemed bright with promise. The trains were running smoothly on their appointed runs.

Kin liked his job. The children liked school, and quickly made friends with the neighbors. If I squinted my eyes just so, the house looked like my dream house. It had a dining room with a bay window, and a living room with a fireplace. The bedrooms were upstairs, with what I referred to as the "sun room" and the "library." In truth, the house was in horrible shape. It had only one bathroom, and the toilet was forever stopping up. The so-called sun room, where Heather slept, was part of a tacked-on addition, and the library was nothing more than an extra-wide hallway where we kept the television. One of the windows in Steven's room was broken and fixed with cardboard. Later, when the cold weather came, plywood replaced it.

Soon, the time came for the love child to be born. The trip from our home in Kansas City back to Atchison and Dr. Brown was made in ice and snow, and below-zero temperatures. Kin ignored the bitter cold he hated so. His baby was about to come into the world. His baby, the child he created. Pacing back and forth, he waited, while Dr. Brown helped me deliver our wonderful, fat, healthy baby girl.

From the moment she was born, Gina was, indeed, a love child. Everyone loved her. Steven and Heather adored their new sister. Kin doted on her. Cards, flowers, and gifts came from the Southlands. Kin read aloud letters from former companions of his, who had once been more than close friends. We felt as if we had proved something that others only hint at in love stories.

I wasn't so in love with this baby, however, that I forgot to have my tubes tied. The procedure made my stay in the hospital a little longer, and my mother, who worked in Atchison, came to visit me every day. She was attentive to me, but her feelings soon became clear that when she talked about her grandchildren, she was not including this new baby named Gina. Mother was the only one who was not in love with the new baby.

When the roads were cleared from the Midwestern blizzard, which had arrived in time to honor Gina's birth, we took her home. Kin had painted the furniture yellow in our bedroom and hung navy-colored flowered sheets on the windows. Every container which could hold water overflowed with daisies. We had a wonderful homecoming.

A nursing baby was in my arms, an endearing, working husband was at my side, and my two children, Heather and Steven, were making friends, and, as always, doing well in school. The trains in my head were all chugging along on the right track, whistles sounding in celebration. It would last. I knew it would. It had to. I needed a break, and it was time, it was my turn.

The day Kin called me from school to tell me he'd be home late, Gina was just over a month old. He arrived nearly three hours later, and went straight to the cabinet where we kept the liquor. He drank two shots before he said anything.

"The teachers are going out on strike."

"That shouldn't affect you, Kin. You don't belong to the union. Besides, it's illegal, isn't it?"

"I don't know if it's legal or not, but I'm not crossing any picket lines. Especially with some of those big mothers they have teaching here."

"Would the union pay you?"

"No, but they're striking for more benefits, and, even if I don't belong to the union, I'll get them."

My heart stopped.

"Oh, Kin, we don't have any money. We can't go even two weeks without a paycheck, and you don't have any idea how long this strike will last. I'm nursing Gina, I can't work yet. You can't strike."

"Don't worry, Jo Carroll. They haven't voted yet. We'll watch the news tonight. But if they do call a strike, I'm not working."

The teachers' union went on strike, and Kin kept his word. He refused to look for other employment, even part time, so I found a temporary job working at City Hall. I'd nurse my baby before I left, express milk at noon, and return home at night, totally exhausted. Kin and the kids, who were also out of school due to the strike, were happy. They spent the days playing games, and covering the walls with outrageous art projects. My trains hurled around the tracks, barely avoiding major collisions. This arrangement wasn't working. Everything was piling up on me. I couldn't handle it all.

Relief came from an unexpected source. Lucy and Jim, a couple who had befriended Kin many years earlier, invited us to spend a long weekend at their home in Eureka Springs, Arkansas, where they owned an antique shop. The drive was about four to five hours from Kansas City, and I wasn't looking forward to it. Weekends were my only time to relax and try to get caught up. The kids usually went to the cheap, Saturday movie matinee, and I took advantage of the time to take a nap. Sex with my husband had disappeared after the baby was born, but, at that point, I really didn't miss it. I wasn't much in the mood myself.

Despite my protests, we loaded up the van and headed to Eureka. Their enormous house, squeezed into one of Eureka Springs' narrow, crooked, hilly streets, was a delightful surprise. The home was furnished with antiques imported from England and France, and merchandise from their successful antique business. Lucy and Jim were the first of Kin's friends I'd met who probably owed taxes at the end of the year.

The kids were in heaven. They spent the weekend running up and down the hills, snooping in the bookstore on the corner, and discovering a rock collection under the porch of the nearby pottery studio.

Alone in the kitchen with Lucy, I thanked her.

"You don't know how much I appreciate you inviting us down here. I almost didn't come."

"Why don't you let Steven and Heather stay and finish the school year here?"

"I couldn't do that. You and Jim don't have any children. They'd drive you crazy."

"We'd love it. There's only six weeks of school left. If you take them back to KC, who knows when they'll finish the year. Besides," she said with a wink, "wouldn't you and Kin like a little time, 'just you and me and baby makes three?'"

I couldn't deny the appeal her suggestion had for me. But what would the kids say? I would be creating yet another change in schools, and I hardly knew these people. But if they went back to Kansas City with us, they would just be sitting around the house playing with Kin, until the strike ended. And, heaven only knew when that would be.

Lucy was in her late 20s, and Jim was at least ten years older. They were stable, dependable, and comfortable. They wore old jeans and sweatshirts, but never seemed to worry about money. I decided that letting the kids spend some time with people, whose grocery cart was filled with good things to eat, would be good.

So, I left my two children in this fairy tale town in the heart of the Ozark Mountains and headed back to Kansas City, with my baby and my husband. I went to work at City Hall every day, and he stayed home with Gina, writing reams of poetry, short stories and plays. He never attempted to get anything published. He said being published might change the way he wanted to write, and he wanted to hang on to his artistic talent. Long hours were spent poring over coffee-stained papers as he chained smoked his Salems. He said he needed space, and I gave it to him.

The only thing that kept me from diving into that deep dark pit of depression was Gina, my baby. Many times I'd come home from work so exhausted I'd take her to bed with me for a nap and we'd still be there in the morning. Kin would write all night. Sometimes, he'd meet with friends at his favorite coffee house, and occasionally he slept in Steven's bed, but he never shared mine.

The strike continued, and Kin realized he might have to end up teaching until fall. Then the newspaper announced the good news, "Union and School Board Reach Agreement."

"I'll finish my contract but I won't live in this God-forsaken frozen tundra another winter. I'm going to take you back to the South, back to New Orleans."

"Kin, that's such an expensive city. We can't afford to live there, especially with a family. Why don't we just go back to the Gulf Coast. It's familiar, we're both comfortable there, and it's a lot cheaper."

"I don't care, as long as I don't have to stay here. I'll find a job in New Orleans, you'll see."

We worked out a compromise. I would move to Eureka Springs when Kin started teaching again, and spend the summer there with the children. In the fall, we would take a chance and move to New Orleans, live among its decadent splendor, and look for jobs. If that didn't work we'd move along the Coast, and, somewhere, hopefully, we could find employment.

However, the strike ended in the middle of May. So, I boarded a Trailways Bus with my baby in tow and left for Eureka Springs. Jim and Lucy were having an old rental house remodeled. The carpenter and his girlfriend lived in one of the downstairs bedrooms. The other was vacant, and Gina and I moved into it. Steven and Heather shared a top-floor room where they spread out their sleeping bags every night.

The weather was beautiful. The town was appealing. Eureka Springs was an art colony, where all the people I met were warm and friendly, and connected with the arts in some manner. They threw pottery, painted pictures, carved wood, or, if they were not artistic themselves, sold someone else's work.

Friendships transcended normal cultural guidelines. The commercially successful and the starving artists dined together. The highly visible gay community mixed easily with heterosexual friends, and children were everywhere.

I was among them, a mother, with a baby strapped to my stomach in a pouch, and two gangly children running wild around town. To make money, I sewed. I made pillows, mended trousers, hemmed skirts, anything to bring in a few dollars for food money. The trains were rolling around in my head without an engine.

I was living in a dream world, and the blackness in my soul retreated, and waited, perched on the horizon, like a vulture. I felt a certain lightness, but I was still watching from the outside.

I would bring my baby to the pottery where the carpenter's girlfriend, Karen, worked, and just watch. I was fascinated by the way they could throw soft clay on a wheel and end up with hard, beautiful works of art. The spotless pottery was next to an immaculate gallery where its wares were displayed on fine European antiques. The owner, Gary, made exquisite pots with Calla Lilies clinging to the sides, while his lover, Sean, ran the business side of the operation.

I was still nursing my baby, and waiting for Kin to complete his teaching job in Kansas City and join us at the end of the summer. I didn't know why. The marriage was beginning to bother me a lot. Kin was sweet and gentle, but I needed someone whose primary goal was to support and nurture his family. Kin was not unwilling to support us, but he didn't seem to know how. Financial support didn't appear to be one of his priorities. He thought we would always get along, somehow, with a little help from friends and relatives. I didn't like it.

Summer ended, and Kin arrived. The time came for us to go to New Orleans. He had no promise of a job, although he was convinced something would turn up, and his sweet-talking once again convinced me. I was ready to go back to the warm South. My trains had no other destination in mind.

I told myself everything will be wonderful, just like Kin said. He'll find a job he likes. I've been too hard on him. We'll live in a wonderful house, the kids will go to good schools and my bed will be warm again.

7 Sunset Limited

Over the last few months, we had borrowed $1,000 from Alicia and Randy, who were now teaching on a reservation school in Arizona, packed our VW van, and moved to New Orleans.

Louisiana can be an oasis in the winter, but in late August, in an un-air conditioned VW, jammed with possessions and children, it was hot as hell.

We quickly rented an old "camelback double," a popular building style in New Orleans, which was a duplex, with a single story in front, and an old-fashioned, curved stairway leading to bedrooms on the second floor. The camelback was on Magazine Street, close enough to the streetcar line to provide transportation.

I was getting tired of not knowing where we would be living from month to month, how much food was left in the cupboard, if there would be gas for the car to get us to work, or if there would be work at all.

I also had not faced the reality of our relationship. I was becoming more like a sister to Kin, someone to share the adventures he wanted to have, but not his bed.

Kin busied himself putting up glass shelves in the kitchen to hold the scraggly plants the supermarket was throwing away. I scoured the classified ads for a job. I found a teller's position at a bank that marked the end of the streetcar line on Carrollton and Claiborne.

Days were hectic, nights were lonely, and the darkness was returning. I'd get up each morning, get myself ready for work, dress Gina and drop her off at a babysitter near the streetcar line. Kin kept the VW to look for a job, and eventually found one in an Orleans parish public high school.

We couldn't seem to get organized enough to even get the grocery shopping done. Every night after work, we'd stop at Schwegmann's Supermarket to buy something for supper. The kids had to do the dishes before they could do their homework. By then, I'd be in bed.

I'd always promised myself that my children would attend public schools. After a short while, I realized New Orleans was not the place to take this stand. Heather and Steven were struggling to adjust to yet another educational system, when they started to get beaten up at school. The problem was not a matter of integration, but a question of survival. More black kids than white kids on our block went to private school. I found a small Episcopal school in the Uptown area that would accept them on a scholarship basis. The kids adjusted to their new surroundings quite quickly. Steven got a huge trophy for outstanding work in the Boy Scouts, and Heather brought home little girls from school for slumber parties. My baby was walking and happy, but every night, I cried myself to sleep while Kin wrote with colored pens in his journals.

Christmas came, and New Orleans was eerie, with the warmth of a Southern city, and all decked out with evergreens, in anticipation of snows that never came. New Year's passed with ships in the river blowing their horns all night and neighbors firing their pistols into the air in celebration.

Then came Mardi Gras. The whole family got excited. Schools and businesses were closed. Everyone had fun at Mardi Gras. But Heather had a toothache, and kept me up the entire night before the holiday. I was sure she'd be better in the morning, and we'd be able to attend the parades.

I was wrong.

Her toothache got increasingly worse, and, on "Fat Tuesday," I couldn't find an open dentist's office in all New Orleans. The entire city was either in the parades, or watching them. Heather was in agony. Something had to be done.

I remembered a dentist I'd taken her to when we lived in Gulfport, and called his office.

"If you can get her here this afternoon, we'll take care of whatever it is."

Before we left, I called my former neighbor, Linda, to see if we could come to her house afterwards. We were going to need someplace to spend the night. The two-and-a half-hour ride was long, but not nearly as long as the night had been with Heather constantly crying.

By noon, I had reached the dentist's office in Gulfport. Heather was lying on the seat beside me, ice pack on her cheek, sucking on whole cloves in an attempt to relieve the throbbing pain. She was still crying. The nurse took her back to the examining room, and I sat in the waiting room staring at the sign, "Payment required at time of service." I didn't have money to pay the dentist and health insurance hadn't made our list of necessities for quite a while. The checkbook I carried was worthless, there wasn't any money in the bank. So, I waited and worried.

I looked up to see the nurse smiling at me.

"Dr. Herman wants to talk to you."

The first thing that came to my mind was that he wanted payment up front.

"Mrs. Wallace, I'm going to have to do a root canal on that tooth of Heather's. How long has it been that way?"

"She didn't start complaining till last night. I couldn't find a dentist in New Orleans."

"Well, I'm glad you brought her here. That wasn't going to go away by itself. I'll clean the tooth out and put a temporary crown on."

"How long will that last?"

"Four to six weeks, then you'll need to bring her back, and I'll put the permanent crown on it. Basically, Heather has good, strong teeth, but you need to find a dentist in New Orleans where she can get regular checkups."

"Dr. Herman."

"Yes?"

"I'm sorry, but I can't pay you today."

"Don't worry about it. Just give us your address, and we'll bill you, or you can pay when I put Heather's permanent crown on."

As it turned out, almost 20 years passed before Heather's tooth got its permanent crown.

Heather was groggy when she reappeared, almost an hour later.

"Here's some pain medication for her, and she probably needs to take a good long nap," the nurse instructed me.

The drive down the coast to Linda's was familiar. Their house had been destroyed by fire after I moved away, and she and Alfred had rebuilt on the same site. The house was different, but the mess inside was the same.

Linda greeted me with open arms. We deposited Heather in a fairly quiet back bedroom with the blinds closed, and calm prevailed. Then, we sat down to catch up.

"I'm so glad to see you," Linda cooed. "You can't imagine what it's been like around here."

She told me how the children had barely escaped with the babysitter, and her oldest son, Robert, had been badly burned in the fire that had demolished their home.

"How's Robert doing?"

"Great. He's so lucky the fire didn't burn his face, and the only scars that show are on his legs, and part of one hand. His temper is worse than it was before, but he probably just takes after his father. He'll be all right."

"And now, you have Andrew, too!"

Linda had gotten pregnant almost immediately after the fire.

"I couldn't believe you had another baby. You and Alfred must be getting along a lot better."

"Not really. My diaphragm burned up in the fire and Alfred was still horny. You know how it goes."

I bit my lip. I wish I did. Kin had been amorous only with his paper and colored pens since our move to New Orleans. He wasn't cheating on me in any way. He just seemed to be totally disinterested in sex.

"Can I use your phone, Linda? I just want to touch base with Anna."

"Go right ahead. I'll be out on the patio working on my tan."

Anna and Merle had been in New Orleans a while back, and stopped by our house, unannounced, shortly after Kin and I had moved there, but I had not seen her since, and I missed her. She was delighted with my unexpected phone call.

"Join us for dinner," she invited.

"Thanks, but I don't think Heather will be up to going anywhere tonight. I'm going to let her rest."

"I bet you haven't been out to dinner for a long time. Let Heather rest at Linda's and we'll take you out someplace for fresh oysters."

I don't know which was stronger, my desire to see old friends, or my hunger for fresh shellfish, but I left my mother's guilt with Heather at Linda's that evening, and went to dinner with old friends.

At Anna and Gordon's house, we were enjoying drinks and catching up with gossip, when I heard a car pull into their driveway.

"There's Merle. I asked him to join us. I hope you don't mind, Jo Carroll. We all miss you."

I smiled at Anna. Her professed innocence didn't fool me. Whether she was a bit mischievously matchmaking or not, I didn't care. I hadn't realized I'd missed Merle, and his awkward nature so much.

We got ready to leave for the restaurant.

"Let me take my car," I said. "I'll probably want to leave early to get back to Linda's."

Anna chimed in quickly.

"Merle, why don't you ride with Jo Carroll so the two of you can catch up. You can ride back with us and pick up your car then."

As we drove to the restaurant, Merle filled the space between us with questions about my kids. Does Steven still build those model ships he was so crazy about? Is Heather's tooth going to be okay? Is Gina walking yet?

He didn't ask about Kin, and he didn't ask about me. He took one of my hands from the steering wheel and held it gently, but firmly. I didn't try to pull it away.

The restaurant was off the beaten path, an old plantation house set in a grove of trees. We were seated in a small, back room, away from the crowd. Flickering candles, sparkling crystal and crisp linen all added to the feeling of elegance romance and, for me, escape. Sitting with Merle and my old friends, sipping a White Russian, the difficult times of the recent past faded, and I concentrated on the here and now. We lingered long after dinner, and when we finally got up to leave, Anna asked me if I would mind dropping off Merle.

"We'll get his car back to him tomorrow, don't worry about it," she said.

"That sounds great," agreed Merle.

"I'd like Jo Carroll to see what I've done to my boat."

Merle and Shags lived on Moon Shadow at the Biloxi harbor. The implicit invitation was enticing.

"I don't know, I get seasick," I said with a foolish grin.

Merle just smiled.

"I've got some Dramamine in my pocket."

"Maybe you should call Linda before we leave."

Anna had remembered my child, not me.

Alfred answered the phone.

"This is Jo Carroll. How is Heather doing?"

"She's okay right now, but when are you coming back?"

"That's what I called about. Is Linda there?"

"Just a minute."

Linda picked up the phone almost immediately.

"Linda, sorry I didn't call earlier. Is everything all right? Could you keep Heather overnight for me? I'd like to spend the night at Anna's."

"I can keep her here, but don't you think you should be here with her? I don't want to get up in the middle of the night if she's not feeling well."

"Linda, I'll explain everything in the morning. I just think I've had too much to drink tonight. It would help a lot if you could keep her. Please?"

"Okay, but I don't think Alfred's too thrilled with the idea of you leaving her here. She seems to have settled down now."

The Dramamine worked, and so did the sex. I felt wonderful spending all night on a boat in the harbor in bed with a guy I'd been attracted to several years ago, and still found very appealing. I knew this was just a dream that would fade when I woke up in the morning. But, meanwhile, I could not ignore the depth of passion that Merle aroused in me.

Too soon, the sunrise peaked through the wide windows of his gently rocking craft "Moon Shadow" and I knew it was time for me to return to reality, to take care of my child, my family and me.

When I left, Merle walked me to the end of the dock, put his arms around me, and turned so I was looking into his very blue eyes.

"You know," he said, gently, "last night was not about fucking. It was about making love. You make it hard to forget."

I hadn't figured out what I was going to tell Linda about leaving Heather with her all night, but I didn't have to worry. By the time I got there, she had left for a meeting and Mae was standing in the door.

"Well, well, well, Miss Jo Carroll. I didn't know y'all was livin' in N'awlins.. You better take care of this chile, she's lookin' kinda peaked around the edges."

"Mom! Why did you leave me?"

I heard fury in Heather's voice.

"Those kids were so damn loud, I couldn't sleep all night. I had to sleep with Aleece, but Robert kept coming in and spying on us, and the baby boy cried all night. He's older than Gina. He shouldn't cry that much."

I fixed a bed for Heather in the back of the van, and she slept all the way to New Orleans. I felt guilty all the way back. I had missed a day's work at the bank, but thought I could at least make use of the time to catch up on grocery shopping, for once, and get the house cleaned up. When I pulled into the driveway, I saw Kin sitting on the back stoop. It was too early for him to be home from his teaching job. As I walked toward him, I saw the half empty bottle of scotch in his hand. He looked at me, and took a long pull on the bottle.

"Guess what? I quit."

"Quit what?"

"I can't teach those fucking idiots any more. Pushing my desk up against the door to keep gang members out is not my idea of a safe place to work."

"Kin, shut up and go in the house. You're drunk!"

"Am not. Am fucking free. Free to fucking breathe. Free to fucking leave that fucking place."

I gave up talking to him, scooted past his babbling, inebriated body, and got Heather into the house.

The half-full packing boxes were scattered all over the house. I'd been gone a little more than 24 hours, but in that short time, Kin had almost stripped the house. Partially filled boxes of dishes lay around the kitchen, and most of Kin's writing materials were packed into crates. I peeked in at Gina. She was asleep in her bed, but her toys were piled into a laundry basket stacked in the corner of her room.

I ran back outside to see if Kin could make any sense of this. He had passed out where I left him, the liquor bottle lying broken on the curb.

Steven arrived home from school, but he didn't know much either, just that, last night, Kin had told him to start packing his stuff. At first, he thought, Kin was throwing him out, and he had tried to call me.

"Didn't Linda tell you I called? Actually, I talked to Alfred. He probably wouldn't tell you anyway."

My insides were screaming. Guilt overwhelmed me. Could Kin possibly know where I had been last night? And if he did, did it really matter? My trains were racing in circles, faster and faster. I was frightened. I couldn't make sense of anything. Did I have this instability in my head because of our money problems or were the money problems a result of my instability?

Figuring out the answers didn't really matter.

If I could get up the nerve to take my neighbor's gun from his unlocked porch, and put it to my head, and pull the trigger...

If I could find some quick way to end this miserable life...sex, money, hurt, darkness would all be things of the past. They couldn't get me any more.

Suicide was a cheap, simple answer to my problems, but it was no answer for Heather, Steven and Gina.

Night came with no solutions. I slept fitfully in Gina's room, and heard Kin stumble up the stairs about 1 am.

The next morning, I buried myself in routine, got the kids off to school, took Gina to the babysitter and went to work. When I got home, the boxes were a bit fuller, and another bottle was nearly empty. Kin was watering his precious plants.

I didn't know whether to confront him or ignore him. I couldn't handle anything else at that point, so I opted for ignoring him, and tried to tiptoe quietly up the stairs. He came to the bottom of the stairs and yelled.

"I can't work there any more. I'm suing them."

This brought me back downstairs quickly.

"Suing them? Suing who? For what? Because you don't want to work?"

"They pushed me down the stairs. I can't walk any more. I'll sue, and I'll be set for life. Workman's comp will pay all the bills. I'm not going back to that insane asylum. We're moving to Ocean Springs where a man can live a civilized life."

8 Coming Round The Bend

I don't know how we got from New Orleans to Ocean Springs, Mississippi. The trip is not in my memory.

Once there, we rented a three-bedroom bungalow. Our new home, located on a quiet, tree-shaded gravel road, was a wonderful, peaceful contrast to the hustle-bustle of New Orleans.

Everything around me seemed to proceed at the stereotypical-slow, Southern pace.

But not me. My emotions were racing around and out of reach. My trains and I were going faster and faster.

And, the much-anticipated settlement from the New Orleans public school was as imaginary as Kin's fall down the stairs.

We had no money.

The dishes weren't even unpacked when the VW died. I managed to get it pushed to a mechanic, who took out the engine, and then announced the cost to fix it would be more than $300. He might as well have told me to push it into the ocean. Without a way to pay the bill, the car sat at the garage, with no hope of rescue.

No one was going to rescue me either, I decided. Kin had a promise of a job at a small city college in nearby Pass Christian, but I wasn't surprised when it didn't work out.

A new Hilton Hotel down the Coast was scheduled to open in a week, and had advertised plenty of jobs. I got a ride with a neighbor and applied for a job, any job. I was afraid I wouldn't have any money to feed the kids if I didn't find work immediately. I was scared to take the time to look for a more conventional job as a bank teller. I couldn't make things happen fast enough to slow my racing trains.

The Hilton hired me on the spot as a waitress in their cafe. I reported the next morning for training. If they had offered me a job as a chambermaid, I would have taken it and spent my days scrubbing toilets in solitude.

I got a ride home with a plump, bleached-blonde with bright red lipstick and a toothy grin, who said her name was Jan. Jan and I would be wearing the same multi-striped uniform by next week.

"You don't look like you've waited any tables before, honey. How come you want this job?" she asked. "Ever lifted one of them heavy trays loaded with food and then had some asshole pinch your butt just as you got it on your shoulder?"

"No. I needed to make some money real quick. I figured the tips on this job would be good."

"You can make good money on tips if you swing just right," she said with a grin. "You got an old man?"

"Yeah, kinda." Suddenly, I wanted to ditch Kin and have some freedom. "He's around, but that doesn't matter a whole lot."

My new friend was driving with one hand on the wheel, and pulling something out of her dirt-stained white purse with the other.

"You smoke?"

I started to say "no thanks," then I noticed the cigarette was small, thin and hand-rolled.

"Sometimes," I said.

Her eyes never left the road as she lit it with one hand, took a long drag, and carefully handed it to me. The smoke formed a bond of friendship between us, and, by the time she dropped me off, we agreed she would provide my transportation to work until the VW was fixed.

I'd been without medication or professional counseling for quite a while.

"I can handle it on my own. I don't need anybody else," I kept telling myself. Gone were the rational thoughts which had guided me to the free mental health clinic after Bruce left.

Jan's smoke had slowed the racing trains in my head for that afternoon. Everything seemed bright, beautiful and peaceful. The older kids were in school, and Anna, who lived in a nearby subdivision, had picked up Gina. Kin was in the back room pecking at his typewriter.

"Hey, beautiful," I yelled, as I swept past him into the room. In a bold gesture, I planted a warm kiss on the back of his neck as he leaned over his writing. I'd been quite hostile to him since the broken whiskey bottle in New Orleans. He ignored me, and the magic smoke was beginning to filter out of my head. I tried slipping my arms down his body so he couldn't move to type.

"Kin," I whispered in my sexiest voice, "let's talk." I bit him gently on the neck.

"Jo Carroll, please! If you want me to get a job, leave me alone. I have to have this application in this afternoon. I borrowed my dad's car so I could meet the deadline. First you want one thing, then you want another. Leave me alone."

I left Kin alone, but the blackness wouldn't leave me alone. The joint in the car had given me temporary relief, but it was no substitute for the prescription drugs I had once taken to lighten and control my depression. I just needed to suck it up. I could handle this. If I had my children around me and was making enough money to take care of them, everything would be fine. I could do anything I wanted to do. As soon as the kids finished supper, I pretended to be tired and hit the bed.

The next day, getting dressed for work, I looked in the mirror. I didn't know what to do. Should I put on more makeup? Did I need the bright red lipstick my new friend used? I didn't have any money to bleach my dark brown hair and the freckles on my face seemed darker because my skin was so pale. I didn't have the energy to make myself look any better. I couldn't worry about it any longer, Jan would be honking her horn any minute.

At the Hilton, we posed for a group picture in our striped multicolored uniforms. I hated it. I didn't know or like what I was doing. I couldn't keep straight who ordered what at my tables and nobody in the kitchen could decipher my writing, even if I managed to spell the entrees correctly. I tried making little notes to myself on my waitress pad, " ...this goes to little fat man in corner..." until I realized I wasn't getting any tips because this was the same ticket the customer got to pay the bill.

In the back of the kitchen, steam tables had been set up for food for employees. The food was not the same as the menu. I soon realized not many employees sat down and ate what I did. One day, I sat next to a waiter from the hotel's elegant dining room that shared the kitchen with the cafe. He had a steak on his plate, the most tender, juiciest piece of meat I had seen in a long time.

My mouth watered.

"Did you have to pay extra for that?"

"Not while I'm wearing this tux. How come you're eating that slop, girlie?"

"I'm hungry, and my name isn't girlie, it's Jo Carroll. What does your tux have to do with that steak?"

"Never worked as a waitress before, have you?"

"No, but I do okay."

"Not if you're eating that crap. Anyone who works where food is served is stupid if they don't eat anything they want. I told the couple I was serving that eating the center of the Chateaubriand was bad luck, so the chef always kept it."

I laughed, and much of my tension disappeared during the next half hour as John, a waiter from New Orleans, who was almost 20 years my senior, told me the rules of how to survive in lower hotel management.

The next day, I traded John cherry burgundy ice cream, which was only served in the cafe, for a piece of delicious steak. In spite of the difference in our ages, I knew his interest in me was not paternal. In the alcove outside the kitchen where water pitchers were filled, his hand frequently found my waist and hips.

I blotted out life at home. Kin had finally found a part-time job at the community college, the kids were in school and Gina was surviving. Anna let me borrow her car until I put together enough in tips to redeem the VW. Kin seemed to have permanent possession of his parents' only car.

And, I had decided John was the unlikely white knight who was going to rescue me. One evening, while I was working, he came in, sat at the counter and ordered coffee. He wore a horrible Hawaiian print short-sleeved shirt and coughed as he chained smoked Camels. I had never before seen him out of his penguin suit. His blue eyes were large and almond-shaped, and his short, black hair held just a hint of gray. At that moment, he looked like the man of my dreams. As I poured his second cup of coffee, he put his hand on my wrist.

"I'm off this weekend," he said, "and I thought you might like to do something, maybe get a drink, have dinner."

"Sounds like fun. I'll think about it."

"Include an overnight bag in those thoughts. I don't intend to take you home."

I smiled at him, but his comment scared me a little. Kin and I had a lax relationship, but I couldn't be gone overnight and not tell him anything. What kind of excuse could I think up that he would believe? The trains in my head were racing around so fast they were jumping the tracks and bumping into each other. I ignored the warning signals and hurled ahead. I could do anything I wanted to.

"Kin, some of the women at work are getting together for a party when we get off. The manager is letting us use a few rooms and we're going to make it a weekend. The kids don't have anything special this weekend. Do you mind if I go?"

I'd rehearsed the speech on my way home, and now that I was actually asking Kin the words almost seemed true. He agreed easily. By this time in our relationship, I don't think either of us wanted to ask too many questions for fear of what secrets might be uncovered. I knew he was as unhappy in the marriage as I was, but I didn't want another man to leave, for any reason. Any husband was better than no husband.

I left my small overnight bag at John's apartment. His French Provincial furnishings were charming, and not at all what I'd expected to find. We went to Mary Mahoney's, a tourist restaurant just down the beach. Nobody who knew me would see me. We ate on the patio under a live oak tree with a view of the moon on Biloxi Bay. John ordered an assortment of hor d'oeuvres, which was fine with me. I was too nervous to eat much of anything. Later, at the bar, I sipped my White Russians while John downed vodka on the rocks. The drinks clouded my brain a little, but not so much that I was unaware we had left without paying.

"John, we forgot to pay the bill."

"Relax, girlie. If a guy who serves drinks in one of these joints in Biloxi can't get free drinks from another waiter, something's wrong. The world ain't what it used to be. Didn't get a bill. Didn't pay a bill. He got a tip. I didn't wine and dine you for you to worry your sweet little head about a bill."

We were just minutes from his apartment and once inside, after only a few long, deep, hungry kisses, our clothes came off. I looked at his lean, hard, bare body. His physic was nice, especially for a man over 50. Suddenly, my eyes just stopped.

"Hey, girlie, something wrong?"

"No, I'm sorry. I've just never seen anyone, who, I mean I've never seen, well, you know, a man who wasn't circumcised."

"Turn you off?"

"Not at all. It's just different."

"Well, it works just as good. Come over here and I'll show you."

He was wrong. It worked even better. We slept late into the morning the next day, and then made love in the shower. The only thing to eat in his apartment was some junk food in the refrigerator. We gobbled it up, and settled down to a lazy afternoon of reading. He lent me Tom Robbins "Another Roadside Attraction," while he read a worn copy of a Louis L'Amour. I hadn't been so completely relaxed for years. I had no guilt about the kids or cheating on Kin. I made believe I had no strings, no responsibilities.

Toward evening, John's poker buddies started to drift in. I knew two of them from the Hilton. John didn't have to tell me this was no penny-ante game. He couldn't possibly have made enough as a waiter to afford this apartment.

"What's the dame doin' here? It's bad luck."

"Women always yap."

I looked at John and started to get up.

"Stay put, girlie. This is my place. She's my luck. Any objections, you can go back out the door you came in."

Nobody left.

I curled up in a comfortable chair about three feet from the table, and kept my expression constant. At one point, when the men were getting themselves fresh drinks, John handed me a pouch and a small pipe.

"It's hash. Go sit in the corner and smoke it, you'll enjoy the game more."

I looked inside the bag. It looked like dark patches of sawdust held together by glue.

"Go easy. It sneaks up on you."

I sat in the corner of the living room until dawn, watching John's poker friends surrender their money, while the vodka disappeared from several bottles. The hash disappeared from the bag, too. It made me feel terrific. Floating without a care, no freight trains were traveling on my tracks that morning, only deluxe cars with vista domes. Funny, though, I never smoked hash again, and that was the first and last time I ever spent a weekend with John. Once in a while I would work a split shift and share his bed in the afternoon. We'd make love fierce and hard, as though it was the last time, ever. John was trying to deny his age, and I wanted to escape my responsibilities. I told myself he was intelligent. After all, he could read a book. And, his hard sexy body was all I needed. But, by the end of the summer, I realized I didn't want to sustain this lifestyle, even if I could.

While I had been sleeping around on the afternoon shift, Kin had let the Persian cat I'd given him as a wedding present die of neglect. I was so mad I couldn't stand it. That was the last straw. Heather and Steven were staying with their father in Indiana. I packed the VW with everything that was precious to me, including my baby.

"Just get out," I told Kin. "I'm going to Kansas to visit my mother, and by the time I get back, I want you out of here."

I'd been at my mother's farm outside Horton just short of a week when Kin called.

"Where are you calling from? Are you out of the house yet?"

"Jo Carroll, please give me another chance. There's a new song on the radio, 'Midnight Blue.' Please listen to it."

I took my mother's car for a drive to hear the song. I twirled the radio dials, trying to bring in a Kansas City station. Finally, I heard,

"...wouldn't you give your hand to a friend, wouldn't you give me just one more chance..Midnight Blue..." This was the romantic Kin I'd fallen in love with. I'd treated him terribly last year, but, maybe, I still loved him.

The next morning I called.

"OK, Kin, we'll give it one more chance, but I can't promise anything."

Once back in Ocean Springs, I knew I couldn't go back to picking tips off tables, while Kin and the kids ate hot dogs. Midnight Blue had sounded good from the fields of Kansas, but once I returned, our life was the same old mess. I don't know who was more irresponsible—Kin with his promises of jobs, or me, trying to find solutions in his promises.

Anna told me I had two choices. I could either check into a mental institution or run away from my present circumstances. I wasn't about to check into an institution, so I decided to run away and Eureka Springs seemed like the best place to go. I ignored the trains bumping together and left all three of the kids in Kin's care.

I'd been home from my mother's less than two months when I remembered my fascination with the pottery in Eureka Springs. I kissed my kids goodbye, boarded the bus and threw my future on the potter's wheel. All the way to Eureka, the caboose in my head kept repeating "Guilt, guilt, how can I leave my kids with someone I don't want to stay with?" The words "guilt, guilt," grated on the rails. I thought of Anna's advice, and figured either way I'd be away from my children, and if I went to Eureka, I might be home sooner and saner to take care of them.

Eureka Springs, Arkansas, might well have been labeled a miniature San Francisco with its steep, winding hills with sharp curves at the top, houses set flush with the curbs, gables and spirals reaching through the fog.

When Kin had visited Lucy and Jim in this charming town, long before we met, his sexual orientation was well known. During that summer I'd spent there with my kids, our marital status was not in question. Now being here by myself, I didn't know how or where I would fit in. Would people think Kin had left me for his former lover?

I shouldn't have worried. You could sleep with anyone you wanted to, and everyone would know at breakfast the next morning, but nobody cared.

I lived with the same carpenter and girlfriend whom the kids and I had shared a house with the previous summer. This time, Karen and Ken lived in a small stucco house on a mountain side, just outside Eureka Springs. Ken worked as a caretaker for the absentee owners, who didn't pay any attention to how many people shared the house as long as their property was taken care of. I slept in a borrowed sleeping bag on the couch in the corner of the living room. In addition to the sofa and me, the room held a big, wooden dining room table loaded with house plants. Karen was nursing through the winter, and a lumpy, overstuffed chair that was too old to be thrown away. My bed was just inches away from the wood-burning stove Ken loaded with wood every night before we went to sleep, but by morning I could always see my breath just above the covers.

Karen and I made the trip into town in her old, red Falcon every morning about 9. At the pottery, Karen proceeded to make beautiful pots. Gary, the owner of the pottery shop, patiently tried to teach me how to wedge clay, start the kick wheel and get the lump of clay in front of me to look like an object of art. Pottery was hard work, much more physical than I'd imagined. Nothing I made looked remotely like anything any tourist who wandered in would want to buy.

Karen was into health foods, so we grabbed some vegetables at the end of every day, drove back to the side of the mountain, and fixed supper for the three of us. A television didn't fit into their budget or lifestyle, but the public radio station and the library kept us occupied, and, on more than one occasion, we dipped into the stash of seasoned weed readily available.

In Eureka, I always had someone to talk to. After the tourists left, the hardcore population was one big family. I had a lot of shoulders to cry on. If I kept my perspective narrow enough to exclude the family I'd left in Ocean Springs, I never felt out of sync. Gary had given me the title "Apprentice Potter," but, judging by the quality of my work that winter, I think he had a soft spot for me. He and his companion, Sean, sometimes took me to lunch at an old, stone hotel on Main

Street, just down the street from the pottery shop. One day, they surprised me with an invitation.

"Why don't you come spend the weekend with us, Jo Carroll?"

"We have plenty of room, and we'll cook something besides vegetables."

I didn't hesitate a minute to accept. I knew where they lived, but I'd never been inside their house. I wanted to peek in on how two gay men lived. Kin had always told me I could ask him anything about his former lovers, but I wasn't sure I wanted to know too much about my husband's past.

"Sounds good to me. Maybe it will give Karen and Ken a little extra time to themselves, too. Sometimes I feel like I'm an adopted child, and they need an empty nest right now."

Everyone I knew in Eureka joked about Gary and Sean having a maid for the upstairs and one for the downstairs.

"Nothing's as clean as a Queen," said one friend. They were giving me an opportunity to see for myself. I was on their doorstep the next weekend.

When I peered through the window at the edge of the door, I could already see the gleam of glass and polished wood. Sean opened the door before I could knock.

"Come on in. Let me take your things upstairs. Gary's in the kitchen."

The house smelled of fresh baking bread and well-oiled furniture. Sean took my overnight bag as I wandered into the living room, gawking at everything in sight. Art nouveau glass figurines covered nearly every surface in this renovated Victorian. No wonder they needed two maids. I sank into a leather chair by the fireplace and looked around. My friend had been right. Everything was spotless.

"Hi, Jo Carroll. Ready for some wine?"

More relaxed than at work, Gary was the perfect host. He smiled, and his eyes sparkled through wire-frame glasses as he handed me a crystal goblet.

Dinner proved to be luscious, and afterwards we rounded out the evening with snifters of Cognac in front of the fire. We laughed about the Christians who flocked to Eureka to see the cement Christ of the Ozarks on a mountainside that overlooked the town.

"No class," Gary said. "The statue's got no class. I've never seen so much ugly concrete in one place in my life."

"But doesn't it bring a lot of business to town?" I asked.

"Are you kidding? These people bring their campers and eat their lunch from paper bags. And then they come downtown to have a tour. All they do is go in and out the doors on Main Street. In and out, hour after hour. It's the closest thing to sex some of them ever have."

Sean was the first to laugh at his own joke, but Gary and I both joined in.

"How about another?"

"Oh, thanks, but unless you want me to sleep on the sofa, you'd better show me where the guest room is now."

Sean led me upstairs and opened the door to the guestroom.

"Just holler if you need anything. There's extra towels over there and the light switch is right here by the door."

The bedroom was like nothing I had ever experienced. The dinner drinks had gone to my head and, for a moment, I thought I'd walked into the latest edition of "Home Decor." The overhead light had been dimmed, and a scented candle flickered on the bedside table. The cover had been turned back on the carved, wooden, antique bed and a piece of Godiva chocolate lay on my pillow. I felt relaxed and pampered.

I undressed, climbed into the inviting bed and tried to go to sleep. I couldn't. The irony of it all had caught up with me. Here I was on a queen-sized mattress, in a couple of queens' home, trying to escape the fact that I had a husband who would probably feel a lot more comfortable here than I did. I didn't know whether to laugh or cry, but a sob caught in my throat and I knew I had to get out of this situation and face reality.

The next morning, I wrote my hosts a thank-you note and slipped out the back door before breakfast. I walked over to the pottery and let myself in. I looked at the stuff waiting to be fired. I could tell it was Karen's work by the graceful ribbon handles on everything. Gary's pots were more delicate, occasionally one here or there was decorated with a woman's face. And then, there were mine. They looked like crude lumps that would have been rejected in any high school art class. Gary kept telling me I just needed more practice, but these things were terrible. Was this the reason I'd left my kids a thousand miles away? My stupid thoughts that I was an artist?

I'd always thought of myself as an artist, exploring different types of art. As a child I'd taken ballet, and I loved being on stage in front of an audience. And of course there was the theater. Art is a form of expression and I had convinced myself that I could express wonderful art images in the clay here in northern Arkansas. I clasped my hands together and rested my head in them. What the hell was I doing here?

I spent the day cleaning the floor and shelves of the pottery, trying to get rid of my guilt. By evening, I had made up my mind. If I couldn't be an artist by putting my hands in clay, maybe I could be successful behind the lens of a camera.

I figured, if I left on the bus the next day, I could still make it back to Mississippi in time to enroll for the spring quarter at the University of Southern Mississippi in good old Hattiesburg. This time no pregnancy would interfere with my studies.

Gary just smiled.

"If you ever decide you want to come back, feel free to. You're not that bad, with practice, your work would sell."

Karen and Ken wrapped their arms around me. Karen told me I was the easiest person to live with she'd ever met. I had pretended for a while I could live their lifestyle, but I had to go home. I missed my kids. If I ever came back, I would have to have them in my knapsack.

Kin and I had kept in close touch, but mostly by letters, neither one of us could afford a phone bill.

What if Gina didn't recognize me? What if Steven and Heather had some horrible problems and no one had told me? What if they were mad at me and couldn't forgive me for leaving them? I had too many what ifs. The trains in my head were colliding.

Nobody knew I was coming, so when the bus stopped in Ocean Springs there was no one to meet me. I dragged my suitcase to the house. It was supper time and Kin was at the stove stirring pots. He looked up and nodded, but the kids were another story. Steven and Heather hit me with hugs so hard I stumbled backwards and sat on the floor. Once I was on the floor, Gina covered my face with kisses. I sat Gina on my lap, and Steven and Heather stuck to my sides.

"Mom, why didn't you tell us you were coming? I wanted to make a banner that said "Welcome" Steven told me. Heather was quiet and just looked at me as tears started to flow down her cheeks. I knew I'd never leave my kids again. Kin looked over in our direction and said, "Supper's ready."

Nothing had changed. Money was tight, but I was determined to get my degree this time. Driving 180 miles round trip, three times a week, photographic assignments, studying, teaching a night class and the responsibility of being a mother kept me from thinking about my relationship with Kin. I still couldn't get the idea out of my head that there was an artist lurking in my body, and I was giving myself one more chance with photography. Kin didn't cross my path very often. He resented having to care for Heather and Steven during my absence and now he retaliated by ignoring them and focusing on Gina. He doted on this child of his, cooing over her and wooing her with trinkets he brought home almost every day, but she was sleeping on a mat unrolled on the kitchen floor because we couldn't afford a bed. Sometimes, she slept with Heather, and sometimes, I would take her into my bed while Kin wrote all night.

My frustration with the whole situation boiled over one evening. My trains collided. The track had run out.

I couldn't stand how I felt any longer and needed to escape.

Without thinking, I walked out the door, but was only able to go to the corner. At 11 pm, the harsh glare of the street lamps lit up the lonely, deserted neighborhood.

Scared and alone, I tried to make some sense of situation.

I was 33 years old.

I had already run away from home.

I wasn't looking for a future, I needed to deal with the present.

And, I couldn't.

I started to cry and couldn't stop.

Finally, I started walking and found myself at the phone booth outside the 7-11 by the Back Bay Bridge. Digging in my pocket for change, I called Anna and asked if one of them could come get me. A rain had started and I was soaked by the time Gordon arrived. I sat in the car and cried. He said nothing. I don't know how long we sat in the parking lot before we left. I do know, by the time we got to their house, Anna was worried. She put her arms around me.

"What do you want us to do?" she asked.

I had no answers. I didn't know what I wanted to do myself. They took me back to my house and I slept on the floor with Gina. I convinced myself my problems had to be physical. I could take care of any mental anguish by just being a little tougher. I made an appointment with my family doctor for a complete physical. I was sure he'd prescribe some extra vitamins, and I would be okay.

At the doctor's office, I tried to figure out whether the opening of the paper gown went in the front or the back as tears started to get it wet. The doctor walked in and started the examination without noticing the tears. He stopped at my right breast, and went over the same spot a couple of times.

"Let me put your hand here. Do you feel that? Is that something you normally feel?"

"I don't know."

"I'm sending you to the hospital for a sonogram this afternoon."

"That's not really what I came in here for. Can't it wait? I have some other plans."

"No, it can't," he said sharply. "I'll have my nurse call ahead for you."

I had the sonogram and pushed it out of my mind. Heather and Steven were leaving in four days to visit their father, and I had to get them ready. And, I had decided to return to Eureka with Gina. Heather and Steven would come later, after they got through visiting their father. While I was in Eureka, Kin was moving us to a larger house just down the block where I could have a darkroom, and the kids could swim in the bayou. But the real reason for the move was for Kin and I to each have our own separate bedrooms.

The day we were all leaving for our different destinations, the phone rang.

"Kin, I thought you had that thing disconnected. We can't afford to pay a phone bill all summer when no one's here."

"I forgot. Can you answer it?"

"Jo Carroll, this is Dr. Haskell. I just got the results of your sonogram, and I don't like the looks of it."

"I'm sorry, Dr. Haskell, but I was just getting ready to leave town. I'll be back in a few months, and make an appointment then."

"I don't think you understand. The test shows that there's a mass in your breast. It might be malignant. I'll see you in my office this afternoon."

I started to scream and cry as I slammed down the phone.

"This can't be happening to me. Nothing ever goes right. I don't have time for this nonsense."

"What's the matter, Mom?" asked Heather.

"Nothing. I'm fine. I'll tell you about it later."

Kin took the kids to the airport and I took myself to the doctor. He wanted to schedule surgery for the next day. Surgery? My mind raced. I still had so many things I wanted to do, so many things to try, so many avenues to explore. I certainly wasn't ready for my life to end. Had I already used up all my options and made all the wrong decisions? The implications of my condition went out of focus.

I was also vain.

"I don't want any scars."

"I'll keep them to a minimum," Dr. Haskell said. "But I can't control what I'm going to find."

The scar was minimal and the tumor was benign, but the procedure had left me very weak. Kin's concern didn't extend to caring for a convalescent, so Gina and I stayed with Anna until I was strong enough to make the trip to Eureka. Steven and Heather met me there.

Jim and Lucy once again offered me free living space, this time above a storefront. The previous tenant had left a gas hot plate. The small room had a toilet and sink, but the shower was downstairs. We slept on sleeping bags between the storage boxes. During the day, Gina went to daycare on the edge of the woods, and Steven and Heather ran up and down the streets. I was actually selling some of my flower pots at the pottery shop.

At night, we went on picnics, swam in a nearby lake, and visited with friends. That summer was the hidden garden of my life. Despite the economic disadvantages, my life seemed perfect. My children were with me, I was surrounded by people I actually liked to talk to, and I didn't have any trouble sleeping at night. The rhythmic clickity-clack in my head was reassuring and soothing.

I don't know how he found me, but one night, John, of my Hilton days, showed up on my doorstep. He didn't look quite so suave and debonair away from the cosmopolitan backdrop of the Gulf Coast and his poker playing friends. He looked grubby. His hair needed cutting, and his face was covered with a 5-day beard.

"Hey, girlie, I thought I'd never find you."

"John, what the hell are you doing here?"

"That's a funny question from somebody who used to smoke my stash and fuck me in the shower."

"Shut up, my kids are in the other room. What do you want?"

"I want to sleep with you. Crawl in your arms and stay forever. I wanna be your lover boy."

"Bullshit! You're just drunk. You can't stay here. My kids are here, and it's not even my place. Get out of here before I call the cops."

"Where am I supposed to sleep if you throw me out?"

"I'm not throwing you out, you were never in. You're a big boy, go find your own mattress."

I slammed the door in his face. I wished I could slam the door on other parts of my life just as easily. Somehow, I had to create a safety valve to keep my past behind me.

My face was wet with tears when I left Eureka Springs at the end of the summer. The place had given me a rest, a bunch of quiet moments strung together for my soul. Now, I needed to go home and finish my degree.

I didn't have any idea what Kin had done to survive financially over the summer. He swore to me he was teaching English at Biloxi High in the fall, and his monthly paycheck would support us. I got my grant money together for school, enrolled in the fall quarter and bought myself an enlarger, so I wouldn't have to spend so much time in the lab at school.

A neighbor was attending classes on the same campus, and we started to car pool. Janet had bright-red hair, and claimed she'd once dated Elvis. She was going back to school so she could find a career in which she could earn enough money to leave her abusive husband. The amount of makeup she wore was exceeded only by her bubbly spirits. I figured if she could hold her life together, so could I.

School had been in session for over two months, and I still hadn't seen a paycheck from Kin. He assured me it was just a matter of time, a "mess of paperwork" was how he described the delay. My grant money and child support were not enough to keep the wolf away from the door, and I was starting to panic. I didn't trust Kin, and I began to nag him about the paycheck he kept promising was coming next week.

"I can't believe you've been teaching all this time and they haven't given you any money. What are we supposed to do?"

"I'll talk to the office in the morning."

"That's what I've heard for two months. I need to know something for sure. I have money for the last installment on my tuition, but I can put it off if I need to take the money and buy food."

"Pay your damn tuition. I can pay the bills. I'll have a check by Friday."

I could tell when he walked in the door Friday evening he didn't have a check.

"Get out. Go. I don't care where. Just get the hell out of here, and leave us alone."

I had no money in the bank and no food in the cupboard. How could I have been so stupid as to trust him and spend the last money I had on my dumb tuition bill? I was so embarrassed, I didn't know where to turn. My kids were hungry, and I didn't have any food in the cupboard. I had never imagined myself in this situation. I went to the house of a friend who I knew wouldn't ask any questions. She gave me two $20s.

"Are you sure this is all you need?"

"It's more than enough. I'll be fine," I lied. "I just need to get some groceries."

I only called my brother once a year on his birthday, so when he heard my voice, he knew something was seriously wrong.

"I'll send you a $500 check this afternoon," he said. He wanted me to go to the county welfare office for food stamps, but I was too ashamed.

My mother and Joe sent another $100.

9 Couplings

"Why don't you let me take you home?" asked Phil.

Phil was a short, stocky Mexican, who claimed to have inherited his Spanish past from a distant cousin I might know, Salvador Dali. We'd just met in a bar. I was out looking for male companionship, or, more truthfully, sex, and I was not terribly discriminating.

"We'll go out for an early breakfast or something," he said.

"No, thanks. It's that 'or something' I'm worried about," I told him.

Four months earlier, I had filed for divorce from Kin. I thought divorcing him would solve all my problems. I was sadly mistaken. I had come to the bar with Maureen, a woman who had taught classes at the same school where Kin once worked. She had moved in with me to help with rent. She had frizzy red hair, and a tall, hard body. She raced sailboats in her spare time. I taught elementary darkroom techniques to keep food on the table. I was enrolled in more classes than I could handle in order to make this semester my last.

Nothing was enough. I never felt satisfied. But instead of cutting back, I took on more.

Back at the bar, Maureen had left early and alone. I stayed, convinced if I didn't meet someone that night, the rest of my life would be ruined. The first time Phil asked me to dance, I told him, "Not right now."

When he came around a second time, I accepted. I rested my head on his shoulder, and we danced the next dance, and the next, some slow, some fast, until we were the only ones left, and I had not called Maureen to come pick me up.

"I'm safe," said Phil. "Look, I'll even let you drive the car if that will make you feel better."

Soon, I was driving his car down the Coast Highway and we weren't going to my house.

"Turn right up there, at the light," said Phil. "You're a photographer, right? I've got these terrific photos I want to show you."

I fooled myself into believing I was following his directions to see how good he was as a photographer. We headed down a dark, gravel road. We pulled into his driveway, and I realized his place was terribly isolated.

"A suicidal impulse must have brought me to this place," I thought to myself. "I must be crazy to drive to a strange man's house in the middle of the night."

I had visions of my body being found in a remote ditch. I went inside anyway. I was relieved when all he wanted was sex. The second time I saw Phil, he asked me to marry him. I said, "No, all I want is sex."

The next Saturday night, Linda invited me to tour the bars. She had divorced Alfred several months ago. I told her I had too much homework, and couldn't afford to pay for food or drinks.

"Honey, don't be silly. Y'all don't have to pay for anything. If we can't find some bubba to pay for the drinks, it'll be my treat."

At the second bar, we found two tanned hunks in their early 20s, surveying the scene. Linda glanced their way a few times and they ambled over to our table.

"You ladies mind if we join you?" the tall one asked.

Linda looked up and giggled. They sat down and ordered a round of drinks. The guys were oil jocks from Louisiana, enjoying a fast weekend on the Coast. I could tell they were much younger than we were, and I didn't feel like babysitting. I got up to leave, but Linda dragged me to the ladies' room with her.

"I don't want these guys to get away," said Linda, "so I'm going to invite them back to the house. The kids are asleep by now, and the babysitter lives close enough to walk home."

"I don't believe you," I said, "after all the crap you gave me last week about going to Phil's house you're going to take these guys home with you?"

"No. We're going to take them home with us."

She licked her forefinger, and then playfully jabbed at my chest.

Linda still lived in the big, beautiful house she and Alfred had had on the beach. I hoped, as we walked through the front door, her house didn't look too ostentatious to these young jocks. Linda and Mike went into the kitchen to fix drinks. I chatted with Tom in the living room. He seemed like a nice kid, bright, clean-cut and just looking for a good time.

Linda was taking much too long with the drinks, so I went to check on her. The kitchen was deserted. I walked down the hallway to her bedroom. The door was closed, locked, with no one in sight. Even if I wanted to go to bed with Tom, this was not the time. I made a date to see him in two weeks, agreeing to meet him at the same bar. He offered to pick me up at my house, I wondered for a second if I would be embarrassed if my kids knew I was picking up young men in bars, but I agreed anyway.

Linda called to say she had enjoyed our night out. A month later, she had a date for me.

"Now, I know you won't want to go out with this guy, but he needs a date for the Jaycees banquet at the Broadwater," Linda explained. "It's a really fancy affair, with great food, and maybe you'll even be able to make some professional connections, maybe meet someone who needs a photographer."

"What's his name? How did you meet him? Why aren't you going yourself?"

"I hear they're going to have a great band, and I believe they're going on a moonlight cruise."

"Linda, stop. Who is it?"

"Alfred."

"Alfred? Your Alfred?" I asked. "The one you just divorced? The one I can't stand? Come on, what are you doing getting him dates for, anyway?"

"We were talking about when he is going to pick up the kids, and he said he didn't have a date for this party. He seemed so lonely. I told him I'd call you for him. It'll just be a one-time shot. You don't have to do anything but go to dinner with him. It's not like you have to marry the guy," she giggled. "I already did that."

I agreed to go. I hadn't changed my opinion of her ex-husband, but I figured my waning photography business could use an infusion of young, professional businessmen who might need their pictures taken.

I borrowed a formal dress from Linda, a pale green color that was not me. But I shouldn't have worried, Alfred was nervous enough for both of us. During dinner, the Jaycees shouted constantly, and he hardly spoke to me. I wondered why he had wanted a date.

The evening did not include a moonlight cruise. The band played all night, and we danced without conversation. At the hotel, we sat down for breakfast at a large, round table, elegantly set with starched white linen, stemmed glasses of fresh-squeezed orange juice and baskets of fancy sweet rolls. We shared conversation with two other couples. Alfred asked me about my photography, classes, kids, and he listened to my answers as he ate his steak and eggs. He'd just been named to an honorary Jaycees board. When he talked about how much this meant to him, his dimples showed.

I was dead tired, but when he invited me to watch a baseball game on TV at his apartment, I surprised myself and accepted without hesitation.

We sat on a small couch and stared at the TV. I felt very uncomfortable. After a while, he scooted close and put his arm around my shoulder.

"You have very beautiful eyes. I noticed them the first time I saw you."

I thought, "Yeah, right." I didn't want this to go any further. I stood up and made an announcement.

"Alfred, I think it's time for you to take me home."

I got no argument from him. His face formed a frown, and then he jokingly blew me a fake kiss. However, when he walked me to my door, he leaned over and lightly brushed my cheek with his lips.

"What if I call you later in the week? Maybe we can go to a movie or something?"

"Sure, that's OK," I found myself saying. He'd been nice and I'd had a good time, but I couldn't forget he was Linda's ex-husband, and all his yelling I'd heard years before echoed in my mind.

The phone was ringing as I walked through my door.

"Where've you been?" asked Linda. She sounded irritated. "I thought the party was over after breakfast this morning. Isn't he an ass? I hope you enjoyed your meal because I'm sure that was the only decent part of the weekend."

"You didn't tell me he was such a good dancer."

"You didn't ask."

After the third date with Alfred, I stopped talking to Linda. I didn't know what to say. "Hey, Linda, your ex, the one I told you to leave, well he's a totally different person with me and he really turns me on."

Alfred and I had a few dinner dates, and one time, we went to the dog races in Mobile. At the end of each evening, our physical involvement never progressed beyond a few kisses. He held me close several times. I could tell he wanted to kiss more than the upper part of my neck. I'd begun to notice he was very sexy when he ate. The way his mouth moved, and how he talked, appealed to me. He wasn't the man I had known as "Linda's husband." He didn't yell. He wasn't aggressive. He had a gentle nature. I wondered if Linda's diamond had smothered his gentle side. Whatever the reason, I liked being with him. I'd decided I wanted more than a platonic relationship.

One night, when the kids were away, I decided to not hold back anymore. My mother had sent me Kansas City steaks and I had saved two luscious strips for a special occasion. In the middle of the afternoon, I called Alfred at his furniture store in Gulfport.

"I was just thinking about you," said Alfred. "Stallone's got a new movie out. Want to go see it with me?"

"Well, he's not exactly one of my favorites. Actually, I had something else in mind. Would you like to come over for dinner?"

"Sure. What can I bring?"

"How about some wine? See you at 7?"

"Great."

I had less than four hours to clean the house, fix the outdoor grill, dust off the wine glasses and find something sexy to wear. The house was easy. I just shut a few doors since Alfred wasn't going to be taking a tour. I put fresh sheets on my bed, moved the photography chemicals to the other bathroom and sprayed the room with a slight hint of Estee perfume. I pulled everything out of my closet before I found the right thing to wear--a long dress of white eyelet with a plunging neckline. It was just perfect for a summer night on the veranda. Too bad I didn't have a veranda. I felt lightheaded and silly, like when I tried on my prom dress. I looked in the mirror and I was flushed. Why was I going to all this bother? I had been married twice, had three children, and I could probably sleep with Alfred any time I wanted to.

When I heard his car pull in the driveway, I fluffed the pillows on my bed one more time.

"I hope you like this wine," he said, as I opened the door.

"Oh, it's fine, I'm sure. I've already got the charcoal going. How do you like your steak?"

I tried to be all business about getting dinner on the table. Alfred had been to my house before, but never with just the two of us, and with me acting so domestic. In spite of what I had planned, I felt a little shy.

I lit the candles as he poured the wine. I'd put a small, white cloth on the end of my big dining room table to make it look cozier.

"When will the kids be back?" he asked.

"In a couple of weeks. Heather and Steven are visiting their father in Indiana, and Gina is staying with Kin."

"I'd like to take you to the beach in Florida before they get back. How about week after next?"

"I don't know if I'm up to that."

"Oh, sure you are. Just the two of us, and the sun and the sand. Maybe we can even find a boat and go fishing."

"The beach sounds great, but I'm not so sure about the fishing part. I get seasick."

Alfred was devouring his steak while I just pushed my salad around the plate. He looked so good sitting across the table from me. I wanted to lead him to my fluffy pillow that minute, but, somewhere, in the back of my mind, I knew I didn't want this to be just another one-nighter.

Dessert started out as a game of kissy face on the couch, to which we had moved after dinner. After several long, deep kisses, I asked Alfred a question.

"Wouldn't you like to do more than kiss me?"

His hands answered my question. The white eyelet sun dress had large buttons for easy removal. Alfred wasn't a teenager and needed no instructions. His passion took my breath away, and some time passed before I realized we were on the mattress in Steven's room rather than reclining on the pillows of my fresh bed. My heart was pounding so hard, I was sure Alfred would ask me what was wrong. Instead, he pushed my hair back with his hand.

"Lovely lady, you make love the best."

Suddenly, the evening was all wrong. I didn't want this man to remember me just for how well I made love. I wanted more than that from him. I had ruined everything.

I burst into tears.

"Did I say something wrong?" he asked. "What's wrong?"

Alfred was as confused as I was. My trains were racing too fast around familiar curves. I could almost feel a wreck approaching around the next bend. I'd been here before: slept with the wrong guy and wanted too much. This time, I didn't want a short, whistle stop. I wanted a life-time journey, but I had no idea what destination I had in mind. I'd planned this tumble into bed with Alfred because I wanted more. Maybe he didn't. Probably he didn't. Love and sex seemed to be riding in the same boxcar. Why couldn't I separate them? Did I really think I needed both? My sobs began to sound like I was losing control of my breathing. Alfred couldn't feel the steel wheels on the tracks, so he just held me tighter.

"I'm sorry. I guess I'm just tired," I said.

"Shhh, don't cry. Let me hold you," he said.

Alfred held me while I cried. Finally, the pillows let us rest our heads, and he spent the night. I didn't untangle myself from his arms until morning.

I waited for him to leave. I was sure he was going to walk out of my life. But, instead, he finalized our plans for the Florida weekend, where we finished falling in love. With the ocean waves rolling onto the beach, and the fine, sparkling white sand sticking to my body, I had no worries, no care, and no plans for the future. Love had melted the tracks and my trains had taken a holiday.

When the kids returned home, I told them Alfred and I were dating.

"I don't see how you can stand him," said Heather. "All he ever does is yell at his kids."

"That's not fair, Heather. He doesn't yell at me, or at you, for that matter."

"Are you serious about him, mom?" asked Steven, his voice was anxious. "You wouldn't marry him, would you?"

"We're just friends. We're dating, that's all. We're taking all of you to the beach next Sunday."

"All of us? Alfred's kids, too?"

Heather and Steven groaned.

"Oh, please, no," said Heather. "We don't have to ride all that way with those kids do we?"

"They're so loud I can't even think," said Steven.

"You won't have to think, you'll be on a picnic. Just be sure to bring your suntan lotion, and everything will be all right."

We took the kids on picnics and dragged them to Jaycees family outings. We pretended to be the big, happy, all-American family. By now, school had started for the older kids, and Gina was in morning preschool. But, my career in photography was just an odd job, and didn't bring home much money. I was afraid our cupboard would again be bare. I didn't want to go through that another time. I examined my options, and didn't like any of them. Taking a full-time clerical job would kill my attempts to establish myself as a professional photographer. Working as a waitress would at least allow a little more flexibility, but that had been a degrading experience for me. I wanted to move forward, not backwards, but I wasn't sure which direction that was. I could also try to talk my mother and Uncle Joe into taking the kids until I got my act together. I didn't want to let go of my kids but I couldn't ask them to suffer through the same financial mess we'd been in just a year ago. In spite of my happiness and growing love for Alfred, panic was beginning to creep back into my life.

Alfred was having his share of problems, too. Whenever I visited his apartment I noticed empty bean cans on the counter or in the garbage.

"Is that all you eat?"

"That's all I have time for. Between the kids, the store, the Jaycees, and now, you," he turned and grinned at me, "I don't have time for anything else."

He couldn't afford anything else. With high alimony and child support, wooing me and my children, and the expenses of a small business, his grocery list was short. One afternoon, I'd just had it. I called Alfred to invite him over, knowing his presence would soothe me, but then I found myself crying so hard, he couldn't understand me.

"The store closes in 20 minutes. I'll be there as soon as I can."

"I'll be okay," I sobbed. "I'm just tired."

"Tell that to somebody else, not me. I'll be there as soon as I can."

I was still crying so hard, I didn't hear Alfred come in the back door. The first thing I knew, he was pressing a cool washcloth to my forehead.

"Jo Carroll, tell me what's wrong. Are the kids OK? Did something happen?"

All I could do was shake my head. How could I admit to him that I couldn't manage my finances, or care for my children? He'd think I was stupid. I didn't want to lose him. But, I told him everything. I didn't know if he would laugh, or run.

He put his hands on my shoulders and pulled me to a standing position. Drawing me near, he whispered softly in my ear.

"Jo Carroll, will you marry me?"

I thought I was imagining things. I didn't say anything. He repeated his whisper.

"Jo Carroll, will you marry me?"

"Alfred, didn't you hear me? I have all these problems. I can't figure out what to do. I don't want to send my kids away, but I want..."

"Shhh. Marry me and the kids will live with us. You'll find a decent job and everything will be all right."

"I don't want you to marry me because you feel sorry for me, or because you feel you have to rescue me."

"Believe me, I'm not. I love you, Jo Carroll. Will you marry me?"

10 Clickity-Clack

Four days after Alfred proposed, we were married by a Justice of the Peace.

The next morning, we awoke to seven children. Usually, just my three were at home, but Alfred's four had managed to wrangle a sleepover the day we were married. Sleeping bags, extra pillows and candy bar wrappers lay everywhere.

My mother sent yellow roses and champagne. The rails were clear. I'd pulled away from my dark days.

When Thanksgiving came, we had all seven children at our feet. For reasons I don't remember, both Alfred and I had to work that day. Maybe his furniture store was getting a jump on the after-Thanksgiving sales. I'd finally found full-time work at NASA's facility near Picayune. As the bottom person on the totem pole, I probably had to work holidays.

But, this was our first Thanksgiving, and I was determined to make sure it was going to be a good one. If we couldn't have my grandmother's pickled peaches, we were at least going to have turkey and dressing, complete with cranberry sauce.

While Alfred and I were at work, each child had a role to play to get dinner on the table. Steven decided, since he was the oldest, it wouldn't be too hard for him to cook a turkey. After all, he just had to stick it in the oven and set the timer. I tried to talk Aleece into making the stuffing, but she didn't want to put her hands down into all that icky stuff, so the job fell to Robert. The can of oysters I'd left on the counter for him to add to the bread crumbs weren't that much different from the snakes and worms he carried. Heather decided she could manage sweet potatoes and marshmallows, while Aleece consented to supply the family with the mushroom soup and green bean casserole. Carol was told her role in this family feast would be making sure Drew and Gina stayed out of trouble and didn't fight too much.

"That's not fair. I'm old enough to cook something," she complained. "The little kids can just sit and watch TV. That's what they always do anyway."

So, I gave her a large package of Jell-O, showed her the directions on the back and handed her some bananas she could add to the mixture. Nothing was too fancy for our first Thanksgiving.

Alfred and I both arrived home early. Before sitting down to eat, I took the kids outside to take their picture. I arranged them in a pyramid, modeled after the popular TV show, Eight is Enough, with Heather, Steven and Robert on the bottom. The second tier contained Carol and Aleece, topped off by Gina and Drew. It was a wonderful, happy photo, the kids laughing, the sun shining and no one had fallen off yet. And, then we went back into the apartment to devour our feast. I opened a can of cranberry sauce while Alfred took his grandmother's craving knife, and, with the first slice into the turkey, he hit something.

"What the hell!" he yelled.

We all peered in the turkey. Inside was the bag of giblets. I'd forgotten to tell Steven to take it out of the turkey.

"Hey, Steven, I thought I was supposed to make the stuffing," said Robert, teasing as he poked his stepbrother in the ribs.

We ate everything, from the turkey to the runny Jell-O with the bananas floating on top. The pumpkin pie, from the local Winn-Dixie, completed the last holiday meal we'd eat in Ocean Springs.

It was time to move again, only this time I was married to a man who had a job before we moved.

Alfred had sold his furniture store and was working as a buyer with Goudchaux's department store in Baton Rouge. I was a newspaper editor in Baker, about 25 miles from our duplex apartment. Alfred's children had stayed behind in Gulfport. I found a good day care for

Gina. My two oldest kids went to Baton Rouge High, a magnet school for bright students when their parents couldn't afford private schools. The amount of homework they had overwhelmed them at first. Chores that I had normally expected them to do were now either Alfred's or my responsibility. Frozen entrees from the grocery store became a staple and Popeye's fried chicken was a treat.

One night, when no one had to jump up to go anywhere, I sliced and diced, grated and chopped, and put all the makings for tacos on the table in little bowls. Cubes of ripe, red tomatoes, crisp, green shreds of lettuce, little rings of black olives, chunky mounds of sweet-red peppers, and spicy, browned hamburger were all waiting for the kids to jam into the taco shells. We all sat down together for dinner.

"Mommy, I think my gerbil's going to have a baby," said Gina.

"Don't be silly, Gina. Your gerbil can't have a baby," said Steven. He thought he knew everything about sex at age 14.

"Why not?" asked Gina. "I like babies!"

"Because you only have one gerbil," said Steven. "You need two to get babies."

"Besides, you're just a baby yourself," Heather told her. "How could you take care of them?"

"Mommy, can you put my taco together?" asked Gina. "I can't do it, my fingers will get icky."

"Mom," interrupted Steven, "if you'd just give me a chance, I could show you. I'd keep my grades up, I promise. Danny works down at the corner car wash and his mother doesn't object. I'd have my own money so I would put gas in the car and then I wouldn't have to stay around this awful old apartment all weekend. Please!"

"Steven, we've been over and over this," I said. "I don't want you to have a job until you're older. We give you money to go to the movies. If you need something else just ask for it. I can't promise you, but we'll see what we can do."

"Steven's got a girlfriend. Steven's got a girlfriend."

"Shut up, Heather!"

"Don't tell your sister to shut up."

"Tell me about your Junior Achievement meeting last night," said Alfred.

"It was OK," Steven mumbled. "But I'd rather have a real job."

A piece of taco lodged in my windpipe. I was having difficulty breathing. I began to cough, and, when that didn't help, I started to hit myself in the chest with a clenched fist. I was light-headed and sure I would pass out any minute. I could feel Alfred on one side of me and Steven on the other.

"Mom, get your head down between your knees."

Alfred pounded me on the back.

"Jo Carroll, say something. Are you all right?"

I didn't feel all right and shook my head from side to side. I had stopped coughing, but I still couldn't talk, and breathing was nearly impossible.

Alfred lay the back of his hand against my cheek and felt my flushed face.

"Heather, you stay here with your sister. Steven and I are going to take your mother to the hospital."

The hospital? Why? I was scared. Alfred was in charge and if he thought I needed to go to the hospital, I wasn't going to argue.

The car squealed into the parking lot of Women's Hospital. I'd always thought this was such a strange name for a hospital. Couldn't they have named it after a special woman, like Joan of Arc, or maybe Florence Nightingale or even someone's wife? But, right now, I didn't care if it had any name. I quickly envisioned myself hooked up to oxygen tanks while a doctor hovered over me trying to figure out how to get the taco out of my throat.

At the reception desk, a nurse in a green coat greeted us.

"When is she due?" asked the nurse.

"My wife's not pregnant. She's got something stuck in her throat."

"Well, then, I'm sorry, but I can't help you."

"What do you mean? She's choking to death!"

"We're only equipped to deal with pregnant females. I suggest you take her to Baton Rouge General. It's only four miles from here."

I tried to remember how long a person could go without breathing, but nothing computed in my mind. Steven's face was so red, he looked like the one who wasn't breathing. He nervously rubbed his hands over the front of his jeans and then began rubbing my hand with both of his in an attempt to keep me alive. I couldn't move an inch of my body. I tried to say something to Steven, but couldn't even get my mouth open. I tried to move my tongue to the roof of my mouth, but even it wouldn't budge. I could hear everything going on around me. Was hearing the last of the senses to be lost? A car horn honked and a delivery truck pulled in front of us. Alfred shifted gears as quickly as the old VW would let him.

At Baton Rouge General, the doctor peered into my throat.

"There's nothing down there," he said. "I don't see any obstructions in the passageway. Tell me again what happened."

I could breathe now, but I still couldn't talk. Alfred explained the sequence of events.

"Well, maybe it does look a little irritated," he said. "Could I talk to the patient alone, please."

When Alfred and Steven had gone, the doctor closed the examining room curtain.

"Is something wrong? You seem very tense and anxious. Are you and your husband having problems?"

I squeaked out my answer.

"My husband and I are fine. My throat hurts. I nearly choked to death."

"I can't find anything wrong with you. I'm going to give you a shot of Demerol to calm you. You need to make an appointment with your family doctor as soon as possible."

I nodded, although, if the taco was gone, I couldn't imagine what a doctor would do for me next week, or even in the morning, for that matter.

By the time we got home, Heather was in a state of panic, Gina was crying hysterically and Alfred and Steven were exhausted. I crawled into bed and ignored the crisis. The trains were hissing and steaming and going nowhere.

The next morning, I called in sick and lay in bed trying to figure out if my concerns about my job related to the taco stuck in my throat. My small newspaper had been bought by a conglomerate which was streamlining operations. I was worried my job would be eliminated. We needed both incomes just to get by. I tossed and turned and worried about what was going to happen.

The following week, unemployment was a fact of life for me. I was frantic and scanned the classified ads. With only two weeks severance pay, I had little time to find a job.

I mailed out 22 resumes and went back to our apartment. I lay down on the bed to rest and the cat and dog both crawled in beside me. The next thing I remember was Steven peering into my face.

"Mom, talk to me."

I could see him shaking my arm, but I felt as if I was watching an old movie on TV. I felt like I couldn't breathe and Steven was in my face trying to get me to talk to him. I tried to swallow real hard, like if I was speaking in front of a crowd and was so nervous I had to swallow before I could talk. But I couldn't swallow, either. My hands and arms weren't working. All I could do was look at Steven and blink my eyes. Steven left my side and I heard him on the phone with Alfred.

"Mom, Alfred told me to take you to the hospital. He'll meet us there."

I didn't understand what Steven was doing or why. My trains had come to a complete stop. I was dying and nothing anyone did would make a difference. Later Steven would say he was afraid he would get a speeding ticket on the way to the hospital, but he was even more afraid I would die on the way.

So was I.

The emergency room was crowded and they put me on a gurney in the hallway. I felt even worse. A terrible plague had taken over my body. A numb feeling had started in my feet and immediately overcame the lower portions of my arms and legs. I was sure my lungs would go next and I wouldn't even be able to take the few short gasps of breath. I started screaming.

Why wouldn't someone help me?

An orderly appeared and quickly moved me into a cubicle where a nurse took a small brown paper bag and placed it over my nose and mouth.

What are they doing? I'm dying and they're playing with a lunch bag?

I heard Alfred's voice. A nurse was speaking to him.

"She's hyperventilating. Too much oxygen. This will slow down her breathing."

But they didn't understand. I wasn't breathing too fast--I couldn't breathe at all. I didn't know how I'd stayed alive as long as I had. A nurse came in and gave me another shot of Demerol and another doctor asked if anything was wrong at home and told me to see my family doctor.

As soon as we got home Alfred called Dr. Richard Robin, an old friend who practiced internal medicine in Baton Rouge.

"Richard, I don't know what's wrong with her. Everything seems to be fine, and then suddenly she can't breathe."

Alfred listened for a few minutes, and then said he would bring me to his office the next morning.

Dr. Robin's office was located in an old, brick building with endless corridors and overflowing rooms. Alfred had taken the morning off from his job to accompany me, but as we waited, he kept glancing at his watch.

"I really don't see why we're here," I told him. "I just need to find a job and I'll be fine."

I didn't tell him that during the night, I had the sensation of being pushed down into a bottomless black pit. That sensation was like a heavy weight bearing down on my shoulders and at the back of my neck. At times, the feeling made walking hard. I tried to think of a physical explanation for why I felt this way, but I hadn't lifted anything heavier than a bed sheet the previous night.

Dr. Robin was a pleasant, unassuming doctor, about five years older than me. He had dark, curly hair, a prominent nose and a dark complexion. Years later, I realized that Alfred hadn't just taken me to a doctor he knew, he had taken me to a Jewish doctor he knew.

For the next hour, Dr. Robin did a complete physical, with the usual blood and urine tests, along with a "see if you can touch your fingers to your nose" test. Then, he wanted to talk to me alone.

"Is there something wrong at home, Jo Carroll? Are you and Alfred having problems?"

He was asking me the same questions as the ER doctors. What was wrong with these doctors? Couldn't they see I had some sort of physical problem making breathing difficult? What the hell did that have to do with Alfred? Alfred certainly didn't beat or mistreat me. He was wonderful. These questions didn't deserve answers.

"Do you mind if I call Alfred in? I need to talk to both of you."

Alfred stood behind me. He held my hand and put it to his lips.

I waited for a death sentence. Maybe I hadn't been able to breathe because I had some horrible cancer growing inside me. Whatever it was, I just wanted him to tell us and get it over with.

"Jo Carroll, I find you to be severely depressed. You're dehydrated, which would indicate you're not eating, and you're not responsive to most stimuli."

I wanted to scream, "Give me another chance. I'll pass your damn test!"

But my mouth didn't work. My brain wouldn't function. I was having trouble breathing again and the pressure on my shoulders was becoming unbearable. A paper bag appeared from somewhere, and I found myself forced to take deep breaths. Its thin sides expanded and collapsed. I was able to breathe.

Alfred's face reflected his concern. His jaw was clenched and thrust forward, and his eyes looked at his friend, a doctor he expected answers from.

"What do you think we ought to do?" he asked.

"I'd like to put Jo Carroll in Baton Rouge General. I don't want to put her in a psychiatric hospital without Frank Silva seeing her. He's the best psychiatrist in town and he just left for a week of vacation. I really want him to treat her. But, in the meantime, she needs to be monitored. I don't want her to have one of these attacks off by herself somewhere. They'll probably increase in frequency until she gets some help."

"What good will hospitalizing her do?"

"If I admit her to the hospital, I can sedate her until Dr. Silva gets back. Meanwhile, it will isolate her from any stressful conditions at home, and, at the same time, there'll be someone available when these attacks occur."

I was aware people were talking about me, but I wasn't interested. I was dying, and no arrangements anyone made could change that. I just wanted to go home and have Alfred hold me until the end came.

"Honey, I don't want to go to the hospital. It won't do any good. Let's just go home."

"Jo Carroll, you heard what Richard said. You need help. I can't live this way, wondering whether or not you're going to be at home or at the hospital when I come home from work. And it's not fair to the kids either. Think about how scared Steven must have been when he had to take you to the emergency room. It's nothing to be ashamed of, but we need to take care of whatever it is and get you well."

"We can't afford for me to be in the hospital. I need to work. I need a job."

"You need to get well first. I'll manage, but I can't manage if I have to worry about you. We're going to do what a very good doctor told us to do. I'm taking you to the hospital."

"Couldn't we just go home first? I need a little time to think about it. Maybe I'm just tired from trying to send out too many resumes. We could grab a bite to eat on the way home, and I promise I'll feel better tomorrow."

"You can't make that promise. This is something you have no control over. If you did, we wouldn't have had to go to the hospital in the first place. I love you. Now, get in the car."

Alfred took me straight to the Baton Rouge General. This time, we parked across the street and entered through the admissions office instead of the emergency room. Alfred told the clerk I'd been there the night before, and an orderly dressed in the usual white quickly appeared and took me to a room. I put on an open-backed gown and was told to get in bed. The cool, crisp sheets felt good. I could die in comfort. But I didn't know what I should do while I waited. A nurse came into my room.

"The doctor ordered this shot for you."

"What is it?"

"Just a little something to make you feel better. Now, just relax. It takes effect almost immediately. If you need anything, all you have to do is press this button. I'll be back to check on you shortly."

She hadn't even left the room before waves of euphoria hit me. I heard my train smoothly running along the rails. And, for the next 7 days, I remained content in a Demerol-induced fog.

I only remember two episodes during that time. Once, when Alfred was visiting me, the IV needle in my wrist came loose. As he called for the nurse, I had another attack. Cold sweat covered my body, and I felt like I was falling into a hole inside the bed. I was convinced everything was hopeless. My veins were closing up inside me. Obviously, the doctors had no idea what to treat me for. Anything they did would be useless anyway, I would die soon if the needle wasn't replaced. I had no idea what kind of concoction was being carried to my body, but I knew it must be vital.

Alfred tried to appear calm. His lips formed an imaginary kiss, and I could hear the sound of the pucker it sent to me. I could tell he was worried. He wasn't saying anything. He wasn't trying to reassure me. Usually, he'd kiss me on the forehead and tell me to try and breathe slower. Maybe he was afraid I was so ill that touching me would make me worse. He must know he was going to lose me. I wondered if he would try to raise the kids by himself. Maybe, if he didn't tell Bruce and Kin I was dead, he could put their child support checks in our joint account and go on as though nothing had happened. No, that would never work. Heather would tell her father. She still didn't trust Alfred, and my death wouldn't change that.

"Jo Carroll, try to breathe slower," said Alfred. "You're going to be all right. Open your eyes and look at me. The nurse has fixed the needle. Nothing's wrong. Open your eyes and look at me."

Alfred was reassuring me in his strong, radio announcer voice. I was afraid to look. What if I opened my eyes and I wasn't in the hospital any more? I wondered if that moment of light comes just before death like some people say. Then, he shook me.

"All right!" I thought to myself. "I'll open my eyes. I can't stand to have the bed jiggle so much. And I have to say goodbye to him."

"Alfred, I love you. Please take care of the kids for me."

"What are you talking about? The kids are fine."

But the kids were not fine. Heather had run away that night. Steven later found her sitting by the side of the road. Alfred had called Kin to ask him to take care of Gina until I recovered. I knew nothing of all this.

The other time I remember a male voice at the end of my bed disturbed me. The voice was thick with a Cuban accent. I struggled to open my eyes. His square body was topped with thick, dark hair plastered flat on his head. His perky nose didn't fit his masculine looks. He kept adjusting the knot on his tie with his left hand as he waited for me to speak.

"Who are you?" I asked.

"Well, we're awake now. I came to visit you to see if you are to be my patient. I'm Dr. Silva."

He asked me a series of questions, punctuated by long pauses, never starting another question until I had completely answered his last one. He didn't ask me if I was having trouble with my husband.

After he left my room, the IV was removed and the Demerol shots ceased. Not long after, I found myself seated in Dr. Silva's office at Parkland Hospital. I looked at the fancy diploma hanging on the wall behind his head. "University of Havana" was written in large, ornate scroll letters arced across the top. I could feel Alfred's presence in the back of the room.

"Jo Carroll, we're going to start you out on some fairly low dosages of medicine to treat depression," he said. "As you get used to the dosage, we'll increase the medication."

I clutched my waist with crossed arms, hoping I could hide my desire to gasp for air.

"When can I go home? How long will it take me to get well? What's the matter with me?"

If I could just sit up straight, maybe he would see I was not sick.

"We'll talk about that tomorrow when I see you. Right now, I'm going to have a nurse take you to your room. Try to get some rest. It will take you a little while to become accustomed to the hospital routine. You'll soon be familiar and comfortable here."

I didn't have the energy to tell him I had no intention of staying long enough to become "familiar and comfortable." Since I had discovered I wasn't dying, I was certain a little self-discipline would cure whatever ailed me. I just needed to try harder.

Dr. Silva walked me to his office door. I gave Alfred a kiss.

"Don't worry. I'll be home soon," I whispered in his ear.

He held me.

"I love you," he said.

A woman was waiting just outside the door. She didn't look like a nurse. Her flowing red hair was gathered into a pony tail which reached almost to her waist. She wore jeans and a blue blouse covered with white daisies. For awhile, we walked silently down the corridors, stopping at each door while she withdrew a different key from the ring that dangled by her side. This scared me. Why would anyone locate a hospital in a neighborhood so bad that everything had to be kept under lock and key?

"Have you ever been hospitalized before?" she asked.

"Of course. I had my babies in the hospital and I just spend 7 days flat on my back in one where they couldn't decide what was wrong with me."

"No, I mean a mental institution."

"I've seen movies," I said.

"Well, we're at Parkland Hospital. It's a mental institution.

"I understand you have a very modern, up-to-date institution," I replied.

I almost gagged on the last word. Was that really where I was? Who would protect me from all the crazy people?

As we continued, she talked about the routine, meals, programs, and the "cans" and "cannots" of life in a mental hospital. She explained how patients earn and lose their privileges.

"We'll be going into your unit next. I'll take you to your room. You won't be expected to participate in the activities until tomorrow. You'll meet your roommate at supper."

"I want a private room."

"My, my, you have seen a lot of movies. Old movies. There are no private rooms here. You'll have a roommate and a toilet. The showers are down the hall."

She unlocked the heavy, metal door to what was to be my home for the next six weeks. I peered into a large room filled with sofas and tables and chairs, but no people. Bunches of plastic flowers were shoved in plastic vases.

"You took me to the wrong place," I said. "This isn't a hospital room, it's a bus depot."

"No, Jo Carroll, come on in," she said. She sounded just like my fifth grade teacher, Miss Cover, who once beat me with a leather strap. Both of their voices were rough and demanding, and sometimes their tongues seemed to be stuck to the roof of their mouths just to emphasize a point.

"This is the informal space you share with the other patients," she said.

The thought of sharing any space nauseated me. Visions of someone peering up my gaping hospital gown flashed across my mind. My trains were chugging around madly.

"You wear your street clothes here. Nobody stays in bed. We have activities to keep you busy all day long," she said

Her thumb rubbed back and forth below her lower lip. I wondered if she had that dry skin that appears under chapped lips or there were hairs there that she had missed in her plucking.

Suddenly, I realized the doors were not locked to keep people out.

I had to leave right now!

Crying and screaming at the top of my lungs, I lunged in the direction of the door.

The ponytail woman caught me in her arms.

"Hey, none of that. Let's just go to your room and rest awhile."

I stared at the pale blue walls of the cubicle and waited for the shot of Demerol. But no shot ever came. Instead, a tiny nurse, with her hair pulled back in a neat little bun, appeared with a small paper cup and two pills.

"Dr. Silva ordered these for you," she said. "Try to get some rest and someone will be back to show you where the cafeteria is. Supper's at 5:30."

I lay my head on the pillow for a few minutes and watched the pill woman disappear through the only unlocked door I'd seen all afternoon. When I opened my eyes, a thin woman in her 50s with a heavy makeup was watching me from the other bed. Loose skin hung from her chin and bony arms.

"Hi, I'm Jane," she said. "We're roomies. Isn't that Isabelle an absolute bitch?"

Her Southern accent made "bitch" into two long syllables.

"I saw her bring you in here. She's the worst nurse on that shift. Come on. I'll show you where to get the slop they call supper."

"I'm not hungry."

"That doesn't matter. You have to go to meals anyway. Push your food around and dump your plate on the conveyor belt. No one will ever notice."

The cafeteria line terrified me. Jane had shoved me in front of her and I bumped into a grossly overweight man whose tight T-shirt rode up, showing his belly button above his too-tight, new jeans. He kept removing his khaki fishing hat, wiping his head with the palm of his hand and replacing the hat, only to immediately begin again. I huddled next to my new roommate for protection.

"You know that line in the Bible about 'Wherever two or more of ye are gathered therefore will I be'?"

I shook my head. I didn't want to remember any Bible stories.

"Well," she continued, "I figured as I'm standin' there in the grocery store with Pete, that's my husband, and I knew damn well he wasn't Jesus, so I figured I was. My mistake was to tell everybody. I couldn't walk on water so nobody believed me."

I put a piece of lemon pie on my tray and nodded to the server who was dishing out the macaroni and cheese.

"Here, sweetie," said Jane. "You'll like these rolls. They're the only thing the kitchen makes fresh every day."

I sat down at the end of a long, empty table and looked at my tray. I vomited.

I woke up back in my room and felt cold compresses on my forehead.

"That medicine didn't do very well for us on an empty stomach, did it?" Isabelle clicked her tongue as she stood over me. "Tomorrow we must remember to eat better."

Tomorrow and tomorrow and tomorrow ran into each other. Some days, I was so depressed, I couldn't breathe. Other days, I could barely walk. My legs felt so heavy I wanted to reach down and move them with my hands.

Dr. Silva tried so many medications the names began to blend together as though they had been ground into one huge apothecary jar. The exception was Melaril. Most medicines were passed out from a pushcart in the central area, but a nurse appeared in my room early one morning with a liquid that looked like rubber cement and baby puke. She mixed it with apple juice.

"Drink it down in one swallow," she said.

In less than 10 minutes, a sledge hammer had knocked all my trains from their tracks. Walking to breakfast seemed impossible, but somehow I managed. I fell asleep beside my eggs. I stumbled to therapy class. I was awakened at the end of the hour. I rolled myself into my room and crawled into my bed.

"Lunch time."

"Activity time."

"Exercise time."

I couldn't move for any of them. Someone had tied weights on my arms and legs.

The next morning, the nurse arrived with another dose of the sticky yellow stuff.

"No, I can't," I protested. "I'll never be able to think again if I keep taking that crap."

"You have to get used to it. Everybody's like this in the beginning. It's meant to slow you down at first. You'll be running around the block in no time."

Meanwhile, I had talking sessions with Dr. Silva. He would see me for 15 minutes to an hour. If I had a lot to tell him, the session was never long enough. I made a list and kept it in my pocket until the next visit.

"No list," he said. "Just tell me what's on your mind."

"But I forget."

"It doesn't matter. You'll remember what's important."

He never took notes, but his long-legged assistant was frequently with him and she would jot in a notebook as we talked.

Then, one day, while standing in line at the pushcart for my afternoon dosage of whatever the current pill was, I collapsed.

"Jo Carroll, off the floor! Get up. You can't act like that."

I couldn't get up. Two nurses carried me to my room and placed me on my bed where I remained for three days. Trays were brought to my bedside, but I didn't eat. I didn't change my clothes, take a shower or get out of bed for phone calls. My body weighed two tons. I was nauseated constantly. I lay on the bed and watched for that light.

On the afternoon of the third day, Dr. Silva and his assistant, strolled in and pulled two chairs up to my bedside.

"I hear it's going to rain." Dr. Silva said.

Was he talking to me?

"Sherrie, what do you think? Can I get in a little tennis before the downpour starts? Jo Carroll, you ever play tennis? Ought to try it. Great game. What's this over here on the table? Oh, my favorite, chocolate-covered almonds. Want some Sherrie? Jo Carroll, these are great. Where were we? Oh, yes, you really ought to try some tennis."

He glanced at Sherrie and they promptly got up and left.

How dare he! I was dying! He was my doctor. If he couldn't find a cure he could at least give me the respect due a dying person. I'd show him he couldn't treat me this way. I threw back the covers, grabbed a towel and headed for the shower.

The next morning, in addition to the regular antidepressant, a new pill, a little gray and yellow one, appeared at the pushcart for me. I would come to find out later that the pill was Lithium and that I had been diagnosed as manic depressive, later to be known as bi-polar. Soon, the food tasted better, I could concentrate and my therapist was starting to sound intelligent. I even grew to like Jane.

But the hospital was not a restful place.   A commotion occurred every day. One morning, terrible shrieks could be heard coming from the hallway.

"What's that?" I asked. "I've never heard anything like that before."

"Oh, don't be silly roomie. You remember Jake. Three times a week, they come get him and take him for shock treatment. Otherwise, you don't hear a thing out of him. He just lies in his room and stares at the ceiling."

"Do they do that with many people? Shock treatment, I mean."

"Nah. The doctors can't find anything else that works on him so they decided to give the old geezer a jolt. Hey, did I tell you I'm getting out of here next week?"

"That's not fair. I thought we made a pact to leave together. Besides, what if they move fat Ella in here with me? I couldn't stand the smell."

"They only put the crazies together, you know that. Tell you what, I'll leave you my brown velvet robe. That'll keep you company till you escape."

My roomie was leaving. I had new medicine. I needed to call my husband.

"Alfred, I want to go home. I'm well now. The kids need me. I need to get back to work. I can't imagine what this hospital stay is costing. I'd rather spend our money on a nice hotel in Florida."

During the first week of hospitalization, I wasn't allowed any visitors and my one phone call a day was closely monitored. After the initial period, Alfred brought me books, held my hand while I complained about the latest new medicine, and when I griped about the meatloaf tasting like burnt wood, he brought me Hershey bars.

"Dr. Silva says we have to wait to make sure the lithium is doing its job and it's not toxic or anything."

"Everything they poke in your body here is toxic. They take my blood every five days to check the lithium level. They could do that as an outpatient. Jane got to go home last week. Did I tell you she left me her pretty robe?"

"Please be patient. I don't want you to wind up here again just because you went home a couple of days too soon. Whatever you want to do, see the kids, go to work, it can all wait."

"How about crawl between the sheets with you?"

Lithium made me gain weight, but it didn't eliminate my libido like the other medications. A long time has passed since Alfred and I had made love. The touch of his hand suddenly excited me.

The next week, I was dismissed. I packed a belt with red hearts stamped around the entire length I made in leather crafts. I had already punched another hole to fit my growing waistline.

I packed Jane's robe last. I knew hospital policy forbid inmates fraternizing after release, but I had promised to call her as soon as I was home.

"I'm Jo Carroll, Jane's friend from the hospital."

"Oh, I'm so glad you called," said her husband. His voice sounded like it was coming from a sewer tunnel, with long echoes after every word. "I don't know what I'm going to do next. Our kids are over here going through her stuff, and I just can't stand it another minute, and the police said an autopsy is required after a suicide, so her body wasn't brought to the mortuary until this morning. The funeral director assured me, however, that visitation can be held tomorrow morning. Who did you say this was?"

I didn't answer, I just hung up. I was too shocked to cry.

It could have been me.

Why would I have a better chance at staying alive than she did?

I had a fatal illness.

I took my little gray and yellow pills faithfully three times a day, regularly went to the outpatient lab for blood tests, and bought larger dress sizes. The lithium helped, but it didn't protect me completely.

During our 12 years in Baton Rouge, our sweet, Southern life was interrupted by three more lengthy hospital confinements.

Years later, they would halt the lithium only long enough to administer shock treatments.

11 Sons of Pullman Porters

"Well, oh, uh, Missus Lewald, I'm Henrietta–Henrietta Ames at the Baton Rouge Community Action Program, or 'BRACA,' as we like to call it. We're interviewin' applicants for the position of public relations director, and we'd like y'all to be here at our office at 5 o'clock this evening, if you're interested. Missus Lewald. Are y'all there? Are y'all interested? Will y'all be there?"

The morning I'd gotten out of the mental hospital, BRACA called.

I hadn't wanted to answer the phone.

I was tired. Leaving the hospital had required as many forms to be filled out as being admitted, in addition to making more appointments with doctors. Now, the kids were in school and Alfred had gone back to work at his office.

"Take a nap, honey," he had told me on his way out.

I was out of the hospital, but I was also out of work. During my month-long hospitalization, I worried someone would call about one of the jobs I'd applied for–especially the BRACA job. What if someone tried to reach me? What if one of the kids said, "Oh, my mom's in the hospital. I don't know when she'll be home." What if they couldn't get an answer and moved on to another applicant? What if I missed my big opportunity just because Dr. Silva thought I needed to stay a few extra days?

After all, my illness wasn't like an infection to be cured with antibiotics. I'd take the pills as long as the medical experts wanted me to, but I felt like if I could just get it together, have one good week where supper got on the table, the laundry got done, the bills got paid, if I could get everything cleaned out from underneath the kids' beds, Alfred's socks would all match and fit neatly in the top drawer, and—I'd be all right.

Sometimes, I thought I just liked the clean sheets someone else had put on the hospital bed, and if I could achieve that feeling of orderliness in my household, any symptoms of mental illness would disappear. I hated it when the daily newspaper would feature a story about how some woman had gone berserk and killed all her children just because she had forgotten to take her medication. On the six o'clock news all the neighbors would gather around the TV camera explaining how they'd never imagined that a killer lived next door to them.

"Why, I saw her take out the trash just last Wednesday. She didn't look like the kind of mother who would drown her baby the next day," a neighbor would tell the camera.

But, there was always one in the crowd who knew. Someone who had spotted the telltale signs.

"I knew something was going on over there. Cars coming and going all times of the day and night. One day, that killer woman came out in nothing but a blue-green robe and just stared over the fence at me and my dog. Glad the dog was there. Who knows what she would have done if I'd been alone? I was just gettin' ready to call the authorities when I saw those body bags being hauled out."

That wasn't me, even if I skipped my meds for a week. I didn't want anyone to find out I took those kinds of medications. I just needed time to pull things together. My mother had told me that my grandmother had a nervous breakdown in the 1930s, and had taken to her bed for three months. I'd only broken a little, and certainly didn't need three months. I needed to get going. My life had been going too fast without getting anything done. The pills would help, but I certainly wasn't going to take medication for the rest of my life. I wanted my kids to know I would be there to take care of them. There would be food on the table. I'd be at Heather's violin recital next week. Steven didn't need to check my bed every day when he came home from school to see if I was having another attack. Alfred got so mad when I told him I was tired. He thought every time I said I was tired I was covering up some depression that had managed to creep out in spite of the pills. But, sometimes I was just tired. Maybe the medications took away my energy. The mania I experienced was not unpleasant, and I missed it. When the trains in my head ran slower, I just felt tired.

I had complained to Dr. Silva about losing my chance to get the BRACA job. It was a good job. It was in my field. And, more importantly, it paid well. We lived in an apartment where most neighbors had at least one truck up on blocks in the front yard and the trash overflowed with beer cans. Inside our duplex, we could hear the adjoining tenants flushing their toilets and yelling at each other. Alfred's desk shared our small living room with the loveseat where we crunched together to watch nightly TV. A trip to the grocery store meant scouring the shelves for bargains that would feed hungry teenagers, buying the cheapest soda available and just skipping the paper towels, an old rag was a cheaper way of wiping up everyday spills. I learned how to soak Camilla Beans, the staple of many Southern families, and red beans and rice became a favorite out of necessity. When second gear when out on the VW bus, we just learned to shift from first to third, with a pop of the clutch.

Alfred's company health insurance had a cap of $10,000 for treatment of mental illness in an institution and, once I was out of the hospital, neither the medicine nor the trips to the psychiatrist were covered. A big sign at Dr. Silva's office informed patients to pay for services before they left, but Alfred always managed to hustle me out the door before the receptionist could ask for a check.

At that point in our marriage, Alfred handled the expenses, and wrote what checks he could from a big, blue checkbook that had three stubbed checks on a page. The checkbook, a remnant of his furniture store days, was kept in the left hand drawer of his desk, and I rarely looked at it. I knew our money situation was tight, but it was years before I learned what a juggling act Alfred preformed each month. Some bills were paid one month, others the next, making everything overdue all the time. We were still paying off my medical expenses years later when Gina started to college.

I'd just begun to enjoy the sense of freedom I felt walking out the locked door of the hospital. The smell of the air was different. The oil refineries along the river in Baton Rouge emitted a sweet, acrid smell that I'd never really liked, until now.

That morning when I left the hospital I ran around the car three times, while Alfred put my luggage and the junk I'd accumulated in the trunk of the car. He caught me in his arms on the driver's side and walked me over and opened the door for me.

"Take it easy," he joked. "Someone might be watching out the window and think you've gone into a manic phase."

He kissed me on the lips before he shut the door.

I kept the window down all the way home. The wind blew in my hair. The world was at my feet. I wanted to fix the kids something they would really like for supper, and then maybe splurge with some ice cream afterwards.

At home, the ringing telephone wouldn't stop.

It was Henrietta.

While Henrietta gave me the directions to BRACA, I worried about what I could wear to the interview. I'd gained so much weight in the hospital, I didn't think I could still get into anything even remotely businesslike. Every different pill that had gone into my mouth seemed to put another pound around my middle. My legs were still skinny, so pantyhose didn't work at all. They either fit my legs, with the top curling down my fat middle, or stretched around my widening waist and hung loose at the ankles.

I raced around trying things on and throwing them in a heap. Finally, I pulled out a plain navy skirt that had an elastic band that reached around my big middle. I settled on navy heels, a plain white blouse and pearls. Someone had once told me there was no wardrobe flaw too large not to be able to be covered up by a small simple strand of pearls.

As I left the house for the interview, the sky threatened rain. In my adopted South, almost every summer afternoon, just when I thought I couldn't stand the heat another moment, the rain arrived. A few blocks from home, the first fat raindrops bounced on my windshield and soon the rain was coming down in torrents. I could barely see the road. I glanced at the map on the seat beside me. I turned on my blinker, moved into the left lane and heard the squeal of tires, the screech of the brakes and the awful thud and crunch of metal on metal. The sultry heat of the Louisiana summer pressed down on my lungs. I could hardly breathe.

I sat very still. What was going on? Did a car hit me or was I having another attack?

My car door was wrenched opened and a strange face peered in.

"Are y'all right in there, ma'am?"

I was so relieved to be having a real car accident and not another anxiety attack.

"I guess so, I guess I'm okay," I said.

"Thank God," said the face whose head was covered by a blue bandanna. A hand then appeared in front of me.

"Here, let me help y'all out, ma'am," said the blue bandanna. His hand was huge and rough and dirty, but the grip was firm, and I was out of the car before I could catch my balance. "Careful there, this same damn wet street that caused the crash can make you fall 'fore you know it."

I found myself standing in the middle of Florida and 22nd, one of the busiest intersections in Baton Rouge. The rain was pouring down, soaking my blouse and skirt. My car was blocking the intersection in rush hour. I ran to the side of the road. I was going to be very late for the interview. Two officers filled out what seemed like endless reports while I sat, chilled, in the back of the patrol car. The confinement brought back memories of the hospital I had just left. The other driver was given a ticket and the cars were towed away. I tried to decide what to do next. Should I call BRACA, call a cab or call Alfred?

"Can we give you a ride somewhere?" asked one of the officers.

I could still make that interview.

Maybe someone would still be there.

Why not give it a try?

Within a few minutes, the police car pulled into BRACA's gravel parking lot. The three-story brick building had been a neighborhood school. The old iron fire escape zigzagged down the south side of the building. Like a used car lot, a high, chain link fence enclosed rows of bright and shiny parked cars, from old Fords to new Cadillacs.

"Ma'am, are you sure you want us to leave you here at this time of evening? It can get mighty dark around this time and you know I'm not talkin' about no sunset," said the officer.

I crossed the parking lot to the sidewalk, stepping carefully so I would not trip on the rain-slick gravel. My hair was plastered to my head and I was soaked through. I remembered the positive relaxation exercises the hospital nurses had taught me about contemplating a beautiful waterfall.

The back door of the building creaked and groaned, and stuck at the bottom from humidity and too few cleanings. I walked down a long, narrow hallway covered in cheap paneling. At the far end, I could hear soft laughter coming from the floor above. Upstairs, I met three black women seated in straight-backed chairs.

"What's wrong with you, girl? You been out walkin' in the rain?" asked the one dressed in a black suit, with white piping that ran around the large round lapels. "I wouldn't go in there lookin' like that. Fact is I wouldn't go anywhere looking like that."

She pulled a pack of Juicy Fruit from her big, mint green straw bag. Without taking her eyes off me she opened the gum and folded several sticks into her mouth.

"Have they interviewed for the public relations director yet?" I asked her.

"That's what we're waiting here for," said the second woman, patting her briefcase.

The third woman had a serious look on her face and did not glance up.

"I'm here for the interview, too. I was in a car wreck," I said.

The woman with the briefcase motioned for me to be quiet.

"Can't you tell there's a meeting going on in there," she said in a hoarse whisper.

The sight of her briefcase made me remember I'd left mine in the backseat of the wrecked car, along with my suit jacket that might have made me more presentable.

"Where's the restroom?" I asked.

"The john's down the hall."

Water squished in my shoes. The bathroom door was open and the odor of stale smoke and strong disinfectant lingered in the air. I never wore much makeup, but what little I'd had on was gone now. My hair was hanging in clumps and my darker roots had grown out. My skin was pale from being in the hospital so long and my eyes were puffy and faded. I stared in the old school mirror. I knew everyone would know I had been ill.

I dug in the bottom of my purse and found an old wand of mascara. I ran it under the hot water faucet, hoping to loosen some of the magic black paint to brighten my eyes. I searched in my purse for a comb, but instead my fingers curled around a pill bottle. I took a deep breath. I decided I didn't need it.

I brushed down my damp hair, put on a light dusting of fresh face powder and some pale pink lipstick. My wet blouse clung to my body and revealed not only the outline of my bra but the lace pattern. I shrugged my shoulders, closed my eyes for a minute and took another deep breath.

I returned and waited with the three women. One by one, they were called into the conference room. The Juicy Fruit woman smiled confidently at the others as she came out. The woman with the briefcase looked defeated as she left and the third had no expression.

A large, black woman wearing a frilly, flouncy pale lavender summer dress motioned for me to come into a small, stuffy room. Twelve black people were sitting around a large, wooden conference table. "Relax," I told myself. They all watched me take my place at the other end of the table.

In an effort to appear more modest, I immediately folded my arms across my chest and leaned forward on the table.

"I've just been in a small fender-bender," I said, "and I guess the rain soaked me good. I assure you I don't usually appear in public like this. If you'd like me to come back another time, when I'm more suitably dressed..."

The woman immediately to my right interrupted me.

"The interviews are this evening. Now if you're ready, we'll start with our questions."

"What was your first job?"

"I worked as a bank teller."

"Where were you employed most recently?"

"I was editor of the Baker Observer," I answered, "until the publisher sold the paper to a big chain. They had their own people, so I was out of a job."

"I hear ya on that one."

"Did you take that picture of my niece at the zoo with her fourth grade class?"

"You put a mighty pretty picture of Cousin Alberta in her vegetable garden right on the front page."

"I've been looking at your resume. It says you graduated from the University of Southern Mississippi just a couple of years ago. You're a lot older than my daughter and she graduated five years ago. Why'd it take you so long?"

"We don't have to know that Maybelle, but what I wanna know is why when the Baker City Council voted to impose a curfew on teenagers your newspaper backed them. Wasn't that targeted at our kids?"

The last question came from a man seated at the head of the table, directly across from me. He flicked the ash of his cigarette off with his little finger and gave me a hard look. The furrows in his brow deepened as he pursed his lips.

"No, I never thought so. Baker was having problems with teenagers cruising on the main street and parking in business parking lots. They were interfering with people who wanted to shop and the kids were also throwing junk out of their cars. The kids weren't just one color. They were both black and white. I think the council was just trying to find a solution to a problem."

"What kind of prejudices do y'all have?"

This question came from the chairman, a heavyset man in his late 60s with snow-white hair, white mustache and skin the color of burnt coffee. The room was silent.

"I grew up in a small town in Kansas where there weren't any blacks, Hispanics or Jews and hardly any Catholics," I said. "A mixed marriage was between a Presbyterian boy and a Methodist girl."

Several people chuckled.

"When I got to college, of course, it was a different story. I was exposed to cultures I'd never heard of before. I've always tried to treat people as individuals. I believe I can accept people for who and what they are without thinking first what color they are or I wouldn't be here. I feel I can represent this agency, its purposes and needs, effectively in the community. If you can accept having a white woman represent you, I would love to take the job."

Everyone began talking at once in voices either too loud or hushed. I felt like a kid getting my first job and not a 37-year-old mother with seven assorted children. The subject of mental illness never came up. I didn't have to fill out an application asking for medical history and no one asked what I did after leaving the newspaper. I might get a new job. I could lead a normal life.

"When can I expect to hear from you?" I asked.

The white-haired chairman smiled, revealing a gold tooth.

"Why, we've already decided. Can you be here Monday morning at eight?"

12 Flares on the Track

Shortly after Alfred and I were married, his ex-wife Linda sued for more child support and Bruce sued for custody of Heather and Steven. Neither was successful. But the lawsuit that almost knocked my trains off the track was the one Kin filed for custody of Gina, claiming I was an unfit mother because of mental illness.

During one of my hospital stays Alfred had asked Kin if Gina could spend a couple of months with him in Mississippi. Kin seemed both sympathetic and delighted. He made the three-hour drive from the Coast and picked up Gina, her bulging suitcase and all the stuffed animals she could cram into the back seat of his car. During the next few weeks, Alfred called several times to see how she was doing and nothing seemed wrong.

Then one day, just after my hospital stay had ended, the doorbell rang.

"Certified Letter. Sign here please."

As I signed for the fat envelope, I noticed it was from an attorney's office. *Linda can't be asking for more money again. Doesn't she realize the well is dry?*

I sat down and tore open the envelope. It was from the State of Mississippi stating that a custody trial was to be held in 10 days for Gina. I didn't know whether to laugh or cry. A gasp was all that came out of my mouth.

I called Alfred immediately, but either he simply couldn't understand what I was trying to tell him or he didn't believe me. He'd been working on overload and was under a great deal of stress since I'd gone to the hospital. When he didn't seem to get it I started screaming.

"Kin thinks I'm an unfit mother. That stupid son of a bitch is telling a judge I'm the unfit one!"

"Jo Carroll, what's wrong? Calm down. Can't this keep until I get home from work? Whatever the problem is, nothing is going to happen in the next few hours. Now go read or watch TV or do something to occupy your mind till I get home. I love you. Everything's going to be all right."

I hung up the phone and waited for the sky to fall. How could Kin do this to me? We'd had all kinds of differences, that's why we weren't married any more. But until now, we'd never been at odds about Gina. How did he think he could provide a proper environment for her, much less a better one than I could? Would some stupid judge in Mississippi agree with him and say that because I had been hospitalized I couldn't raise my daughter? It was a dumb thought, but I couldn't ignore it. My trains raced around in my head then slowed to a more normal pace as reason took over.

Wait a minute--Kin had openly admitted he was a homosexual. I knew it had never made a difference in his parenting of Gina, but he knew my bouts of depression had never made any difference either. If he wanted to play games, I could too. He wasn't going to take my baby away from me.

Heather and Steven got home from school long before Alfred came home from work, but I decided not to tell them about the letter. It was a mistake. I wasn't very good at hiding things. My kids could tell just by looking at me if something was wrong.

"Mom, are you okay? I mean, I don't want you going back to the hospital or anything, but did you forget to take some pills?"

Steven was always concerned about my medicine. He needed to know what kind, when and how it was to be taken.

I gave them each a hug.

"I'll talk to you after supper, but I promise the problem is not with me. I need to talk to Alfred first. Don't you have homework?"

When I heard our car in the driveway, I went outside to meet Alfred.

"Hi, honey," he greeted me with a kiss. "What's all this about? You were so upset on the phone I couldn't figure out what you were talking about."

"Come in the house. I've got the letter in the bedroom. I'd rather not talk about it in front of the kids."

"It's not a secret is it?"

"No, but I want us to talk about it first."

The kids had gone into their rooms and shut their doors so we didn't even get any funny looks when we headed straight for our bedroom. Alfred removed his suit jacket and inserted his forefinger in the loop of his tie as I handed him the letter.

"Jo Carroll, there's nothing to worry about. I'll call Norm in the morning and we might not even have to go to court. Kin's crazy, but he's not this crazy. He can't be serious about this. People don't lose custody of a child just because they've been in the hospital. I don't want you to worry anymore. It's ridiculous. Now, what's for supper? How about that little spaghetti place around the corner? Tell the kids to get ready while I change my clothes."

Norm, Alfred's attorney in Mississippi, didn't take the matter so lightly. He told Alfred that all the proper forms had been filed. Gina would have to stay in Kin's custody until after the hearing and we would have to come to Mississippi to testify. When Alfred gave me the news the next day I couldn't control my tears.

"Alfred, I'm scared."

"I told you before, there's nothing to worry about. It's just going to be a little more trouble than I thought. Norm's a good attorney. He knows what he's doing."

I stared at Alfred. We'd both been burned by attorneys.

"Alfred, I believe in truth, justice and the American way, but not attorneys."

Out of the windows of my trains, I could see the arms of women reaching for children they had lost through the court system. All you had to do was turn on the TV. Every day courts took children from their mothers. Every day, adopted children were snatched from the only home they knew and handed over to strangers whose sole claim to them was physically giving birth. Every day, children were removed from their homes because someone accused the parents of abuse.

"I'm not going to let him raise Gina. I don't care what anybody says. Wait till the judge finds out he's gay."

"Jo Carroll, believe me, it won't go that far. Saying that in court won't do anyone any good. Norm said we need a statement from your doctor that you're OK. We need to tell the kids what's going on. The court date is next week and they're old enough to spend the night here by themselves."

When we explained the situation to Heather and Steven, they were adamant about their feelings.

"I can't stay here."

"No, me neither."

"But I don't understand. You kids baby sit and spend the night alone then. What's the big deal about staying here by yourselves?"

"Mom, you don't understand."

"We want to go with you. We could tell the judge what a good mother you are."

"Who does that stupid old Kin think he is, anyway?" Heather was close to tears.

"Well, you have to remember that he is her father and he loves her and he probably does miss her, but I think she'd be better off if she lived with us."

"She's not going to live anywhere else!"

During the following week, we didn't say much about the scheduled court date. I couldn't talk about the possibility of losing Gina. Alfred and I arranged our work schedules so we could be gone, and I sent the school written excuses for the kids to be absent "due to a family emergency."

I wasn't getting much sleep at night. I tossed and turned wondering what I would do if some damn Mississippi judge gave Gina to Kin. There was no way my mind would accept the image of her growing up in Biloxi with Kin, and me having "visitation" every other weekend. I began to develop a plan in case something went wrong.

Our attorney explained the schedule for the day of the court appearance. We could pick Gina up from Kin's home for an hour's visit before court. Then we were to take her to a mutually agreed upon day care center while the court determined who would pick her up and raise her for the rest of her life. I had already decided that there were some things worth fighting and lying for. My child was certainly one of them.

It was still dark when we left Baton Rouge for Biloxi. We had to see our attorney before we picked up Gina and the court session began at 11. Alfred tossed the keys to Steven and helped me into the back seat. I started to protest until I saw the mug in Alfred's hand filled with lemonade and vodka. The two teenagers turned the music up loud and for once no one yelled at them. I took my little white pill, hugged my pillow and watched Alfred sip from his favorite New Orleans Saints mug.

We arrived at the pillared white porch of the attorney's office on time and with reasonably clear minds. Steven and Heather were scared to death. All their brave words about what they would tell the judge dissolved when they were confronted by a real live attorney who was telling them not to say anything unless he asked them.

"Now, I want y'all to understand you can only see the child for an hour and then I'll see you in court. Alfred, I know I can trust you."

Southern lawyers seem to come in only two flavors: Fresh-scrubbed, fresh-faced, straight from Ole Miss or white-haired, smiling cigar smokers. Norm was straight out of Ole Miss.

"We might have to argue the case you mentioned to me on the phone. Do they know?"

He nodded slightly in the direction of Steven and Heather. I suddenly realized I had never told them that Gina's father was gay.

While I had always been open with my children and taught them about the birds and the bees, I had never thought it necessary to talk to them about any one's personal sex life, especially mine. I held Alfred's hand a little tighter. I turned to the Ole Miss poster boy.

"Do you have a room where I can talk to my children for just a minute?"

"Sure. Right through here."

The three of us squeezed onto a tiny blue-flowered couch in a small room decorated so completely in blue I thought for a moment we'd gone underwater. I hugged them and cried.

"Mom, we're not going anywhere. We love you. Has the judge already decided something?"

I took a deep breath, "Do you know what a homosexual is? What a gay man is?"

Steven wrinkled his nose in confusion at my question.

"Of course, mom, but what...?"

Heather just nodded.

But I wanted to be sure.

"Say it so I know you know."

"He likes other men," Heather replied.

"Mom, we know," Steven added. "But what has this got to do with today?"

"Kin is gay and if we're forced to, we'll tell the judge in order to get custody of Gina." There it was, all out at once.

"Are you sure?"

"How do you know?"

"But you two were married. When did he change?"

I gave them the best mother's hug I could.

"I'm sorry, there's really not time to explain all that now. We'll talk about it later. I promise. Right now, getting Gina back is the most important thing and we have to do what the attorney says."

When we got back in the car this time, Alfred drove. Kin's house was not far from the beach. Steven and Heather remained in the car while Alfred and I went to the front porch and rang the doorbell. I could hear Gina before I saw her.

"Mommy, Mommy!"

The front door opened and I could see her hugging her favorite teddy bear, Pinkie. Kin opened the screen door and she came bounding out and threw herself into my arms. I caught her and she smothered me in kisses and hugs.

Kin had her suitcase and a small satchel.

"I'll just take these to the car," he said "My attorney said it had to go to Lindy Lou's Day Care with her."

"I'll take those," Alfred said firmly, as he started toward the car.

By this time, Heather and Steven were slamming car doors and racing to see who could get to their sister first. Steven won the race and grabbed Gina and swung her around.

"Come on kids, let's get out of here."

I herded them back into the car and we drove to a playground on the nearby beach where we drank Cokes and watched the clock.

I pulled Alfred aside and held his hand to my cheek.

"Gina's not going to Lindy Lou's Day Care."

"We have to go to court, Jo Carroll."

"I know, but she's not going to be where he can find her if something goes wrong."

"Where do you want to take her?"

"I called the day care I used when I lived in Ocean Springs. They're expecting her."

"Do they know what's going on?"

"No, they just know there's been some trouble. I told them no one but me was authorized to pick her up."

First, Alfred smiled, then he gave me a big kiss.

"There's nothing wrong with your motherly instincts."

"Come on kids. We need to get back in the car. Careful. Shake the sand out of your shoes. I wouldn't want you to take this whole beach back to Baton Rouge with us."

So, it was over the bridge to Ocean Springs to deposit Gina and then back again to Biloxi to see what the judge would say. The trains in my head were gone, the pressure was so great it had melted all my tracks.

We stood up when the judge entered, but Alfred never let go of my hand. The judge was the white-haired, cigar-smoking variety. What if he thinks I belong on a funny farm? What if he thinks... But the what ifs were interrupted when the judge called the two attorneys to the bench. The three talked for what seemed an eternity so the what ifs began all over again. What if they wanted to see Gina?

Steven tapped me on the shoulder.

"Mom, what's going on?"

I shrugged. I didn't know any more than he did.

The judge's gavel pounded several times.

Then he announced in the sweetest southern drawl I've ever heard, "Case dismissed for lack of evidence."

Our attorney did a fast shuffle and got us all out of the courtroom before the questions started flying.

"What happened?'

"Does this mean we get Gina?"

"If there wasn't any evidence, why did we have to come here in the first place?"

"Can we just get Gina and go home?"

"Can he do this again?"

Norm said the judge had taken one look at the petition Kin had filed and found that the fact I had been in a mental hospital didn't make me an unfit parent.

The vodka stayed in the trunk, and Alfred drove the 200 miles home as we all sang any song Gina wanted to hear.

In the years that followed, Kin saw Gina off and on, and continued to provide support until she was six-years-old. Then, one weekend, he brought her back, kissed her goodbye, and we didn't hear from him again.

Two years later, when the court contacted him during Alfred's procedure to adopt Gina, he made no protest, either legally or emotionally.

13 Shalom Zephyr

"Why is this shiksa sitting in front of me?" Without turning around I knew who had uttered this question just slightly above the volume of the Rabbi's sermon. The Rabbi didn't pause, and no one answered the question, but more than one head turned in my direction.

I had noticed this old man deeply engrossed in a small black prayer book, as Alfred and I slipped into the wooden straight backed pew in front of him, just before the regular Friday night services at Congregation B'nai Israel, in Baton Rouge. With a completely bald head and a wrinkled suit that was too big for him, he looked as old as the congregation itself, which predated the Civil War. I could hear him mumbling the prayers in Hebrew before the services began. Even though I was a shiksa, a four letter word for a non-Jewish woman, I had learned to recognize the sing-song inflections of the classic biblical language. I couldn't understand a word he was saying in Hebrew, but the language had a certain sound I had come to know.

I'm not Jewish because I was born to a Jewish mother. I didn't hear Yiddish lullabies as a child, I heard Methodist hymns. I remember learning two songs in Sunday school: "Jesus loves me, this I know, For the Bible tells me so," and "Ring around the Rosy, pocket full of posies, last one down is a nigger baby." By the time I was ten I didn't believe the words to either song. By the time I was 15, I'd learned that one was acceptable, one was not. At summer camp when I was 16, I fell in love with two boys. One was black, the other was Jewish. My background hadn't prepared me to really understand anything about either one of them.

My mother took me to church on Sundays while my father slept in.

"Why isn't daddy going to church with us?" I asked her as we got in our brand new Nash. The hood ornament was so shiny I always went around front and grinned into it to see if I had anything stuck in my teeth before I pulled the handle down on the door.

"He works so hard at the store Saturday nights he's just too tired to go with us," my mother answered. I'd always question why I had to get up on Sunday mornings and go to church while daddy could sleep in. I figured if it were so important he'd be going too. In our little 50's bungalow I could hear my daddy snoring as mother and I and sometimes my brother Jack tiptoed out the door. "Maybe next week he'll go," she'd reply.

Next week never came unless it was Christmas or Easter Sunday. I remember one Christmas morning, sitting between my mother and daddy at the First Methodist Church in Horton, Kansas. Jack was 8 years older than me so he got to sit with the older kids on the front row and could go to the bathroom anytime he wanted. The only bathroom in the small church was located in the basement and you had to walk through the nursery to get there. It was a great way to escape if you didn't like the song the choir was singing or the minister was preaching too long. On Christmas morning, however, everyone wanted to stay in their seats because the minister was calling all the kids names and everyone could go up and get a present. I was waiting for my name to be called, Jack had already got a balsa wood airplane, when a lady ran in and whispered something in the Minister's ear and he called my daddy's name. "Orell, Orell Shelton" There was a slight pause and then the whole congregation laughed. Presents were only for children. What was he doing calling my daddy's name? Maybe he meant me. "Orell, there's a telephone call for you in the office." My daddy was out of the room when I got my present, a ball and jacks game. Why couldn't I get an airplane, I already had jacks at home. When daddy came back into the sanctuary he picked up his hat off the pew and whispered to my mother, "Got to go. Hank Ladding's fridge has gone out and he's got 15 people coming for dinner." My mother caught his hand, "Can't it just wait, just this once?" Daddy pulled his hand away, telling my mother, "I'm sure the Dentons can give you a ride home." The short ride home with the Dentons was quiet. Actually we could have walked, it was only four blocks. Mother was fuming mad. She slammed the door shut, "Just once, just one time, that's all I ask him to go to church and he has to make the whole family look like a laughingstock by leaving right in the middle of the service. I'll Orell Shelton him, when he gets home he's going to know what's what." My daddy didn't come home for several hours and by the time he opened the door, with his now greasy hands, my mother was all over her huff. He said, "Sorry Smack," and kissed her on the cheek. Smack was his nickname for her, and when he said it, it just made her melt. "It's okay," she replied, and then they both intoned together, "The customer always comes first!"

My daddy ran an appliance store in Horton, a town of only 1,800 people and two appliance stores. He had a customer base who demanded service. His quests weren't religious, but business related. He bought a two-seater airplane, a Piper Cub, painted "Shelton Appliances" on the side of it and flew low over the small farming communities that surrounded us, throwing advertisements out of the open window. Just after World War II, when washing machines were still almost impossible to get, he found two box cars full and bought them. The problem was that the machines didn't have any motors. No problem for him. He knew his customer, the small farmer, always had a spare motor in his barn. Daddy sold out in 10 days. The reading material on his bedside table wasn't a Bible, it was the business section of the Kansas City Star.

As a young married woman in Atchison, I tried to fit into the social set by going to church. Bruce and I had our two babies baptized in the First Methodist Church under the hopeful eyes of adoring grandparents, but nothing happened in my social life. I coaxed Bruce into joining the Episcopal Church where I thought the social set was more active. My mother gritted her teeth and said, "They're too much like the Catholics, you'll regret it." My daddy simply smiled and said, "Any religion that makes you a better person is the right religion for you." I liked the garments the Priest wore and the way they lit so many candles. Bruce and I did get invited to a few wedding receptions, but nothing spiritual ever clicked.

Kin and I were married by an Episcopal priest, but I never knew what religion Kin grew up in. Kin's mother must have believed, for if something was wrong she would roll her eyes to the sky and say, "Oh Lord, This World and then another one, too."

I knew Alfred was Jewish. I simply never noticed he did anything different until he came over one day, before we were married, and put a paper bag on the counter.

"What's that?"

"A bottle of Jack Daniels and some pickled herring."

"Yuck. I'm fixing hamburgers for us, but peanut butter sandwiches would be better than that."

"It's Yom Kippur. I always break my fast with whiskey and herring."

"What's Yam.....however you pronounce it?"

"It's a Jewish High Holy Day. We fast. I haven't eaten since last night. I stayed home today, didn't open the store."

Here was a man who was on his own and practiced his religion because he wanted to, not because someone else thought he should. I was impressed, but I didn't ask him about it until we moved to Baton Rouge. It didn't seem to matter to him that I wasn't Jewish. He was always checking to make sure that Linda was giving his children a Jewish education, while at the same time being nonchalant about the fact that he and I didn't attend any services. None of my children were receiving any religious education, formal or informal. While I'd been married to Kin, Heather used to tag along with some friends to Sunday School for social purposes and Steven's Boy Scout activities had taken him inside some places of worship. Gina liked presents at Christmas and hunted eggs at the park on Easter, but I steered her away from children's bible stories at the library.

Once we moved to Baton Rouge, we were only a couple of hours from New Iberia, where Alfred's parents lived and operated several women's clothing stores. I knew his mother had called him several times to urge him to join the local Temple, but he refused, saying he wasn't ready yet. I told him I didn't care. It didn't matter to me. I also thought it was kind of odd for someone whom I knew was serious about his religion to not want to worship with others of his faith. He could go to the services on Friday nights, while I took the kids to a movie. "Half of being Jewish has nothing to do with going to services," he told me, while he continued to tell his mother no. In April his mother called with an invitation to a Passover Sedar at Gates of Prayer, the Temple in New Iberia. "It's on Saturday," she argued. "I know you get off work at noon. Bring Jo Carroll and her children. You can spend the night."

So we went. I had no idea what to expect. I knew Alfred had grown up in this Jewish Temple, in the middle of the Catholic Cajun country. What I would learn later is that his great-great-grandfather helped build the building in 1904, where we would be celebrating Passover with his family. As we turned down Weeks Street in New Iberia, a town of 30,000 located just north of the Gulf Coast, I could see the red brick building. It looked like a cross between an old one-room school house and a Baptist Church. The front section was long and narrow, the door located in the middle of the short end, with the sides having several long tall windows. The windows were stained glass, and as we came closer I could see a person's name was part of the design at the bottom of each window. A large square building had been a recent addition to the Temple and this was where we were to have the Sedar. I was sure this was a very formal affair and I didn't know if I had dressed appropriately. Alfred still had on his suit and tie he wore everyday to work. The kids and I had put on our Sunday best. Alfred was carrying Gina, who had fallen asleep in the car and I was holding Steven and Heather's hands as some one opened the door for us. The noise of about 50 people talking at once sounded like 200. Someone recognized Alfred and told him his mother was in the kitchen. We wove our way around the tables, topped with white tablecloths and filled with table settings and wine glasses.

"Oh, I'm so glad y'all made it," Carolyn said to her son, as she pulled at the sleeve of a woman who was stirring something on a huge stove. "Look who's here, Jo. Alfred, you remember Jo Wormser, don't you?"

"Of course. Nice to see you again." More introductions and then it was time to find our seats at the correct table.

Place cards decorated with little blue six-pointed stars were sprinkled on every table. I found myself between Alfred and a woman he had gone to high school with, and the kids were sitting across the table from us. Chatter still filled the air, until the a woman at the head table ran a glass bell to get everyone's attention. "Who's that?" I leaned over to ask Alfred.

"She's the Rabbi. She comes out here every month from Cincinnati because the congregation can't afford a full time Rabbi."

"You're kidding!" I could hardly keep my voice down to a whisper.

"No," he said, "There's not very many members now, and nobody seems to have a lot of money." Alfred was totally unaware that I was surprised that the Rabbi was a woman.

Haggadahs, books explaining the story of how the Jews escaped from the enslavement in Egypt centuries ago, were handed out to everyone. They contained beautiful illustrations, songs and word games. Everyone told turns reading, there were special parts for children and silly songs where everyone tried to sing faster and faster. And before the evening was over, four glasses of wine would be drunk by all the adults. Laughing and having a good time, I felt more like I was at a birthday party rather than a religious rite. And then the food began. Hot matzo ball soup, with elderly women loudly discussing whether good matzo balls should float or sink. The delicious charoses, a mixture of apples, nuts, cinnamon, and wine that was served on the flat matzo crackers was clearly my favorite. Plates of roasted chicken appeared surrounded by the spicy vegetables you find only in New Iberia, where Tabasco sauce is made. The meal ended with flourless rich chocolate cake that resembled a torte. And the service ended with the people singing a song I knew very well, "America."

As we crawled into Alfred's parents' hideaway bed, the bump in the middle of the mattress didn't bother me at all. I was full of good food, sweet wine and had enjoyed my first peek at a religion my husband revered.

As I wrote my in-laws a thank you note I mulled over what had happened to make the Sedar so special. No one shouted Hallelujah or bowed their heads in respect. And other than the small sips of wine my grandmother would take at the altar during Catholic communion I'd never seen wine consumed as part of a religious ceremony. People talked while the Rabbi was speaking and no one seemed to be bothered. Fire and brimstone didn't exist, everyone was having a good time. I wanted to know more.

I had a million questions I wanted to ask Alfred, but I wanted to wait for just the right time. But timing was never one of my strengths and so one night while we were watching TV the questions began.

"Alfred, what can you tell me about Judaism?"

"That's like asking me what can I tell you about sex. I don't know what you want to know. Where do you want me to start?"

I banged the copy of newspaper I had in my hand against the back of the couch. It didn't make much noise, but I got my point across, he knew I was mad. "If I knew where to ask you to start I wouldn't be asking you the question in the first place."

He left the room and quickly returned with a thick book.

"Here, have you read this?"

"Is this a Jewish book?"

"No, but it's a good place for you to start."

I read the book he had handed me, "The Source" by James Michener, and I never stopped, reading everything I could find on Jews and Judaism. I went to the library, I went to bookstores, I looked everywhere. Alfred's parents had a lot of books, but their Jewish books tended to be only prayer books, with no explanation of what was going on. From the Baton Rouge Library I picked up books that explained the three main branches of the Jewish religion in the United States. The Orthodox movement, where women always covered their heads, bathed in a ritual bath after their periods and obeyed their husbands. The Conservative branch, where women were treated more as equals, but weren't allowed to be Rabbis and finally the Reform movement where women were treated as equals. I knew Alfred had been bought up in the Reform movement, where the majority of American Jews practice their religion.

Most of the books I read didn't explain what branch of Judaism the author was talking about, so the more I read, the more confused I got. I constantly asked Alfred questions. "Did you have a Bar Mitzvah?" This was a formal rite of passage for a young boy into the adult world of his religion. I just knew his parents would have thrown the biggest party in New Iberia for Alfred. His father had struck me as a braggart and there was always a servant somewhere in the background at their home. "No of course not. No one in my family has for generations." Okay, back to the books, I must have read something wrong.

"Alfred, why did you marry me if I wasn't Jewish?"

"Because I didn't plan on having any more children." I had just read that most devout Jews only marry other Jews, but I hadn't expected this answer from him. I wanted him to tell me something like, "Because I love you so much."

"Oh, really," I answered back "I thought our love was more important than what religion your children are."

"Jo Carroll, I don't want to get in to this conversation. You had a tubal ligation after Gina was born, and my four children were born from my first marriage. It's not an issue," he said as he walked out of the room. Back to the books on intermarriage. .

I always thought that books could solve all the problems of the world, but I'd doubted the sincerity of religious books. Now I seemed to be unearthing a vast amount of history with an emphasis on ethics in day-to-day living.

All I knew before I starting reading about Jews that there were the two Jewish merchants in Atchison who had different holidays and didn't believe in Jesus. I'd also been told my great-grandmother, Regina Struass had been Jewish, but raised her children Catholic because her dominating German husband, Albert, had demanded it.

I had always wanted some answers. Why are only some people moral? What did people believe before Jesus? Maybe these weren't the questions most people wanted from religion or that religion claimed to answer, but they were my questions. If Alfred could be so confident in his religion surely it would have the answer, fill the void in my spirit. If I became a Jew, maybe I could get my trains on the right track, resolve all my problems and never be sick again.

How hard could it be to become a Jew? I wasn't giving up one religion for another or substituting the trappings of one for another. I hadn't felt anything remotely spiritual in years and the last time I'd been in a church was to attend a potluck.

Baton Rouge had two synagogues. I wanted to talk to a rabbi.

"Call Temple B'nai Israel. That's where my parents belonged when they lived here. The other one is kind of an offshoot, started after Israel became a country in the late 40's."

"What should I say?"

"Tell the rabbi you would like to talk to him about Judaism. Ask for an appointment."

"Will he ask me if I'm Jewish?"

"Of course not. Rabbis talk to everybody."

A week later, I was ringing the doorbell by the back door of Temple B'nai Israel. A slight, pleasant, unassuming man a few years younger than I opened the door.

"I'm here to see Rabbi Brahms."

"You must be Jo Carroll. Please come in. And call me Jan," he said, leading me into his office. Bookshelves lined every inch of the wall and newspapers, magazines and more books covered every horizontal surface.

"Would you like a Coke?"

I had expected the rabbi would be older, rounder and much more formal. He didn't even have a beard.

"Yes, a Coke would be nice."

He disappeared for a moment and came back with two familiar red cans. "You must be Robert and Carolyn's daughter-in-law."

"Yes, but that's not why I'm here."

I took a deep breath.

"What do I have to do to become Jewish?"

"You've just done it."

"What?"

"You've come to see me and expressed an interest. That is the first and most important step. Rabbi Hillel said, 'What is hateful to you do not do to your neighbor. All the rest is commentary. Go and study.' I have a class that starts in a couple of weeks. Why don't you join us? It will help you decide whether you really want to become Jewish."

I couldn't wait to tell Alfred about my adventure.

"You're not going to believe this but he didn't even wear one of those little black beanie things."

"Why did you think he would? I don't."

"But you're not a rabbi."

"Even if I were, I wouldn't. My grandfather told me never to trust a rabbi who wears a yarmulke."

"You're kidding! Oh Alfred, I'm so excited. I know already I want to be Jewish."

"Honey, slow down a little."

But I couldn't. I had found something important to me and I couldn't wait to embrace it. Alfred and I attended the class together. I had to start from scratch and learn the basics. Alfred offered support, joined in the discussions and reinforced what he already knew. The class of about a dozen was a mix. Some, like me, were anticipating entry into Judaism. A couple from a nearby church were brushing up on the Old Testament history. And a few members of the congregation were checking to be sure this young rabbi was giving out the right information.

Nel and Louis introduced themselves after the first meeting. Their clothing was a mixture of leftover hippie rags and the latest threads from Land's End.

They lived on Lou's old family plantation across the Mississippi River where they were trying to grow enough food to eat.

"Lou's family's been lighting candles on Friday nights forever here in the South. I was raised a Methodist, but I figure what he has is what I want."

Our husbands had forever been Jewish, but Nel and I soon discovered we were core Jewish. We both found in this religion, new to us, many of the fundamentals we already believed. Judaism justified our ethical beliefs and gave them a rationale and a structure.

Ethics and goodness were at the center and to find them I had to look inward to my soul. I had always known deep down that children and family came first and after death you live on in the memories of others. But I needed to have someone say to me that's the way other people believed, too. Judaism did that for me. It enabled me to hold on to and strengthen my beliefs and know that I was not alone.

In preparation for my conversion, we joined Congregation B'nai Israel and started attending Friday night services. The first night Gina went with us she got a little confused. "Mommy, who is that man up there?" she whispered to me, pointing to the bima, the lectern where the rabbi stands. "That's Rabbi Brahms," I told her. "But Mommy, I thought only women could be rabbis."

After three months of classes, attending Friday night services, reading books Rabbi Brahms had supplied about Reform Judaism I was about to become a Jew, or as the old man with the small black prayer book would say, "A member of the Tribe." My formal conversion to Judaism took place in a private ceremony on a Friday night after services were over at Temple and everyone was gone. I'd never been to a conversion ceremony, my first would be my own.

"I still don't know how to read Hebrew," I told the Rabbi.

"I know," he nodded.

"I have to read the phonetic pronunciations to recite the blessings over the candles."

"So...."

"I just don't want to stand in front of a big crowd and do this, but I want to be a Jew.

"I don't see any problem there," Rabbi Brahms assured me. "We can do it anytime, a Wednesday afternoon, a Friday night after services, whenever is convenient to you and Alfred."

I nodded my head, but sat there a moment. "There's something else. My older children were raised without any religion, I don't want to raise Gina that way. If I convert and raise her Jewish, will she be Jewish too, or does she need to go through a ceremony?"

"If she's Alfred's child she's already Jewish. Reform Jews accept either the father or the mother's lineage," he explained.

"Well, she's not quite his. He's adopting her, but the papers aren't final yet. I haven't heard from her birth father for two years."

Rabbi Brahms rested his chin on his thumb as he rubbed his forefinger across his lips. "Let me see," he said. He swiveled his chair around to face his bookshelves and pulled a book out to lay on his desk. As he thumbed through the thin parchment like pages he must have read my thoughts, "Don't worry, it's just not something I have come across before. I just need to look something up. I don't want to give you a wrong answer."

Sitting in front of his desk, I tried to strike a pose, with my hands in a ladylike position while I waited. It didn't work. I ended up sitting on my hands, my sweaty palms against the leather seat.

He closed the book and looked at me with a big smile, "Jo Carroll, she'll be Jewish because Alfred will be her father and you're her mother. But I think it would be nice if you and Gina went through the conversion ceremony together. All you and Gina need to do is recite the first two lines of the Shema in Hebrew, the most important prayer in Judaism, before the Torah and two witnesses. I can be a witness and so can Alfred, or if you'd like to invite someone else, you may. They just need to be Jewish."

Later that evening I talked it over with Alfred. "This was a very private decision for me, I'd like it to be a private moment when the actual ceremony takes place."

He kissed me on the cheek, "However you want to do it."

"The Rabbi told me I needed two witnesses. Who should I ask? Nel and her husband?"

Alfred brushed his hand through my hair. I'd never been comfortable with anyone else touching my hair. It had always sent shivers up and down my spine. With Alfred I just felt the love.

"I think my parents would be honored if you asked them."

"Really?" I asked as I pulled my head away from his hand. "I never got the impression your mother liked me that well, and I can't tell about your father because he's always drunk. And, besides, Gina's going to be going through the ceremony with me, and you told me your mother didn't want you to adopt her."

"She just said she hated to see me take on any more responsibility That's just my parents, my mother doesn't show her emotions and my father drinks. I still think they'd be honored. They're Jews. Converting is a big deal. Invite them for me."

So there we were, Rabbi Brahms, Alfred, his mother, Carolyn, and his father, Robert with Gina and my voices echoing into the large empty sanctuary.

Sh'ma Yis-ra-eil, A-do nai E-lo-hei-nu, A-do nai E-chad

(Hear, O Israel, the Lord our God is One.)

Ba-ruch sheim K'vod mal-chu-to l'o-lam va-ed.

(Blessed is the Name of His glorious kingdom forever and ever.)

I knew it was an honor to stand before the Torah, a scroll written in Hebrew that contained the first five books of the Bible. It was kept at the back of the bima in an ornate niche called an Ark. With the Ark opened I could see it was lined with ornate fabric and three Torahs rested against the back. Silver moldings fit over the top of each Torah scroll, with a faceplate hanging down to match. It looked very heavy. I sneaked a look at the empty seats in the sanctuary. I had just the tiniest hint of regret that I hadn't invited anyone. The Ark's doors had been opened while Gina and I recited the prayer, but now Carolyn and Robert reached up to slide them closed. Carolyn gave me a kiss, Rabbi Brahms said, "Congratulations."

"This is it?" I asked him. "It's that simple? Don't you have any questions you want to ask me?" The Rabbi just smiled and shook his head. Then he leaned down and gave Gina a kiss on the cheek.

It was over. Gina and I were Jewish. Alfred's parents discreetly handed the Rabbi an envelope containing a check, and drove home to New Iberia. It was Friday night and they had a women's clothing store to open in the morning. Alfred picked up our daughter and carried her to the car, while I put my arm around his waist. We went straight home. He had to be at his desk early Saturday morning.

Alfred never pushed, but once I got started the religious oneness added another layer to our relationship. We went to services on Friday nights together and came home and discussed the pros and cons of the sermon. Although I'd gotten a really late start, we looked at Judaism in a very similar way.

"Alfred I can't believe the choir. The Temple hires Christians to sit behind a curtain and sing Jewish hymns. Either you sing songs or you don't, you don't hire someone else to do it for you."

"I couldn't agree with you more. One thing you have to remember is that every Temple does it differently, but this is kind of the norm in the South."

My new religion didn't solve my problems. Many days I was so depressed I couldn't get out of bed and the trains roared so loudly they sometimes woke me in the middle of the night. Nor did I find real acceptance in the small Jewish community of Baton Rouge. I got a Temple roster and started going down the list, calling every name I recognized to see who wanted to go to lunch with me. I got no takers, everyone seemed to be busy seven days a week.

I remember as a child seeing a man in his 60s who was baptized at a revival-tent meeting. After the preacher announced, "I baptize you in the name of the Father, the Son and the Holy Ghost" the congregation gathered round him, raised their hands in the air and picked him up and carried him all around the tent. The celebration went on for days. There were picnics at Mission Lake and potlucks with mac-and-cheese and fried chicken at Mrs. Hawk's. I know because I pretended to be a member of the congregation so no one would yell at me when I snuck in to eat chocolate cake. Parties and celebrations to welcome him lasted for days. Every church member invited him to attend services and social gatherings and considered his participation an honor.

My conversion included no festivities. No one in Baton Rouge seemed to notice. I had embraced the tenets of Judaism, made the commitment and converted. I didn't look different, I didn't sound different and if you didn't notice the small Star of David that I sometimes wore around my neck, you'd never know I was Jewish. I felt more connected to Alfred and wanted him to know that being Jewish was very important to me.

I remember my Catholic grandmother, Nana, used to tell me about her Jewish mother, Regina, who would cook for the Jews in Atchison. Regina had learned to cook in her native France, and, although her husband would not let her practice her religion, she was able to profit by it by selling the foods she remembered from her childhood. When I looked up Regina's obit in the archives of the Atchison Library, I was not surprised to see it mentioned her cooking abilities. Nana died 20 years before I converted. I think she would understand why I was Jewish, like her mother. Nana, who wore a crown of long braids swirled around the top of her head, spoke to me often of how much she loved her mother, and how precious her mother was to her. In the next breath, she would tell me how precious I was to her and how I should never cut my hair, for a woman's hair was the crowning jewel of her soul.

But being Jewish was not so easy. The Shabbat challah, the special loaf of bread served on Friday night, was foreign to me until someone brought it to Gina's Bat Mitzvah. I kept confusing the Kiddush, the prayer for wine, with the Kaddish, the prayer for the dead. Although the prayers sound very different and the Kiddush is sung, while the Kaddish is chanted, the names sounded alike to me. The Rabbi had given me the honor of saying the prayer over the wine, the Kiddush, and I called him on Friday afternoon and asked him when he wanted me to do the Kaddish. He hesitated a moment and then said, "Oh, Jo Carroll, you must mean the Kiddush. Don't worry, just sit in the front row and I'll let you know when it's time." I was so embarrassed, I hoped he didn't tell anyone.

I sent Gina to Henry Jacobs, a Jewish camp near Jackson, Mississippi, with a Bible of mine I had hastily grabbed off the shelf. When she came home three weeks later, it was the first thing out of her suitcase. "Mom, I can't believe you sent me with this." I picked it up and ran my fingers over my name which was embossed in gold. It had been given to me when I was confirmed in the Methodist Church many years before. "Mom, it has the New Testament and the Christian version of the Old Testament. Several kids saw it before I could hide it."

In my heart I was Jewish. Many years later in Omaha, Nebraska, Rabbi Azriel, my favorite Rabbi ever, would tell me I had a "Jewish soul." At the moment, however, I felt the need to look, dress more Jewish and sound more Jewish to make this small southern congregation accept me as one of them. Maybe if I had this acceptance I wouldn't be ill again.

I tried to look Jewish by pulling my hair back in a tight bun and wearing pearls, but my Irish eyes I'd inherited from my Daddy were no match for a different hairdo. Alfred would point someone out in a crowd or on TV and say, "They're Jewish." "How can you tell?" was always my reply. He had several different answers. "Look at their name, it's a Jewish name," or "Look at him. Can't you see he's Jewish?" I couldn't. I didn't recognize Jewish names even if it was something obvious like Goldstein. And just when I thought I knew what Jewish people looked like I approached a woman at a meeting and asked her what synagogue she belonged to. Turns out she was Greek-Orthodox and very insulted that anyone would mistake her for a Jew.

I decided to stick to my foolproof method. I looked at the jewelry. On an airplane trip, flying home to see my mother, I noticed the familiar six-pointed star, the Star of David, around the neck of my seat partner. "I just love your necklace," I told her. "I have one very similar at home, I don't know why I didn't wear it on this trip." Her face broke into a wide smile, "Oh, there's not too many of us yet, but just you wait. Soon every Jew in the land will know Jesus was the real Messiah." Was this woman crazy? I looked more closely at her necklace. Behind the Jewish Star of David dangled a Christian Cross. "What's the cross for?" I asked her. She patted my arm with her diamond-encrusted fingers, "I'm a Jew for Jesus, honey." In my readings I'd come across this name. It was a right wing Christian movement. I mumbled something about being sorry I misunderstood and stuck my nose in my book, avoiding her eyes and her questions.

I started wearing my small gold Jewish star more. If I had started up a conversation with a stranger because I thought she was Jewish, maybe someone would do the same with me. I constantly scanned the jewelry of strangers, looking more closely this time. Every time I spotted the Star I would smile and nod, but I got no more reaction than I would have with any stranger. Maybe they thought I looked too much like a Jew for Jesus.

I'd heard several people at Temple sprinkle their everyday conversation with Yiddish words. I found a dictionary at the library on commonly used Yiddish words, but since I read by sight and not phonetically, I couldn't learn to pronounce the words. Alfred had grown up in a family where Yiddish was looked down on, so he didn't know any and didn't see why it was important for me to learn any.

"Remember, you're an American Jew. There's no reason for you to be concerned about it."

Then, to my surprise, one day Carol, the president of the Temple Sisterhood, asked if I wanted to hold an office on the Sisterhood board.

"We need someone to handle public relations, call the newspaper about our fund raisers and stuff like that. The Rabbi said you have a degree in journalism. Would you be interested? It wouldn't take much time."

I hoped I hadn't answered her too fast, for when I hung up the phone I spun around and shouted "Yes" to the ceiling at least 20 times. Attending the board meetings would give me an opportunity to know the Jewish women I wanted to look like and, maybe, they'd be friendlier toward me. I attended a few meetings, acquired a few recipes and one woman asked me to lunch. The Baton Rouge Advocate had just published my article on the Sisterhood's annual Rosh Hashanah dinner when my trains derailed again. Laxly monitored medication combined with my manic tendency to try to do too much had done it again.

I first met my mother-in-law years ago when I was Alfred's neighbor. We'd gone to visit her and Alfred's father, Robert, on most of the Jewish holidays after we were married, but I'd never been able to establish a good relationship with Carolyn. Her upcoming birthday would be a good opportunity to change that. I decided to have a party for her. Alfred and I had just bought a house in Baton Rouge and before I could entertain all those relatives, I wanted to completely repaint the inside. Not have it "done," paint it myself. I wanted to do every room. There was only a week before the party, but my manic self told me I could do it. Alfred tried to reason with me. "Jo Carroll, don't try to do all this, you'll make yourself sick. No one will even look and if they do who cares?"

"I care. I'm going to get Heather down here to help me. I've just got to get that chocolate paint on the living room walls." With Heather's help, I finished the painting, got all the food prepared. The brisket smelled wonderful and it had just the right amount of crust on it. I made a rice casserole dish because no one in Alfred's family, including Alfred, ate potatoes. Too bland, they said. But the eggplant dish wouldn't be too bland. Made of eggplant, Swiss cheese and black olives, I'd spiced it up with cayenne pepper.

The door bell rang. "Alfred, will you get that for me. It must be your mother. Heather would you help me get this out of the oven, my leg is still hurting." All the time I'd been painting my right leg had been hurting. There were no bruises or marks so I was ignoring it, but now it had begun to throb. "Heather, go get Alfred."

"Jo Carroll, what do you want? My parents just got here and they brought my cousins from New Orleans with them. Come out and talk to them."

"I can't. My leg hurts too much." By now I was sitting on the kitchen floor. "I think I need to go to the hospital."

"Well this is one time I can't take you. I've got to stay here and be with my mother."

"Mom, I'll take you." It was Heather. She'd help me paint, get everything ready and now this. I wanted everything perfect and it was, everything but me.. The party took place as scheduled, but without me. That day I was readmitted to the hospital.

The stay was only three weeks. At first the doctor thought I had a blood clot in my leg, but this proved to be false. It was only a symptom of my depression. At home, I wandered through the rooms. I didn't feel like reading, I'd never watched soap operas and my sewing machine wasn't inspiring me to whip up any new curtains. My doctor had advised me to take it easy and not go back to work right away, but I had to do something. I checked my calendar for the next Sisterhood meeting and called Carol.

"I wasn't at the last meeting and I was wondering if there was anything I needed to know before tomorrow night's meeting."

"Like what?"

"If there's anything you need me to do? Are there any public service announcements to be written or any photos that need to be taken?"

"Well, Jo Carroll, I wasn't going to tell you this yet, but since you brought the subject up, the board has decided to relieve you of your office. It's obviously too much for you and our organization has a reputation to maintain and can't afford to have a board member who is, well, who is ill enough to be put in a," Carol paused for a moment, "in a hospital. I hope you understand. Of course, if it were just up to me, we're here for you whenever you need us, but we have to put the needs of the Sisterhood first."

My jaw dropped so fast and far it made hollows in my cheeks. I wanted to scream, "I'm fine. I'm not crazy. And I can run rings around any stupid PR you want done."

But hot tears tolled off my cheeks as I silently hung up the phone. At supper, I told Alfred about the phone call.

"Those fucking idiots! You're 10 times more capable of doing that stupid committee work then they are. I hope you told them where they could go."

I called Nel, my companion in the conversion class, for advice. Her sister-in-law was active in Sisterhood. I could make her understand my mental illness was over now. I wasn't crazy, dangerous or contagious.

"Damn them, let it go," said Nel. "Those narrow-minded bitches aren't worth it. Come and help me. I'm working with some teenagers and I know they'd love to have you."

She was a good friend. But the rejection still hurt. I felt I was in high school and no one picked me to play on the softball team, and the coach has assigned me to another team. Finally, I thought, "I'll be part of the team and be accepted." But I was not. My "team" disliked me even more because I was forced on them. I felt lonely and afraid, only I wasn't 13 anymore, I was 40.

I never again attended a Sisterhood meeting in Baton Rouge. In their eyes, I wasn't "really" Jewish or Southern and I had been to that awful hospital. I was afraid of the power and influence I imagined them to have.

Then I realized I could be Jewish without them. When the Rabbi asked for volunteers to work with the Minister of the First Christian Church to start a soup kitchen, I took the job. Together we founded The Holy Grill in Zion City, a community just north of downtown Baton Rouge. I volunteered to take photos of the religious school picnic and gave the 8x10s to the Temple. Alfred and I attended Friday night services and sat with friends of his from work. Once a month he and I sponsored a preteen group where Jewish values were taught. We'd been sitting on the back row in Temple one night with Gina, when friends of hers from the other Temple in town came in with their children. We motioned for them to sit with us and at the Oneg, a reception held after services, usually with light refreshments, they asked if we could help them with some preteens. Someone had picked me.

I finally decided that I couldn't please everyone and I should just be content knowing I did the right thing for me. The conversion would make me a better person and that was the most important thing. After all my mother doesn't care if I'm Jewish, my in-laws think I'm a little Jewish, my children are proud I'm Jewish and Alfred doesn't need to look at any little star around my neck to know I'm Jewish.

And then there was what my daddy had taught me years before, "The right religion for you......" and I felt Judaism made me a better person.

14 Great Western Flyers

I longed to see Alicia again.

I wanted to be physically close to her and restart our friendship. We had been so close in our thoughts. I wanted to visit with her for days and talk about wanting to lock yourself off from everything. Alicia knew. She had been there. I wondered how doctors could know if they hadn't ridden that train.

I begged Alfred to take me to visit her. Alicia and her husband were teachers on the Navajo Indian Reservation in Chinle, Arizona. Alfred had never met them and wanted instead to take the kids on a fishing trip and stay in a cabin. But when he realized that I wasn't enthused about this idea and neither were our daughters, he relented to this great Western journey I wanted to take to see my friends. Steven, 19, stayed in Bloomington, Indiana, with his girlfriend, but our other six children were going on a week-long, 2,000 mile trip.

We piled into a pale yellow Ford station wagon, borrowed from Alfred's parents. We used every inch of space in the car. Seat belt regulations had not yet become the norm, so the back space was folded down for Gina and Drew. That left room for the other six of us: Alfred, Heather, Robert, Aleece, Carol and me. This Country Squire (isn't it funny how companies give the fanciest names to the plainest of cars) had an automatic transmission, but roll down windows. Alfred and I had driven it back from New Iberia and thought the seats were comfortable, but that was before we put eight bodies in it. The luggage was stored in a pop-up tent trailer we pulled. I had borrowed it from Alice and Al, friends I had met while working at BRACA. She was a

Red Cross nurse and jokingly asked if I wanted her to come along in case her expertise was needed.

About 15 minutes into the trip, as we were leaving Baton Rouge heading west across the Mississippi River Bridge, Heather yelled at Gina and Drew, "Be quiet -- you're coloring too loud!" I closed my eyes and imagined we were in a covered wagon trudging along the Santa Fe Trail, "Never would have made it past Kansas City," I thought.

Robert, Alfred's oldest son, was riding in the back seat. He and Heather had been friends since childhood but now Robert kept to himself and always seemed to be immersed in a Hemingway novel. His rough external appearance and short stubby fingers hid his love of oil painting. He wore his hair unstylishly short. He didn't care what he wore as long as it was comfortable and didn't smell too much.

Robert's next younger sister, Aleece, insisted her clothes be clean, ironed and match. She disliked using the bathroom at rest stops and carried her own roll of toilet paper. Her laughter and giggle reminded me of her mother. She had traveled with friends before, but never family and was excited to be on this trip.

Carol, just 14 months younger than Aleece, had a totally different personality that mirrored their hair. Aleece had curly, almost fuzzy blond hair and Carol's locks were black and straight. Carol didn't much like me, and aligned herself with Robert. She read most of the time too, not even looking up to see beautiful scenery when her father pointed it out to her. She was a beautiful young girl, but her mouth stayed in a pout most of the time.

I was so excited that Heather was making this trip with us. She had been living with her father in Indiana and I missed her. I saw my eyes when I looked at her eyes, the smiling Irish eyes of my daddy's. Her very poor eyesight was hidden behind her contact lenses.

"Just throw your jeans in here and I'll do them all together," I told the kids. I ignored the screams that they didn't want their clothes to be washed together. "I'll never be able to find my favorite pair," Aleece protested. "Oh, don't be silly. Look at all of you," I said, referring to the four teenagers. "You're all different sizes. Aleece, you're way taller than anybody else, Carol, you're the shortest, and Robert, you and Heather are about the same height, but Heather's way skinnier."

When I pulled the jeans out of the dryer I had a fight on my hands. It seems, although they were short and tall, skinny and chunky, they all wore the same size jeans!

We stopped the first night in a family campground in Abilene, Texas. This was the first time we had set up the tent without the ideal conditions of our cement driveway. The wind blew the sand, dirt and dust so hard I thought the pop-up tent might become airborne. I was tired, Alfred was grumpy, and everybody was hungry. We ate Dinty Moore stew straight from the can and shoved candy bars into the kids' hands and told them to go to bed. Nobody argued. Alfred and I put our air mattress in the car. Then I went back to the tent to check on the kids.

"My stomach hurts," said Carol. "It really does. Oh, my head hurts, too."

"Mom, go back to the car," said Heather, straightening out the bed covers. "We've got a flashlight and if we need anything we can come and get you. I'll give Carol some of that pink stuff and she'll be fine."

I smiled, and then fastened the door hook from the outside, locking the door so the wind wouldn't blow it open.

"How are the kids?" asked Alfred.

"Fine. Carol has a stomach ache, but I think she'll get over it. And the usual headache." I thought she needed to be loyal to her mother and tended to exaggerate her complaints in order to annoy me

"Listen honey, sometimes it just takes time. She'll come around. If Heather can change her mind about me, Carol will about you, too."

"I don't think so, but I'm too tired to argue tonight. I'm taking my medicine and going to bed."

Alfred grinned. "No fooling around tonight? The kids are too far away to hear us."

"Are you serious? I've been eating sand for the last hour. I'm so tired I can hardly stand up and there are no curtains on the windows and at least 50 campers within eyesight."

He took my hand, and the last words I heard were "I love you." A few hours later, I awoke to my own screaming. I shook Alfred and tried to find a flashlight. Someone was trying to break the window of the car. Alfred told me to relax as he rolled down the window.

"I'm throwing up," said Carol. "Two times. I threw up two times."

Alfred got out to take care of Carol. I rolled over and went back to sleep. The next morning, Carol was eating Pop Tarts with Heather.

"I thought you were going to take care of things last night, Heather."

"I did."

"Why didn't you come down to the car with Carol? She could have gotten lost and ended up at someone else's car."

"Mom, I couldn't believe you'd locked us in. Carol threw up the first time in the tent because I couldn't get the door open. I got the door unlocked before she barfed the second time. I just waited to hear you scream. If you hadn't screamed, I would have gone out to look for Carol. You always scream."

Back on the road, the land continued to roll out before us: flat, hot and dry. We looked out the window at the never-ending west Texas landscape. The six kids squabbling got on my nerves. I reached for my bottle of pills, then changed my mind. I'd need more help later. I needed to ration myself. I thought about Alicia's soft feather mattress, the one that had been on her bed when I was pregnant with Gina. I wondered if she still had it. Her promise in her last letter to take the kids for a hike through the woods sounded like heaven.

Hours had passed since we'd seen a decent rest stop and everyone was getting hungry. I squinted my eyes and thought I could see the mountains, but no one else could.

"Mom, if Alfred's not going to stop for lunch, can I have a candy bar?" It was Heather, tapping on my shoulder and keeping her voice to a whisper so the other kids wouldn't hear.

"Alfred, how soon can we stop for lunch?"

"Have you seen a place to stop, Jo Carroll?" he answered me. "When there's a place I'll pull over."

"Okay honey, but maybe we should not wait for the perfect place. Maybe just a wide spot in the road so we can feed the kids."

Alfred stopped at the next possible place, which was just a wide patch of gravel beside the highway.

"Hot Dogs again? Yuck!" said Aleece. She wanted peanut butter and jelly. Robert decided his main course should be potato chips. Gina complained of an upset stomach. Alfred tried to make a fire using dried sagebrush. He gave up and cooked the hot dogs over wadded up newspapers.

"Kids," I announced, "Right after lunch we'll be going up the steepest part of the mountains, where they'll really look like mountains. Andrew, there's a place with a whole big nice view and we can stop and get out and look through the telescopes. Just wait. You'll love it."

Heather asked to use the camera to take a picture of the mountains. Gina moaned. I relaxed against a rock and remembered a trip with Bruce and our two kids and my brother and his three. We were in two cars and the trip started out innocently enough with some gentle teasing about a box of cookies my mother had given us and who got to eat it first. We were headed to the Colorado Mountains from Kansas. The home movies of that first night show the kids splashing and having fun in the motel pool. Mid afternoon of the next day we arrived at our destination and something happened. I have no idea why, but my brother hated it and without a word he took his children and left early the next morning. He's never mentioned it, never said why he left. It hurt my feelings because I had been looking forward to a nice vacation with our two families.

The sound of the kids arguing about who would get to sit where interrupted my daydream. I let Robert and Aleece share the front seat with their father while I rode in back and held Gina. The passing scenery of Colorado was beautiful, but the kids weren't looking..

"I have to go to the bathroom," said Heather.

"Just wait," I said reassuringly. "We'll be at the Continental Divide in no time and there'll be plenty of places there."

Miles went by and, although I could tell we were climbing in altitude, we saw no Continental Divide or places to stop. Then, suddenly, without any fanfare we saw mountains, with steep winding curves and leftover snow. Alfred turned off the air-conditioning and the kids quickly rolled down the windows. The Rocky Mountains were as lovely as I remembered.

"Mom, I'm not kidding. I have to go right now."

"Tell her she'll just have to wait. I'm first when we stop."

"You're last. You always leave the seat up."

"I don't see any stuff. Where's the Divide?"

"Alfred, just stop along the side of the road," I said, trying to appear completely calm.

"I can't. There's no place. We're on the side of a mountain, for God's sake."

"Please," I pleaded. "Just pull over at the first opportunity. Gina is throwing up in my lap."

"There's a towel in the back, have one of the kids hand it to you. I can't stop here."

When we did stop it was at a rundown gas station located at the top of the Divide. The tin bathroom door, located on the outside, was swinging in the wind. An old cafe, long closed, stood beside the station.

"This is awful. I don't want to go in there Mom." Heather whined.

"It's there or nowhere," Alfred told her.

"But what happened to the places Jo Carroll promised?" This time it was Carol.

"I don't know. It was a long time ago. Maybe a forest fire or something. This isn't what I remember...."

I let the kids use the bathroom, and then I wet a towel and tried to sponge off my shorts. It didn't work. I got into my suitcase and pulled out another pair and just looked at the pair I had taken off. I threw them in the corner of the restroom. There wasn't any trash can.

Our next destination was "The Four Corners," where Utah, New Mexico, Arizona and Colorado intersect. But the land was a flat and featureless desert. And The Four Corners turned out to be a square cement slab with two intersection lines and the name of each of the four states -- and no flushing toilets. The kids, however, were excited and wanted me to take their picture.

"I want to step on all four states at once first. It's my turn."

"It's always your turn first, Andrew. You're such a baby."

"Oh, Carol, leave him alone. Your foot's so big you won't have any worries."

Andrew almost fell over as he tried to cover all four lines with his feet. Robert hung in the back as though he couldn't be bothered with this routine tourist attraction. The sky was blue and everyone was squinting a bit in the bright light. For one moment, everyone paused in the activities to allow me to take their picture.

"Come on everybody," I said, herding them back into the car. "We've still got a ways to go this afternoon. Let's get moving."

Everyone found their pillows and managed to fall asleep. I dozed a little, too, waking every now and then to assure myself that Alfred was still awake and driving.

"Are you okay? Do you need me to drive for awhile?"

"No, Jo Carroll, go back to sleep. Once we get to Randy and Alicia's you'll be so excited you'll never close your eyes tonight."

My friends taught at a school in Chinle, but spent their summers on their ranch just outside of Greer, a small town in the White Mountains. Back in New Orleans, when Alicia was pregnant, she had been so enamored with the way Randy had described the New Mexico and Arizona countryside she had named their son "West." Now that she was living here, I wondered if she liked it. She and Randy had been so supportive during my marriage to Kin. I couldn't wait for her to meet Alfred and see my new, normal lifestyle.

Alfred turned off onto a dirt road and pulled up to an ugly barren fence.

"God, how can anybody stand to live in this forsaken place," I thought.

Alicia's daughter, Anna, ran out to meet us. She was pretty and had long braids. She had the same big brown eyes I remembered she had as a toddler.

"Mama said for me to take you inside."

We followed her into the long, low stucco building that looked like it belonged on the set of a Roy Rogers movie. Lodge poles overhung the edges and the roof was flat enough to walk on.

"Oh, Jo Carroll. I thought you'd never get here. What took you so long?" said Alicia. She nearly squeezed the life out of me before she even saw anybody else. She looked and sounded the same as I remembered. Her tiny body was overwhelmed by an enormous smile and big round eyes. Years of being apart from my dear friend melted away. My train was running smoothly on a parallel track with hers.

Finally, she let go and, with the gleeful voice of a little girl said, "Now you just have to tell me who everybody is!"

Randy stepped forward and shook Alfred's hand.

"Glad you could come. Alicia's really been looking forward to it. We've got a picnic supper all ready to go as soon as y'all get settled." Other than a tan and a few more wrinkles around the eyes, Randy was still the same gentle man.

We piled into two cars and drove to a picnic spot by Canyon de Chelly, a National Monument entirely within a Navajo reservation.. Randy had outdone himself with a beef stew everyone gobbled up. Then, with Randy acting as a guide, all the children and Alfred climbed down the steep canyon wall to peer at The White House, the famous pueblo cliff ruins. The minute they disappeared from sight, Alicia leaned over and gave me another hug.

"I'm so happy for you. Alfred's really in love with you. I've been worried about you. How are you feeling?"

"Better, much better. I'm not sure the stress of this trip was the best thing for me, but for now, the depression is gone. There's no blackness right now. The medicine helps. I don't think I'll ever get used to it and I don't like the weight it puts on, but I'm feeling pretty good. Now, tell me about yourself."

Alicia laughed, "Today, I have diarrhea, like always. But my life is improving. Randy and I have a better relationship. West and Anna enjoy the school and the mountains so much, but the demons do come back sometimes. I wonder how that can ever happen when I'm so happy in my beautiful spot here in the mountains, but it does. I can't explain, but there are days, you know, we've talked about the...." Her voice trailed off for a minute, and then she continued. "I know things have changed for both of us since we were first friends. But I don't think our basic sameness will ever go away. Those demons, depressions and darkness we share."

By the time we reached Alicia's mountain home, the stars had come out in full force. Alicia instructed everyone to leave their shoes in the mud room just off the front hall. The kids were tired and got ready for bed without any fuss. Sleeping bags were unrolled in West's and Anna's rooms. Soon, all was peaceful and the four adults went outside. Alicia and I made ourselves comfortable on the porch, while Alfred and Randy wandered off to talk. "Jo Carroll, I've never seen you so happy. How do you do it with all these kids?"

"Oh Alicia, they aren't all around all the time, Alfred's kids live with their mother most of the time. And I'd had enough of that free love stuff, it certainly doesn't put food on the table." Alicia put her arms behind my back and gave me a understanding hug.

When I couldn't stay awake any longer, Alicia led me to her bedroom, a quiet, simple retreat with an old iron bed that still had the feather bed on it, a handmade quilt, braided rug and a rocking chair. Alicia handed me a big nightshirt that must have been Randy's and kissed my forehead.

"I'll have Alfred in here in a minute," she said.

A quick hot shower relaxed me completely. I had just closed my eyes when I felt Alfred nuzzling my neck. He kissed me hard on the lips.

"The kids--" I said, but he put his finger to his mouth and motioned me to be still. Sliding out of bed, he made sure the door was locked and then took off his shorts and T-shirt. His hands aroused me under the borrowed nightshirt, and soon it was off and the children were a 1,000 miles away. I closed my eyes as he entered me and deepening spirals of joyous colors filled my head. I whispered words meant only for him and soon we both slept soundly.

The next morning, I awoke to sunlight and someone beating on the door.

"It's me, Carol. Aren't you ever going to get up?"

In the kitchen, the kids were eating breakfast and running in and out of the house. Alfred had promised the last two days of the trip would be spent at Astroworld in Houston. After a few quick hugs and tears, we were off again. Trying to hide my disappointment at not being able to spend more time with Alicia, I went right to sleep in the back seat of the car, oblivious to the chattering and commotion around me.

The afternoon was spent riding through mountains. We stopped at a campsite near Taos, New Mexico, for the night. I started to fix supper, while everyone else began to wander. The camp stove was in the middle of the cramped pop-up tent and the burners were turned up high to make macaroni and cheese.

"I have a little surprise for you," said Alfred. He reached into a storage seat and pulled out a bottle and two wine glasses.

"To celebrate our future," he said. "To us."

Our glasses clinked and we kissed.

"Dad, come see! Come see!" one of the kids yelled.

"I'll be right back, Jo Carroll. Try to hold this moment."

Glass in hand, I turned back to my cooking.

"Jo Carroll, Jo Carroll, where's your camera?"

"I don't know. I'm busy cooking."

"Look, mom, there's a deer in our camp!"

"Hush, you'll scare him away. Jo Carroll, get your camera."

I whirled around to see, knocking over the boiling pots on the camp stove. My wine glass broke and the macaroni and cheese was on the floor of the tent. I grabbed the camera and leaped outside, but the deer was gone. I got one photo of the deer's white tail.

After we cleaned up the mess, a supper of cold sandwiches tasted good. Later, I curled up next to Alfred in the station wagon and cried.

The next day, we had only been on the road a few hours when I saw two horses galloping.

"Alfred, stop the car!"

"What's wrong, lovely lady? Can't stand the traffic any longer? You don't have to yell, I'll stop if you need to pee."

"No, No, back up. Look -- they're almost the same color as the desert. They look just like streaks. Robert, give me my camera, quick. Alfred, stop. Let me out."

I jumped out and aimed my 35mm at the wild horses rapidly moving further away.

"Oh, what's that damn thing on my foot? Ow, ow. It's an ant!"

I had stepped on an ant hill.

"Somebody take my camera. You know I'm allergic to ants. I get giant red welts that itch like crazy."

"Mommy, you squashed it."

"I hope so. Robert, put my camera away. Gina, why don't you sit on my lap for a while? What are you doing?"

"Heather 'n me are writing postcards to Grandma."

"Oh, damn, damn! God damn it! Shit!"

I handed Gina to Heather and stripped off my pants.

"There's another ant biting my knee. Robert, get me some ice out of the thermos. Damn, don't spill the water all over!"

"Jo Carroll, what's going on? It's hard to drive with all that commotion."

"Alfred, please, one of those things bit my knee and I'm going to die, I know it. I told you we should never have taken this trip!"

"Jo Carroll, Jo Carroll, listen to me, NOW. Listen. Say 'I hear you.'"

"I hear," I said faintly.

"Maybe she can hear you," said Carol, "but I can't and I don't want to get blamed for something just because I didn't hear. I've got enough troubles of my own."

"Shut up Carol, Can't you see daddy's trying to save Miss Jo Carroll's life? Daddy, you can go on now."

"Alfred, please drive on the right side of the road, or could we just pull over for a little."

"SHUT THE FUCK UP. Jo Carroll, listen. Long smooth breaths, in, now hold, then slowly breathe out. Robert, get Jo Carroll the paper sack in the first aid kit."

"You mean this one under the back seat with all the gunk on it?"

"Robert!"

"Well, we have so much junk in here we could have two for all I know!"

"Heather, help your mother put this paper bag over her face."

"Why?"

"Just do it. Around her mouth and nose, it will help her breathe better."

"Robert, get out the A and D ointment and a Band-Aid. Heather, that's enough with the bag. Help your mother put the ointment on. Gina! Get your finger out of the ointment."

I realized I was naked in front of the kids.

"All right everybody except Alfred close their eyes while we go though this real dark tunnel." I yelled as though nothing had happened and pulled up my pants.

"There wasn't any tunnel. You lied."

The late afternoon sky was cloudless and the sun's heat radiated in waves from the pavement creating mirages of water ahead in the road. Robert pestered his father to let him drive.

"I'll never to able to get my license if you don't let me practice."

Aleece thumbed though the latest issue of Seventeen. Carol huddled over her diary and wrote. Andrew made all his Matchbox cars zoom down a highway created out of pillows. Heather and Gina returned to writing postcards to Grandma. I spotted an ant on top of Heather's card. I rolled the window down and threw the cards out the window.

"I can't believe you just did that," said Heather. "I paid 25 cents for that card and I already put a stamp on it. I want out of this car right now."

Gina huddled next to her sister. "Mommy, I had just finished writing on that card. I can't write very fast."

"Jo Carroll could you settle things down. I might be able to control my headache if things could just calm down for a little while. Would that be too much to ask? Can't you just look at the scenery for a while?"

My knee throbbed.

"Everyone just stop it. Shut up and stop it. If we ever get back to Baton Rouge I'm not taking you anywhere again ever."

After 12 hours in the car, we had reached the southeastern corner of New Mexico. The sky was dark and no lights could be seen on the horizon. And, we had not seen any campsites. At the next gas station, we asked the elderly clerk for permission to camp. She looked at our car full of kids and told us to move on. Alfred consulted the map. The next tiny town was Melrose, where we found a motel with a campground. A few trailers were wedged in between the individual units, all trimmed in pink. The motel's neon sign flickered and trash blew across the yard. After setting up the tent, we went to the town's one cafe. The kids ordered hamburgers and I ate scrambled eggs and cherry pie. We paid the bill and drove back to the motel. We heard a loud wailing sound.

"Run for cover, run for cover,." Robert jumped out of the car yelling.

I grabbed his shirt. "Robert, what is the matter? Shut up. It's almost 11. Everyone else is, or at least was, asleep."

"But I know what that is. Listen to me. It's a tornado siren. I just took a class in civil defense. I know it's a tornado siren."

"No, it's not. Now just shut up and get in the tent."

"Dad, listen to me. We're all going to get blown away. We've got to find cover."

"Alfred, he doesn't know what he's talking about.".

"Oh, all right Robert. Go over to the office and see what the siren is."

"He doesn't know what he's talking about Alfred. Why do you indulge him?"

"Indulge? Just let him find out what's going on and then we'll be able to get some sleep."

Minutes later, Robert was running back across the dimly lit parking lot. All the children crowded around him.

"What'd they say?"

"Where can we hide?"

"What's making the noise?"

"Oh, they said they didn't know what it was we heard, they're so stupid they'll probably just blow away."

The deafening sound had stopped. I gathered the kids in a circle and nodded toward the sky.

"You see all those stars up there? Look, you can even see the Big Dipper. That's what makes this night so pretty and it also lets us know there won't be any tornadoes tonight. Tornadoes come from low rolling clouds that are easy to see and would block out the beautiful stars."

Giving them a special hug I added, "Besides, when a tornado is close, you'll know it. It sounds just like a freight train."

Around 4 am a freight train roared by. In the dark we had unknowingly set up the tent right next to the tracks. The kids thought they were all being swept up in a giant tornado. Carol and Aleece were trying to come out the door at the same time and Robert was shoving Gina and Andrew out a tent flap. We woke up everyone in the motel and the campground. Alfred cranked the tent down and we took off over the hill for Astroworld.

I reached into my purse, got a little white pill and took it with a sip of lukewarm pop.

15 Mourning Train

When I feel the worst, time has no meaning. I sit and stare out the window and think an hour has gone by. When I check the schoolhouse clock on the wall, it has only ticked away three minutes. My father bought the clock for me when I lived in Atchison. He'd gone to an auction, where a one-room school was closing down, and came home with this wall clock: a Seth Thomas original. I glance at the clock again, thinking another hour has gone by, and the hands have actually moved two hours backwards. What is happening to my head? The clock begins to turn black; everything is black, even the force pushing down on my shoulders has a color and it is black. I can't move; I feel the blackness taking over my blood. I am sure my lungs have collapsed from the pressure. It is so hard to breathe. The trains in my head only travel into dark holes from which they can never return.

"Robert's dead."

Alfred was speaking to me, but his words didn't register. I'd never heard him call his father by his first name.

"How? Was he fishing? Where's your mom? Is she all right?"

I started to cry. Alfred reached down, lifted my face to him and kissed my salty eyelids.

"My son. Robert. My child."

My mind came to a complete halt. My trains were silent.

Earlier, my heart had stopped when I heard Alfred's voice. The time was 9:30 a.m. He'd left for work less than two hours before. He rarely called to chat or leave messages until the middle of the afternoon when work at Goudchaux's tended to settle down a little. Although he was an executive at the large department store, his office was a doorless cubby hole, tucked into a storage room with only a folding screen for privacy. His typical morning included meeting with the advertising department, giving his buyers directions on what to purchase from the various vendors who would call on them and putting out any fires that had started the day before in his retail world. The only piece of humor that occupied his day was the stuffed raccoon that sat atop the boxes that enclosed his desk. He never told me where he got it, each of us had secrets from our past life. It looked like it was going to jump on you if you talked to Alfred too long.

He had said, "Jo Carroll, there's something I have to tell you. I'll be right home. Stay there."

I started to tell him not to be silly, that he could tell me anything over the phone, but something changed my mind.

"Sure, Alfred, I'll be here. Is there anything you need me to do?"

"Just be there," he said.

I took a quick shower and hopped into a pair of jeans before he got home. When I was in-between jobs I always liked to linger in bed way after Alfred had left for work. My kids got themselves ready for school at a very young age, and breakfast for the family had always been whatever was on the lowest shelf.

When he called I had been watching my daily dose of "Good Morning America," and eating half a grapefruit, covered in sugar, with a piece of jellied toast on the side. I left my breakfast and quickly gulped down the rest of my Coke. A million images raced through my mind. My trains picked each one up and made a wreck of it. Had my mother been in an accident? Had Alfred's father gone fishing in the Gulf and not returned? Had Alfred quit his job? He'd certainly been complaining about work lately. He thought Goudchaux's was trying to phase out the housewares department where he worked and give more space to fashion clothing.

A side effect of a medicine I took made my mouth dry, but only when I was upset or afraid. Now my mouth didn't have enough saliva for me to swallow. I pulled my lips apart and put some toothpaste on my tongue, hoping this would help. My mouth felt like Play-Doh.

I tugged a sweatshirt over my head and heard the car door slam in the driveway. I ran down the hall barefooted and opened the door just as Alfred opened the screen.

He wrapped his arms around me and held me for an eternity.

"What happened? Was it a robbery? How did he die?"

I looked at Alfred's face, searching for any answer. There were no tears in his eyes, just blankness. But when he began tugging at his tie, trying to loosen it, his hands trembled. I tried to help him, but he shook me off. He lowered his head until it fit into his hands. His whole body began to shake silently.

Then I heard his sobs. "They said he shot himself. He put a gun in his mouth and shot himself. That's all I know." He wiped his bottom lip with the back of his hand and pulled his head upright. I took his hand and led him to the couch. He sat down automatically.

I took his shoulders in my hands and turned him so that we faced each other. "Alfred, who told you this? Did a Highway Patrolman come to the office? How do you know? Maybe it's not true."

"My father called me."

"How does he know? Maybe he's just drunk again."

"Robert didn't show up for work," Alfred yelled as he stood up. "My father went to his apartment and found him dead in bed." In a fit of anger Alfred walked over to the door and slammed his fist into the wall. He missed the door frame, but his hand went through the sheet rock. His hand was bleeding, but above the sounds of my screams I could hear him hitting the wall again.

"Please don't," I pleaded with him.

He whirled around at me, his face in a sneer, "Don't what? Just once, just once, let me get it out. Don't make me have to think about you. You're not the center of attention this time. Robert's my son. He's dead. What the fuck do you want me to do? Pick up a phone and call a shrink, or maybe better yet, pop a pill."

I grabbed his hand and tried to stop the bleeding with the tail end of my sweatshirt.

"What the hell are you doing? Just stay out of my way, I've got to call Linda, and if you're going to get sick, I don't want to know about it."

My chest hurt and I knew it wasn't depression. Alfred had never talked to me that way before. I'd experienced open jealousy from his children, he and I had even joked that I wasn't one of his mother's favorite people, but he'd never spoke of my illness in a negative way. Under pressure was he telling me what he really believed?

My thoughts were interrupted by loud thuds from our bedroom. I went to the kitchen sink and splashed my face with cold water so I could think better, then hurried to see what was happening in the back of the house.

Alfred had dumped one dresser drawer on the floor and now he was dumping the contents of his jewelry box on our half made bed. I stood in the doorway and watched, almost afraid to come near him, afraid I would set off his temper again. He rummaged through the stuff from the box and went back to take out the second drawer when he saw me standing in the doorway.

"What are you looking at?" he yelled at me as he pulled out the second drawer and dumped the contents in another pile on the floor.

"Did you lose something?" I asked him very quietly.

"Yes, my son. Now leave me the fuck alone."

I went and sat on the couch in the living room and tears ran down my face. Alfred had lost his son, but I'd lost a stepson and now I was losing my husband. Why wouldn't he let me comfort him? Was he afraid of me? Was he afraid I couldn't handle it? That I couldn't be there for him like he always was for me?

"Jo Carroll," he yelled, "I need your help. I can't find Linda's phone number."

"I love you sweetheart, I have it. Just give me a minute."

I brushed by Alfred and went to my vanity drawer and reached way in the back for a small wooden box with a trick top Heather had given me the first year she was in college. It contained the last necklace Bruce had given me, my wedding ring from Kin and a piece of paper with the phone numbers of all our ex spouses. I took out the piece of paper, reached for a clean towel and ran back to Alfred.

"Here, and wrap your hand in this. I'll clean it up for you after you call."

Alfred put his other hand on the back of my neck. His hand was firm and hard and for a split second I forgot who he was, I was afraid. But he used the hand to pull my head against his chest. "I'm sorry.." he whispered. I held my fore finger in front of his lips. "Shhh..." I answered. As he released my neck I started to walk away, to give him some privacy with Linda. "Stay here," he pleaded. "I need your help. I can't do this alone."

He looked at the piece of paper I had handed him and tried to punch the numbers into the phone with his forefinger. He kept getting wrong numbers.

"Here, read this number to me." He tried one more time and Linda answered on the second ring. He collapsed on his back on the bed while he told her. I lay down by his side and as my arm tightened across his chest I could hear Linda's cry ripping through the telephone lines.

Hers was a mother's pain. I couldn't help her. I loved Robert, but I was just a stepmother. All I could do was hold Alfred.

My stomach hurt, like a pit had been carved out of my body, but that was of little or no consequence now.

"Is Carol there?" I could hear Alfred asking Linda as he sat up.

"Yes, of course that's all right." he replied to a long pause. "It'll be easier for you to tell her since you're with her."

Easier, I thought. Shit, there's nothing easy about this.

"No, no I haven't made any arrangements yet. Probably in New Iberia, we'll be there in a couple of hours. I'll call you as soon as I get there."

As soon as he was off the phone my thoughts turned to our other kids. We had to get to them before they learned from someone else. Linda would tell Carol, but Andrew and Gina were at different schools here in town, Aleece was just minutes away at Louisiana State University and Steven and Heather were in Indiana. What if it was on the news before we got to them? And Robert, my mind went to how we would tell Robert before I realized he wasn't in the circle anymore.

I called Andrew's and Gina's schools to tell the administrators that there had been a family emergency and please have them in the office so we could pick them up immediately. Alfred and I decided to bring them home and tell them together. I don't know if this was better for us or for them. We only had enough energy to repeat the words, "Robert's dead" a limited number of times.

I picked up Gina, and Alfred picked up Andrew, who was 13. On the way home I tried to keep from crying, but I could barely see to drive. Gina had just turned 11 and knew something serious had happened.

"What's wrong mommy? Stop crying long enough to tell me what's wrong? Are you going to have to go back in the hospital?" The last question really stung. Is this what my children were conditioned to when something went wrong in the family?

"No Sweetheart, something has happened and I don't want to talk about it till we get home and your daddy and Andrew are there too." God, I prayed, don't let this make me sick. I have to be stable for my family now.

With Andrew and Gina seated on the couch, we told them the bare facts. We said Robert was dead of a gun shot wound, Grandpa and Grandma had found him this morning in his apartment. Gina burst into tears, while Andrew sat in silence a moment then asked, "Who shot him?" I caught Alfred's hand as I answered, "We're not sure exactly what happened."

"Are the police looking for the killer?" This time it was Alfred who replied to his son, "I'm sure they're taking care of it. Right now we all need to get some clothes together and get to New Iberia as soon as possible."

I looked at Alfred, "Aleece, we've got to get Aleece before she learns it from some stranger. And Steven and Heather, we've got to tell them." They were in Bloomington, Indiana, where Heather was in her senior year in college and Steven's head was into a computer maze.

Andrew and Gina and Alfred and I had gathered on our king size bed in the back bedroom, to begin making the phone calls when Aleece burst through the front door. Crying and screaming she met Alfred in the hall with her overnight bag slung over her shoulder.

"Oh, dad, how could this happen? What's wrong with Robert that he would do this?" Aleece was almost as tall as her father, but she buried her head in his shoulders and wept for her older brother.

Obviously someone had called her before we had a chance to. Her mother? Her grandmother? Her aunt? It didn't really matter, we just all needed to be together.

Aleece joined us on the bed, kissing and hugging Andrew and Gina, while I picked up the phone to call Heather.

I ignored the smaller children and just blurted out, "Robert's dead. He shot himself." The words brought a pause over the phone lines, but the kids on the bed began to scream and moan. How could I have been so stupid to say that? Gina and Andrew didn't need to hear it that way, and I didn't know for sure what Aleece already knew.

"Mom, what's going on there? Who's there? Why? Why would he do that? I don't understand!" Heather yelled through her sorority phone from 800 miles away.

"Honey, we don't know, we just don't know," I said. My trains had been going a million miles a second trying to think of why.

Robert had lived with us his junior year in high school. He was handsome, with straight thick black hair and a stern chin. He was short, but had a muscular build and like most teenagers his uniform of the day was jeans and a T-shirt. He smoked, but denied it to us. He was street smart and didn't seem to care about any subject at school except art.

We had a Great Dane who was locked in the kitchen when she was a puppy and made a mess. I remember yelling at Robert and bawling him out about it, making him clean it up even though it wasn't his fault. I should have fussed over him more, instead of at him. Let him know how much I loved him, how much we all loved him.

I treated him like a stepson, not a son. I know I would have done more for Steven. I would have made sure Steven went to school activities, that he'd gotten involved with the right people. Not like the boy down the street that I let Robert hang out with who had a tooth missing and worked on his car in the front yard every Saturday afternoon.

Robert had made the drive from New Iberia to visit us just two weeks ago and played baseball with Andrew and Gina in the park. I talked to him about how Andrew was doing in school. Why hadn't I asked him more about how he was doing? I knew he had a girlfriend.

Why didn't I ask him to bring her up so we could meet her? Robert was 21, old enough for us to recognize he might be married soon.

I knew he liked the freedom of having his own apartment, but why hadn't I asked him the little important questions like, What are you eating? Can I send you home with some of this food? Do you really like working for your grandparents or do you think there's too much family pressure there?

Robert had been badly burned when he was only 7 years old. Huge scars from skin grafts covered his left forearm and his whole left leg. Most people had said, "Oh, how lucky, he's such a handsome child, the fire didn't touch his face." The fire burned the entire house down. Nothing material was saved. The babysitter had escaped with Robert's siblings, wearing only their underclothes. Robert was found walking along the water that ran in back of the house by a neighbor. He was in shock and spent the next six months in the hospital.

The origins of the fire were suspicious and never completely solved. Robert had been playing in an enclosure at the rear of the garage that contained the water heater when the fire started. He claimed he didn't remember what happened, but I don't think anyone, even Linda, really believed him. He was a child who liked to experiment and didn't think of the consequences.

Was that what had happened now? Was that what ended his life? Was he experimenting with drugs and out of it when he put the gun in his mouth? Or did he still feel guilty about burning the family's home down so many years ago?

I was receiving all this help, all these doctors' appointments, all this medicine, why hadn't I, of all people, seen that Robert needed help too?

"The funeral will probably be the day after tomorrow," I said. "How soon can you and Steven be here? No, come to New Iberia. Ask your Dad if you can borrow his car. Do you have money for gas? I'll give you some when you get here."

"Mom, does Steven know?"

"I called you first."

"I'll tell him then. He's just down the street."

"Now don't drive too fast and if for some reason you can't make it call me back at Alfred's mother's house."

"Mom, for God's sake, we'll be there. Let me talk to Alfred."

I turned my attention back to the bed, where Aleece had buried her head under the covers while Gina was screaming incessantly and covering her ears. Andrew lowered his head. Tears dripped on to the floor.

Robert had left no note, no explanation. Because he had always been fascinated with firearms some of the family speculated it was an accident. I knew it was a suicide.

Robert put the barrel of a loaded handgun in his mouth and pulled the trigger. There is nothing accidental about that. But why? I didn't know. I had no clue what could have been bothering him so deeply, even though we'd had, I thought, a close relationship. We had no indication anything was wrong. After he graduated from high school Robert moved to New Iberia, his grandparents' hometown, where he went to work in their small chain of women's dress shops.

For the whole family New Iberia had been a place to go back and visit grandparents, to go fishing in the Gulf or to kick back and simply relax. It would never feel like that again. We got in the car for the hour and a half trip across the Atchafalaya Basin when I remembered I had not called Rabbi Weinstein yet.

"There'll be plenty of time when we get there," Alfred said. "There's nothing he can do right now anyway."

No one talked during the ride. There was no aimless chattering. Only Gina's occasional big, gulping sobs broke the heavy silence.

As we drove I relived event after event in Robert's life as the trains in my head rattled around the tracks clacking, "What if...? What if...? What if I had spent more time talking to Robert when he visited? What if I'd asked him if he was really happy, not just the usual, Are you doing okay? What if I'd invited him to come back and live with us?"

The year Robert had lived with us had been a hard year. He was rebellious when he came but by the end of the year we had developed a deep, mutual affection and respect -- so much so that when Andrew, his younger brother, had come to live with us, I sought Robert's support.

"You not only have my support, you have my gratitude. It will be good for Andrew to live with you and dad. I know it was good for me." He promised to come and spend time and family holidays with Andrew and he did. And when he visited, Gina and Andrew were both his siblings as far as his affections were concerned. Gina's heart-rending sobs were a constant reminder of their closeness.

What if...? What if...?

"Alfred, do you want me to drive?" I'd been so engrossed in my own thoughts I hadn't even thought about him.

"No, it's okay. We'll be there in a few minutes. Besides, driving gives me something to concentrate on."

"Do you think we'll stay at your folks? The kids are going to need something to eat as soon as we get there. Nobody ate anything before we left, you know." If I concentrated on mundane, practical matters, maybe I'd make it through the next few days.

Alfred didn't reply and we continued driving in silence. We pulled into his parents' driveway and filtered slowly, mournfully into the house. There was lots of hugging of grandchildren but few words. Nobody knew what to say. And Gina was still crying.

"Can't she stop that?' my mother-in-law, Carolyn, asked.

I didn't answer her, but put my arms around Gina and led her into the kitchen with me while I called Rabbi Weinstein. He listened as I told him what had happened and immediately said, "I'll be right there. Just give me directions."

"No, wait and come tomorrow. There's no need to come today."

"Could I talk to Alfred?"

I found Alfred and quickly moved him toward the kitchen.

As Alfred took the phone, Carolyn grabbed my arm. "Who's Alfred talking to?"

"Rabbi Weinstein."

"Is he calling about Robert? How did he find out so quickly? I guess maybe one of my friends called him."

"I called him." Rabbi Weinstein had come to the pulpit in Baton Rouge after Brahms left for Tennessee.

"Why? Why did you call him? What made you think you had the right to call him?"

Carolyn and my relationship had never really improved very much. We were certainly not close, perhaps civil was the best way to describe it. Now, in her current high-strung state, she thought she had found someone she could attack.

"It just seemed like the right thing to do," I replied.

The Rabbi would come tomorrow Alfred announced when he hung up the telephone. If plans could be completed, the funeral could take place as soon as tomorrow afternoon.

There were so many details to be worked out. What time would the funeral be? Who else had to be called? Stupid details like what clothes should be put on Robert's dead body.

Why did it matter? What difference did it make? He was dead. And the trains in my head reminded me I'd been here before. A 21-year-old boy had killed himself again for no reason. Only this time I was in New Iberia, Louisiana instead of Atchison, Kansas.

The place didn't matter. The pit of my stomach felt the same. I could feel the blackness trying to envelop me. I needed to be close to Alfred. I followed him into the living room.

"There's nothing wrong with his car. I'm going to give it back to the bank to sell. Considering all the business our family's done with them, I'm sure they'll handle it for us."

The damn car! Why was this grandfather standing there talking about Robert's car instead of grieving?

Now my mother-in-law joined the tight circle of conversation. "The funeral home just called. They said someone needs to come down and pick out the casket."

Alfred and his father turned and silently headed for the front door.

"Alfred, I'm going with you."

"Are you sure? You don't have to, you know."

I knew I wasn't staying there. "Yes, I'm sure. I think you need me to go with you."

The funeral home director outlines the various services they offer, shows you the caskets and then discreetly withdraws, leaving you to wander alone among the death boxes.

The sight of rows upon rows of caskets never changes. How do you pick out something for your child to rot in?

My mind wandered, my trains jumped the track. It was almost 15 years ago and we were picking out Bill's casket in Atchison. When I tried to think of Bill's face, Robert's image was transposed over it. Both young men were stocky brunettes who, for the most part, avoided sports and read in their spare time. Was it me? Had I overlooked or avoided some signal they might have given?

"Jo Carroll, what do you think of this one?" Alfred's voice jolted me back to the present.

"No. It's too cold."

I remembered Bill's deeply burnished, smooth, simple wooden casket. There had to be another one like it. I walked along the rows of caskets until I spotted it near the end.

"Here, Alfred, here's the right one."

It was a dark shade of polished walnut. He and his Dad agreed with my selection. Robert had loved the warm tones of wood. It would be appropriate, if anything is ever appropriate for a dead son.

We went back to Alfred's parents' house, to a house full of children who understood even less than we what had happened. We arranged to stay in a motel nearby for the next few days. The mood was too intense and the house was just too small for the assorted needs of two additional adults and seven, no, now six, children.

The undercurrent in my in-laws house was all wrong. People arrived with food and the phone rang constantly bringing expression of sympathy. It was as though Carolyn and Robert's son had died. People were expressing their sympathy to the grandparents, not Alfred, not the grieving father.

Carolyn unleashed her pent-up anger over Robert's death at me again.

"I don't understand why you had to go to the funeral home. Alfred and his Dad could have taken care of things. Why don't you just take your child and go to the motel. Alfred and his family will join you after supper."

"Alfred and I are the same family."

"Not in my house you aren't. You're just trying to take over everything. You always have, and I don't like it one bit. And I can't stand the way you treat Alfred's children."

I had no idea what she was referring to, but in my pain and grief I couldn't handle any more and I began to cry. I started for the front door, looking around frantically for Alfred.

"Look here, you don't belong here. We don't need you here."

By now the fist that Carolyn had been shaking at me found my shoulder. "Do you hear me? Do you hear what I'm saying?" She continued to scream as her voice and fist followed me out the door.

With my eyes full of tears, I stumbled down the concrete steps and ran blindly into the yard. I don't know how far I would have gotten but I didn't have to think about it. A pair of strong, gentle masculine arms surrounded me. Rabbi Weinstein engulfed me with his compassion and I lay my head on his shoulder and sobbed.

"I thought maybe you might need us before tomorrow," he said. Both he and his wife, Linda, had quietly appeared in the front yard.

My mother-in-law, who had followed me out the front door, stopped chasing me when she saw the Rabbi and his wife but she still could not control the anger inside her.

"I hope you can talk some sense into her. Better yet, just get her out of here, out of my sight."

Alfred had come out of the house just a few steps behind his mother and when I looked up from the Rabbi's shoulder, he was trying to get her to go back into the house. No longer yelling, she wilted against her son as he helped her back inside.

Holding me gently at arms length, Rabbi Weinstein said quietly, "We're here to help you. No one should be treated the way Carolyn is treating you. Robert's dead, nothing will change that. But it's nobody's fault.

"Why don't you come back to Baton Rouge with us? We'll bring you back tomorrow for the funeral," Linda said, putting a supportive arm around my waist. "I don't know what's going on in there but you don't need to be subjected to it."

The front door slammed and Alfred rushed out to join us. I hated to see him spring boarding between his mother and me, trying to act as a buffer. He had too much on his mind, too many details to handle, too much sorrow. I had to let him know I would be fine and could handle myself in this grief-stricken atmosphere without getting sick.

"We thought it would be good to take Jo Carroll back to Baton Rouge with us."

Alfred gave me a soft kiss on the forehead as he said, "That's a good idea. The kids and I will be fine. You need to take care of yourself."

"Your husband needs you, your children need you," my trains sent a message. They needed me now more than ever before, and I needed them. I declined the offer, and returned to the house to help comfort my family. My in-laws I avoided.

After a while, I pulled Alfred aside. "Honey, I'm going to take Andrew and Gina back to the motel. You come whenever you're ready. I'll see you later. I love you."

The motel room was wall-to-wall roll-away beds topped by soft, soggy, lumpy mattresses with white sheets and fuzzy blankets that surrounded an equally lumpy double bed. We had intended to rent a couple of rooms but no one wanted to be separated so we decided to cram into one space.

The television filled the air with mindless reruns of formerly funny shows. After a while, Alfred joined us with Carol and Aleece. He had waited for Carol to arrive from Florida. Linda was staying with her sister in Lafayette but someone had brought Carol to her grandparents' home.

We ordered pizza and then passed around an overly-rich chocolate pecan pie someone had dropped off at Alfred's parents. The pizza was only half eaten and hardly anyone touched the pecan mess. Any eating that was done was purely mechanical. We couldn't eat and we didn't know what to say.

Around midnight we went to bed though no one really settled down for the night. I couldn't tell if the kids were crying themselves to sleep or crying in their sleep. Steven and Heather arrived in the middle of the night and managed to wiggle in some empty spaces left in the beds. Before morning, Gina had crawled into bed with Alfred and me. By 7 a.m. the bathroom was overcrowded with kids trying to brush their teeth as Alfred attempted to shave.

I was trying to find the pair of dark hose I thought I'd brought with me when Heather tapped me on the shoulder and said, "Mom, is this all right to wear?" She was holding up a dark print dress which, on any other occasion, would have looked lovely on her. I burst into tears and hugged her as we both cried.

There's really nothing right to wear to a funeral, especially the funeral of a young suicide victim. Somehow everyone managed to get dressed and we were headed for the car when I realized Gina was missing.

Running back to the room, I found that she had locked herself in the bathroom.

"Gina, please come out."

"I can't do it. I can't go to Robert's funeral. It's just not fair."

She continued to talk but her sobs covered her words.

"Honey, please. I know it's hard on you. It's hard on everyone. I'm not asking you to quit crying, just come out of the bathroom and get in the car. Please. Robert would want you to be with everyone else."

The doorknob turned. "You don't know what Robert would want," she said as she came out of the bathroom.

She was quite right. I didn't know. I thought of all the times I'd made him scrub the floor when he lived with us, how I'd badgered him about his homework, how I'd teased him about wanting a new car, how I lectured him about his girlfriend who wasn't Jewish. At that moment I couldn't remember any nice thing I'd ever said to him.

We drove straight to the funeral home. The mortuary was a large concrete building designed to look like a plantation home. In this part of the South there are no Jewish funeral homes, no separate funeral facilities. The parlor room had a wreath of gaudy red roses woven into the carpet and the garish chandeliers shone even in daylight. I tried not to look at the crosses on the wall.

We were the first to arrive. Only the casket, which was closed, and the assistant funeral director greeted us.

"We have a little room off to the side if you want some privacy," he told us.

"No, this is fine," Alfred replied. "We'll be out here with everyone else."

The first people to arrive were friends of my in-laws and I didn't recognize them. Then some people who worked with Alfred at Goudchaux's arrived.

The room was crowded before I saw Linda come in. I tried to rehearse in my mind what I would say to her but nothing seemed right, nothing worked. "I'm sorry" didn't cut it, nothing seemed appropriate. Aleece saw her mother about the same time I did and ran to her for a tearful reunion. I froze.

One of the greatest regrets of my life is that I did not go to her, put my arms around her so we could weep together. Instead, I busied myself accepting condolences from friends and didn't even speak to her.

There is a certain formal order to a funeral service, something to concentrate one's thoughts on so the otherwise potentially overwhelming emotions don't totally take over. The immediate family always occupies the front row. Alfred and Linda took their places on the first hard pew with Carol, Aleece and Andrew seated between them. I sat on Alfred's other side with the rest of the children squeezed between me and the end of the pew. Behind us, Alfred parents sat next to an assortment of aunts and uncles and cousins.

"Are you okay, mom?" Steven asked as he put his arm around my waist. He was being sweet but I was aware the whole family was afraid this nightmare would put me over the edge and make me ill again.

I wasn't afraid. I had begun to realize that the darkness enveloping me at this time was normal, that nobody's trains are on the right track when a child dies. I would be abnormal if I didn't feel this pain, this sensation that my body couldn't hold my insides together any longer. Total self-control and calm shouldn't come to anyone now.

Gina began to cry again when Rabbi Weinstein began the service. I was in my own world and wasn't really listening to him but as Gina's sobs got louder and louder, I reached over Heather to try to comfort and quiet her. Alfred looked over and, with a quick gesture of his hand, indicated he wanted Gina with him. I whispered to her and she slipped out of her seat and quickly snuggled against him.

As I looked around at the people who had come to pay their respects to Robert and his family, I realized that most of them were at least as old as Alfred and me. Perhaps it is too harsh a reality for young people to attend a peer's funeral. I remembered it had been that way at Bill's funeral too. Two lost lives, two young men whose own pain was so intense they could think of nothing and no one else. They would never know what their actions had done to their families.

I looked at Alfred with Gina all nestled up next to him. One thing I knew with complete certainty, no matter when or how often my dark demons appeared or my trains jumped their tracks, I could never put him through this again. Nor could I leave that as a legacy for my children. I would never let my own pain get so out of control it would result in my taking my own life. So much pain. So many people hurt.

In Atchison, it had been covered up. But not here. The small daily paper's headline had blared, "Local man takes own life."

The Jewish cemetery was surrounded by the traditional iron fence and inside was a pile of dirt by the freshly dug grave waiting for its new occupant. I listened to the prayer Jews recite when they bury their dead, the Mourners' Kaddish, "Yitgadal, veyitkadash, shemei raba..." and then watched as the casket was slowly lowered into the ground.

Along with the others, I grabbed a handful of the damp clay earth and tossed it on the gleaming wooden coffin below.

Carol had to be restrained as she tried to throw herself on the casket. "I'll never forget you Robert. Never. I'll name my son after you, I promise."

Death is only final for the dead, I thought.

When Alfred and I would meet new people they would inevitably ask how many children we had. We never knew how to answer them. "Six," I would say at the same time he answered "Seven." The people usually just stared or laughed and I could almost hear them saying, "Don't these people know how many children they have?"

One night we sat down and talked about it. It was one of the few talks we had about Robert after he died. We agreed that to answer the question with the number six denied an aspect of our lives and committed Robert to oblivion, as though he had never existed.

"But what if people ask us where our children are? What they are doing?" I loved Robert but I didn't want to get into a deep conversation about his death with a stranger at a cocktail party.

"Don't worry about it," Alfred reassured me. "Start with one of the other kids. Nobody really listens to what other people are saying about their kids and no one will keep track of how many you are talking about."

He was right.

It was more than twenty years later before I heard Alfred mention his son's death again. His cousin's husband had just committed suicide by stepping in front of a mass transit train in the San Francisco area.

Alfred took her aside and said, "You know the hardest part is that they're just not here anymore. Robert's gone. I can't talk to him, I can't see him. He's not here. I don't think I'll ever get used to it."

16 Midnight Express

It was Omaha and I was afraid and Alfred was afraid. Mental illness is very scary. It's not like they can take a blood test and know how much you've improved or how many treatments you still have to take.

I watched Alfred's mouth draw tight, and the furrows around his eyes grew deep.

"Do what you want," he said, "but if you persist in this foolishness of yours and don't finish your ECT treatments, I'll leave you." His eyes didn't leave my face.

What was happening to my soft, loving husband?

He took hold of my right arm and shook it to make sure he had my full attention.

"Alfred, you're hurting me," I said. "Let go of my arm."

He released his grip and immediately yelled at me, "I love you, but not like this."

"I love you, too!" I screamed back. "But you're not the one who has to go through these damn shock treatments wondering if I'll come out sane or not -- wondering if I'll lose all the memory I have of you and my kids. What good does it do if you love me and I don't remember who you are?"

"Oh, Jo Carroll. Don't be ridiculous! Has the doctor or anyone else for that matter, ever told you you're about to lose your memory?"

"No, but have you ever completely believed what any doctor told you when they were trying to get you to do something? There's always money in there for somebody. Doctors make money the more procedures they put you though."

"I can't believe you're really saying that," said Alfred. His voice had toned down a little.

What nerve he had to be questioning what I was saying! He had just threatened to leave me. No, he said he would leave me if I didn't take more shock treatments. I should be the one in disbelief. How could all our love come down to the knowledge of one or two doctors? What could they have said to Alfred that would make him even consider leaving me? Did they tell him I was a danger to the children?

He started to turn away, but this time, it was me who caught his arm.

"What did the stupid doctors tell you?" I asked, "that I'll hurt someone? That I would hurt the kids? You know that's not true."

"The only one you're hurting is yourself," he replied. "And I can't live like this any longer. You're not the woman I love when you're in deep depression. You've tried all the medicines and none of them do the job. Shock treatments are the only alternative left, but I'm not going to go to court so I can sign the papers. You're going to have to sign the papers yourself. Just remember, if you don't do it, I'm going to leave you."

His words went around in my head like a whirl-a-gig, "The choice is up to you. The choice is up to you."

What if I could get well without the treatments, but afterwards there'd be no Alfred?

Why would I want to get well without him at the end of the tunnel?

I didn't want any more treatments.

I was so scared.

I pulled his arm towards me until he was close enough so I could put both my hands behind his neck. I whispered into his ear.

"OK. I promise when they bring the paper in, I'll sign it. Just promise me you won't leave me if I do this -- if I do this and I loose my mind anyway."

I only knew, right then, at that moment, I couldn't go on without him. I gave him a hard, open-mouth kiss. He lingered at my mouth and then set his hands on top of my shoulders.

"You're not going to lose your mind, you're going to get well. And I'm not going anywhere, ever."

The faces of the nurses, Frick and Frack, are the last thing I remember before going under.

The first two years in Omaha, I was plugged in about 36 times. Not that I can remember the count. I've gone back over records and reread the daily jottings I made during my various hospitalizations.

Three years after Robert's funeral, Alfred took a job in Omaha, Nebraska. Drew went back to live with his mother in Florida. Alfred and I and Gina moved to a large garden apartment in Omaha. Gina attended Burke High School just across the street, and Alfred's office was within two miles. My trains chugged securely along the nice, flat plains of Nebraska and their regularity was soothing.

We attended Friday night services at Temple Israel, the congregation Rabbi Weinstein had served prior to moving to Baton Rouge. I felt at home. The first night, I met a woman who took me to every Jewish organization in town, even Sisterhood. When we toured the Jewish Community Center, she introduced me to Morris Maline, the editor of a weekly Jewish newspaper.

"How'd you like to do some writing for us?" he asked. "Some feature articles from time to time?"

Soon, I was busy with my writing and photography. But, I began to stay in bed too late in the morning and soon I didn't get up at all. My trains derailed.

After each hospitalization, I returned to our spacious, comfortable apartment with four bedrooms, a fireplace and two walkout patios dug into the hillside. We enjoyed the convenience of no yard work while still having some outdoor living space.

One night, Gina screamed so loud our third floor neighbors came running. She had seen a man masturbating onto our window. The police answered our 911 call, but the man was not found. Gina was afraid to stay alone in the apartment. We rented a small house in nearby Millard and Alfred got a Shepard-mix puppy from the pound that he named Eleanor Roosevelt. When winter came, Gina rolled in the back yard snow with Eleanor and then snuck her into her bed at night.

But I hated our house. It wasn't my style. I didn't like to invite friends over because, somehow, it embarrassed me. So many of this type had been built in and around Omaha, no one had to ask where the bathroom was because everyone knew: up the half-flight of stairs, first door on the right. The house reminded me of the place in Atchison where Bruce and I had lived. I felt as though I'd been thrown back 25 years, back to my Midwestern neighborhood of gossip and recipes.

The trains in my head weren't colliding, but they weren't running smoothly either. I attended a therapy group every Tuesday evening, but the cycle was starting again, and I was pulled back into the black pit.

I hated the hospital. I despised the shock treatments. I wasn't going to do that again. But I couldn't ignore the fact my illness was returning. I didn't want to be locked in a hospital room again waiting for shock treatments, under someone else's total control. I also knew something had to be done. My doctor, Sarah Jones, wanted me to enter that pale-green sanctuary again, to be plugged in again. But after much discussion, she let me stay at home and see if medication and rest would bring me back to normal. She told me that I was taking a big chance. She could not promise I would get better at home. She said I might get worse -- a lot worse. But, the thought of returning to the hospital was making me worse. I believed maintaining a sense of control over my own life would help make me well.

Alfred agreed to let me try staying at home, but he was going to watch my progress carefully. I promised to admit myself to the hospital if my condition deteriorated.

Dr. Jones called twice every day. Some days, all I could do was tell her about my last meal. But I kept talking. I tried several medications. I hated the drugs because they made my thoughts feel like too thick syrup. I had to do everything slowly or my mind couldn't focus. Anything above fifth-grade level seemed to be too hard for me to understand.

After several months, I began to come out of my depression. I no longer stared out the window at nothing for long periods of time, I answered the phone on the first ring and even initiated calls to my friends. I broke through the fifth grade mentality and began reading, instead of just watching TV.

I'm not sure which helped the most -- the rest, the right drug or just the love and concern of my family and friends.

Gradually, I returned to my routine of freelance writing and photography. I volunteered on Temple committees. Gina was attending classes at Indiana University by now so sometimes I traveled with Alfred when his job took him out of town. I tried not to overextend myself.

But when he was away without me, I could not bear to be alone. My friends opened their homes to me, and joked that I was "sleeping around." A dear friend, Dorothy Kaplan, who worked at the Jewish Community Center's Library, invited me for a simple supper and to spend the night. After drinking our tea together, we retired, she to her master bedroom and I to the guest room. My room was cozy, well decorated and complete with good light for reading in bed. As I folded down the plaid bedspread, I discovered an electric blanket lay underneath. It frightened me so much. I bit on my fist to keep from screaming.

What if it shorted out during the night?

Would the electricity kill me?

How different was it than what they did in the hospital?

I unplugged the blanket and crawled in between the sheets, but I could still feel the weight of the electric coils against my body. I got out of bed, tugged at the blanket demon and folded it on the floor. I slipped an extra pill in my mouth and fell asleep.

Alfred and I lived in the Omaha house for about two years, and then we moved to Bellevue, a small town just south of Omaha on the Missouri River. The house had a soaring two-and-a-half story family room and wonderful windows to let in light. I curled up in front of the fireplace during the cold, snowy Nebraska winters. I whiled away summer days in a small, private tree house deck high in the woods.

After Omaha, we lived in Dodge City, Kansas, for a short time. Yes, the same one Wyatt Earp made famous. And, just like Wyatt, Alfred and I ended up heading west to California. We'd never worked together, but we opened a shop in Cambria, a small village on the central coast half way between San Francisco and Los Angeles. I decorated "The Best Little Home and Garden Shoppe in California", while Alfred got good deals from vendors he'd ordered from for years. We worked six, sometimes seven days a week, with little help.

We loved it.

Alfred taught me how to be a buyer and we went to shows in Atlanta, Las Vegas and Los Angeles to seek unusual and popular items for our shop. I researched current trends in colors and styles, making a notebook of items we wanted to carry that would fit into four or five themes I could arrange in our shop. When I would fall in love with an item at the market, Alfred would remind me, "If you can't think of a place to display it in the shop, it probably doesn't belong there."

My confidence grew as I became a good citizen in the little seaside community. Many people lived there simply because they wanted to, not because they had to make a living. Shopkeepers also had a certain status and I enjoyed that. I joined a Rotary Club, while Alfred took a place on the Chamber of Commerce Board. We lived in the house of my dreams, west of Highway One, with windows overlooking the Pacific Ocean.

The day after New Year's, Alfred took a load of boxes home from the Shoppe at the same time the phones went out. Cambria sat in a pine forest, and whenever high winds blew, the shallow-rooted trees toppled over and hit power lines, and we would lose phone service and electricity for a couple of hours.

The shop was busy with tourists in town still from the holidays. We had a backup battery for our computer register, so when we lost electricity that day no one had to quit shopping.

I didn't notice how long Alfred had been gone, but it had seemed like a longer time than normal. I couldn't call him because the phones were out and our cell phone didn't work at home. When I glanced past the customers, I saw Alfred walk in. He appeared to be in a daze and was moving slow.

Despite being in his 60s, Alfred was in great shape. He swam laps at Cambria Pines Lodge three times a week, and unloaded all the trucks that came to the back door of our shop. Some of the extra merchandise was then transferred to our garage at home.

"Oh, my God," I thought to myself. "Something bad has happened to one of the kids. Nothing else could make him look like that."

I ran around the counter and rushed up to him to take his hand. It felt like ice.

"Jo Carroll, I don't feel good. I think I need to go to Dr. Gong."

I didn't even glance back at the customers. I had to get Alfred to the car and the six blocks to Dr. Gong's office.

In the elevator to the second floor office, Alfred told me he couldn't catch his breath. Guiding him by his arm, I opened the office door and screamed.

"Help! Help me! Alfred's having a heart attack."

Alfred survived his heart attack and, and a couple years later, I survived breast cancer.

In the years that followed, when any decision had to be made we'd always say to each other, "Well, what's the worst that can happen? It's not cancer."

Our kids always teased us that we'd never make it to 25 years of marriage, so on our 25th anniversary, they all showed up in Cambria and threw us a hell of a party. Alfred and I renewed our vows on the beach and dined at our favorite restaurant in the afternoon.

When the economy tanked, we locked up the shop, sold my dream house and moved to Hot Springs, Arkansas. We were looking for a small town, below the snow line, in the middle of the country with a full-time rabbi, closer to family. Our home is located in an old neighborhood. The facade is lined with boulders that match the two fireplaces inside. In back a deck runs the length of the house and supports a tree house and a hot tub. A huge fig tree hangs over the left hand side and there's nothing better than a juicy warm fig picked fresh from the tree. Our grandchildren love the back yard.

We live just a day's drive from New Iberia. Alfred's father died many years ago. His mother, Carolyn, has visited us in Nebraska, California and Arkansas. During these visits she and I have found many things to like about each other and she adores her Jewish granddaughter, Gina.

For my mother's 95th birthday, I returned to Atchison for her party in the basement of the Methodist Church, the same church where my Grandfather Harry had gone to Sunday School over 100 years ago and the same church that Bruce and I had attended when we were first married. My mother had years earlier buried Uncle Joe, then married a high school friend, Gerald, and later buried him also. She moved from her farm into the house next door to the home in Atchison Bruce and I shared so many years ago.

At her party she's dressed in a bright yellow dress and the sheet cakes, heavy with icing, are decorated with candy yellow roses. You see when my Uncle Joe fell in love with her he told her yellow roses stand for love, and yellow has been her favorite color since then.

Her friends have come for the party, some from the old neighborhood I used to live in.

The large room is crowded with family and friends.

Funny, I never thought of my family as being large, until I look around this room. My brother, Jack, is here. My nieces have come with their families who include sons and daughters and even a grandchild. Guess that makes me a great-great-aunt.

My children are here too,

After a stormy first marriage, Steven married an elegant professional woman from Nebraska and is happy. His two children, Zach and Becca, are in college. Steven and Alfred finally bonded when Steven would come to California to help us at the Shoppe with computer problems. Although his hair is no longer red, I still think of him as my red-headed son.

Heather was married in a lovely, elegant outdoor ceremony in a small Minnesota town. In the receiving line, I stood between Alfred and Bruce. I decided this beautiful, happy bride with freckles showing through her makeup happened because Bruce and I once loved each other, not because we once hated each other. She has twins I've cuddled and snuggled with since they were babies.

Gina's conversion to Judaism really stuck. She received two graduate degrees from Hebrew Union College in Los Angeles and now teaches at a Jewish school in Houston. She married a Jewish guy from Brooklyn and together they keep a kosher home. She complains about the heat, and Texas, but the last card she sent me shows their two children astride a live bull at the rodeo.

Of Alfred's children, Carol went to Holland and fell in love -- with the country and the man she married. When they came back to the States they parted ways, but not before having two beautiful children. And yes, one is a boy she named Robert after her brother. Carol pursued a graduate degree in anthropology at Chapel Hill and Dr. Lewald now teaches on the East Coast.

Aleece settled in the South and used her people skills to become an advertising executive. She is married to Kevin, a liberal Southern Baptist who votes the straight Democratic ticket.

"I could marry a non-Jew," she once told me, "but never a Republican." Their son, Connor, calls me, "Ma Jo."

Andrew came to live with us again after we moved to Omaha, but unlike Alfred and me, he never left. Now he's working in the tech industry. He and Alfred are avid Saints football fans and they meet once a year to go to a game. He married a Nebraska gal and their little girl, Ava, came to visit us recently and couldn't decide whether she liked the horses on the trail or our hot tub best.

Gina occasionally hears from her birth father, Kin. He attended her wedding in California. Alfred had taken care of his room at the hotel, but when Kin checked in and the clerk asked him for his card, he gave them his library card, not understanding the clerk meant a credit card. He was the craziest, most romantic madman I'd ever known. I'd fallen in love with him like I would have a novel by Truman Capote. He'll always be that fictional part of my life that maybe didn't exist, except for Gina.

Bruce died in 2009, after a long battle with cancer. About a month before he died I wrote him a letter that said:

"You were my first love, and after I got over the hate and anger of our divorce, and as you knew it took me a while, I remembered you as that, my first love.

Parts of our marriage were beautiful and are still reflected in the faces of Steven and Heather and our grandchildren. You and I went on to have much better lives apart then we ever would have had together...."

Last night, on the eve of my mother's big party, as I lay in the narrow bed with yellow rose patterned sheets with Alfred at my mother's house, I heard the long low whistle of a train. It wasn't in my head. It was the Midnight Express, heading north to Omaha.

If Alfred gave me an ultimatum now, my answer would be different. I love Alfred, and I'd miss him terribly, but I make my own choices now. I don't want to, but I could live on my own.

I'll probably be on some kind of maintenance medicine for the rest of my life, and one of the passengers in my trains will have to be a psychiatric counselor.

Although my shock treatments were years ago, and, while I may have lost some specific memories of that time, I still can smell the electricity and antiseptic mixing in the air.

And, I remember my fear.

Made in the USA
Charleston, SC
27 June 2012